Presumption of Innocence in Peril

Presumption of Innocence in Peril

A Comparative Critical Perspective

Anthony Gray

LEXINGTON BOOKS
Lanham • Boulder • New York • London

Published by Lexington Books
An imprint of The Rowman & Littlefield Publishing Group, Inc.
4501 Forbes Boulevard, Suite 200, Lanham, Maryland 20706
www.rowman.com

Unit A, Whitacre Mews, 26-34 Stannary Street, London SE11 4AB

British Library Cataloguing in Publication Information Available

Library of Congress Cataloging-in-Publication Data

Names: Gray, Anthony (Law teacher) author.
Title: Presumption of innocence in peril : a comparative critical perspective / Anthony Gray
Description: Lanham : Lexington Books, [2017] | Includes bibliographical references and index.
Identifiers: LCCN 2017046391 (print) | LCCN 2017039079 (ebook) | ISBN 9781498554114 (Electronic) | ISBN 9781498554107 (cloth : alk. paper)
Subjects: LCSH: Presumption of innocence | Burden of proof. | Comparative law.
Classification: LCC K5469.P7 (print) | LCC K5469.P7 G73 2017 (ebook) | DDC 345/.056--dc23
LC record available at https://lccn.loc.gov/2017046391

∞™ The paper used in this publication meets the minimum requirements of American National Standard for Information Sciences Permanence of Paper for Printed Library Materials, ANSI/NISO Z39.48-1992.

Printed in the United States of America

Contents

Introduction

This book calls for the return of the presumption of innocence as a fundamental, pivotal human right in the criminal sphere. One who simply looks to international human rights instruments will see the presumption of innocence apparently enshrined in express terms. Most who cherish the United States Bill of Rights will understand its commitment to due process, and assume that the presumption of innocence is protected as part of that broader right. If a non-expert were asked whether their legal system protected the presumption of innocence, most would say that it did, and indeed it should. Most people have an ingrained, innate sense of what Australians call the "fair go" and justice, and understand, at least at some level, the importance of the presumption of innocence as part of this "fair go."

However, this book will show that the reality is somewhat different to the romanticized ideal. It will show that legislators across the common law jurisdictions studied are actively undermining, circumventing and limiting the presumption of innocence. The book will demonstrate with numerous examples how various legislators are doing this. It will demonstrate that, often, courts have acquiesced in the face of such legislation. As a general rule, they have failed to uphold the presumption of innocence from attack by legislators. Its future in common law systems is threatened. Courts must stand up for this fundamental right. The book will suggest how they might do so.

Chapter 1 of the book will establish the fundamental importance of the presumption of innocence in our legal system. It will do so by firstly discussing its ancient lineage, and its acceptance across a range of legal systems over millennia. It will demonstrate how the presumption came to be acknowledged in the United Kingdom as the "golden thread" running through the criminal law. It will acknowledge the use of a presumption of guilt in medieval England, often associated with trial by ordeal. It will show that it was the introduction of the jury system, and the cessation of divine determinations of guilt, that sharpened concern over decisions that an individual was guilty. In the Middle Ages decision makers grew extremely wary about making an incorrect decision about a person's guilt. They feared for the consequences, if they made an incorrect decision. As a result, logically they were reluctant to determine that an individual was guilty of alleged wrongdoing, in the absence of compelling evidence. And logically, a principle such as a presumption of innocence fits well within this paradigm. If in doubt, the safest path was to do nothing. While Whitman has linked use of the reasonable doubt standard to notions of "moral comfort," it is the thesis of this book that use of the presumption of innocence can also be seen as a manifestation of this attitude. That judgment of another is a very serious thing to do, and that where it is not certain, or virtually certain, that a person is guilty of that of which they are accused, the default position should apply, and the default position is innocence, not guilt.

It will be argued that the main justification for historical acceptance, and continued acceptance, of the presumption of innocence should be the kind of "moral comfort" needed before deciding a person is guilty. Now, originally, this moral comfort might have been confined to the original juror. It can still be seen this way, or it can be seen more broadly, as the kind of moral comfort that we as a society must feel about our legal institutions, and the outcomes they achieve. We must generally believe that the outcomes of our legal processes are fair and just, and correct. This provides the basis for essential public confidence in our public institutions, including our legal systems. We must have moral comfort in the decisions that they reach. If we believed that the innocent were being convicted, our moral comfort would be interrupted and disturbed. A presumption of innocence can be protected under this theoretical framework, as chapter 1 will demonstrate. The chapter also discusses other theoretical rationales for the presumption of innocence, including the stigma associated with conviction, the resource disparity between the state and an accused, the risk of error, the respect for the autonomy and dignity of individuals, and its link with other fundamental due process rights. However, the presumption of innocence is best seen through the prism of the moral comfort that decision makers must feel about a decision on the guilt or otherwise of an individual.

Chapters 2 and 3 contain a description and critique of existing case law in the common law jurisdictions that have been chosen for comparison purposes. The choice of jurisdictions to compare is easily justified—they share a common British tradition of adherence to rule of law, due process and fair trial, and abhorrence of arbitrary exercise of power. These Enlightenment values are inherent in the United States *Bill of Rights*, Canadian *Charter*, *Magna Carta* and *European Convention on Human Rights*. Australia lacks a comparable instrument, but has adopted an amalgam of the English and United States constitutional traditions.

It is considered that, before the state of jurisprudence in a particular country can be meaningfully critiqued, that jurisprudence must be set out. It is particularly important to do this in a comparative work, where readers may have greater familiarity with the case law of one or more of the jurisdictions, than of others. As a result, chapters 2 and 3 both commence with a succinct description of the important cases and developments over the years, in terms of recognition of presumption of innocence, and assessment of the constitutionality/legality of departures from it. And critique must be informed by an agreed basis of "fact"—the succinct description of the case law aims to provide this factual floor for the analysis to most meaningfully occur.

From this comparison, a number of pathologies with existing jurisprudence will be identified, some of which are common to a range of jurisdictions. It will be seen that through a range of means, legislators have attempted to circumvent, undermine and limit the presumption of innocence. Specifically, the extent of reverse onus provisions, casting onuses on defendants, will be noted. The extent of inference provisions, allowing one fact to be inferred from others based on notions of "rational connection," will be noted and critiqued. The critique will support the use, in Canada and elsewhere, of tests based on whether an accused could be convicted of an offence despite the existence of reasonable doubt as to their guilt. This is considered to be a very useful guidepost in determining the constitutionality/legality of a provision undermining the presumption of innocence. It ties in with notions of "moral comfort," which is argued in this book to provide the theoretical basis for the presumption of innocence today. Simply, where an accused can be convicted despite the existence of reasonable doubt as to whether or not they were guilty, this fatally compromises the decision—the decision maker can have no moral comfort in the decision they have reached, and society can have no moral comfort in the decision reached on its behalf. In turn, public confidence in public institutions is challenged. This must not be permitted to occur. The critique in chapters 2 and 3 also rejects other claimed justifications for departures from the presumption of innocence, such as that it is easier for an accused to disprove guilt than for the prosecutor to prove guilt, or where an accused is more likely to have access to the necessary evidence. Even if that were the case, it would not affect the moral comfort that the decision maker, and society more generally, must have in decisions in criminal cases.

Chapter 4 will focus on another manifestation of legislatures' desire to limit or sideline the presumption of innocence, by changing the rules of engagement in the criminal law. They might do this by re-defining crimes by transferring what were traditionally elements of an offense (to be proven by the prosecutor) to defenses (perhaps, to be proven by the accused at some level). They might do this by gutting the definition of particular crimes, taking out some of the traditional elements that prosecutors might otherwise find difficult to prove but which traditionally buttressed criminal prosecutions. In particular, a requirement of mens rea. In so doing, they might "overcriminalize"—criminalize behavior that most individuals would not reasonably regard as being criminal in nature. This forces us to consider whether a substantive or procedural approach should be taken to the criminal law. Specifically, are there any constitutional/legal limits on the ability of legislators to define crimes in the manner they wish? Does anything go in terms of framing an offense and defenses? Or are there meaningful, enforceable limits? And, if so, what might those limits be?

Chapter 4 considers this question, including the extensive case law and academic commentary on the question of whether a procedural or substantive view should be taken of the criminal law. It concludes that, while deference should be accorded to the right of a legislature to craft its criminal law in line with the wishes of the people, there are or should be defined limits or parameters within which legislatures must operate. The court should police these parameters. It will be suggested that articulated limits should include requirements of an act, that it be voluntary, that the accused have knowledge the acts were criminal, they knew or ought to have known the acts were wrong, and that the defendant's actions were sufficiently "morally blameworthy." It is conceded that the precise meaning and contours of this doctrine are contested; however, factors such as history, Mill's harm principle and principles of proportionality would be useful in providing content to these rules.

The concept of only permitting criminal sanction for conduct that is "sufficiently morally blameworthy" is considered to be consistent with the theoretical framework for the presumption of innocence as articulated in this book—that it ensures that there is moral comfort around a decision to find someone guilty of a crime. As an extension of this moral comfort requirement, decision makers should be morally satisfied that actions which they are asked to declare to be a breach of the criminal law, and worthy of criminal sanction, are in fact generally deserving of that kind of opprobrium. Again, public confidence in the administration of justice pivots on observers being generally satisfied that it "works." It is considered to "work" when only the guilty are convicted, and only those considered to be engaged in conduct worthy of the attention of the criminal law in fact come to the attention of the criminal law. The courts have a supervisory role to play here.

And finally, chapter 5 considers another way in which legislatures might seek to circumvent, undermine and limit the presumption of innocence—by claiming that proceedings are in fact civil in nature, rather than criminal, in order to sidestep criminal due process protections, including the presumption of innocence. The lessons from chapter 4 are equally applicable here—unless a substantive view is taken, there is an unacceptable risk that a legislature will effectively neuter the presumption of innocence, by claiming that proceeding which are in substance criminal are civil. Again, this has implications for the moral comfort that decision makers and society might feel about the outcomes of such a process.

Another theme that ties various chapters together is questions over separation of powers principles. Each of the jurisdictions studied accepts, to a greater or lesser extent, the constitutional importance of a separation of powers among the legislative, executive and judicial arms of government, to provide the needed checks and balances against tyranny and arbitrariness. Separation of powers concerns are real when legislatures seek to compel or influence courts to conclude that an element of a crime has been established, when the facts might suggest otherwise, circumventing the presumption of innocence. Some argue that if a substantive, rather than procedural, approach to the criminal law is taken, this is an infringement of the separation of powers principle, because it represents an unconstitutional incursion by the judiciary into what is truly a legislative sphere—the right to craft offenses and defenses as the legislature wishes, at least in theory reflective of the wishes of the people in a democracy. On the other hand, it can be argued that courts play a pivotal role in our system of constitutional governance, a role that includes only punishing those who are truly guilty, and only those guilty of conduct that warrants criminal sanction. Judges and courts are not mere automatons there to unthinkingly apply the legislatures' laws and criminal processes; their role transcends this. They are protectors of the people from arbitrary government, and arbitrary exercise of power, including punishment. On this basis, a substantive view of the criminal law can be supported.

So why did I write this book, and what does it bring to the debate that is new? I hope it is evident from the content of the book that I have read widely in this area. There are some highly theoretical accounts of the presumption of innocence; there are some authoritative historical explanations of its development through the ages. Significant works have been written on whether a substantive or procedural view should be taken of the criminal law. Books have been written on so-called civil forfeiture and civil detention, and about overcriminalization in our criminal justice system. Few books that I have accessed discuss the case law on attacks on the presumption of innocence in detail, let alone adopt a comparative approach to the discussion and critique.

I have not read a book that focuses collectively on the various ways in which our legislatures and courts are undermining the presumption of innocence through use and acceptance of reverse onus provisions, deeming provisions, a procedural rather than substantive view of the criminal law, and "civilization" of the truly criminal. I have not read a book that argues that the notion of "moral comfort" about decisions that an accused is guilty needs to be re-asserted, at the level of individual decision maker and society more generally, to provide a theoretical framework to support the ongoing application of the principle of presumed innocence. This theory supports an approach asking whether challenged legislation can lead to the result that an accused can be convicted despite the existence of reasonable doubt as to their guilt. Where this is the case, the decision is not "morally comfortable" and cannot be supported. It undermines fundamental institutions of our society. And similarly, where a court is required to treat a person as criminal where they are not sufficiently morally blameworthy, our institutions are being stripped of their moral authority, fatally undermining their credibility and strength. My modest hope for this book is that it will cause others to realize the extent to which the presumption of innocence is being undermined by legislatures, with general acquiescence by courts, and why this should matter to, and concern, all of us. That awareness can provide the basis for action in response.

ONE

History of Presumption of Innocence

The first point to note is the long history of acceptance of the presumption of innocence in legal systems around the world, acceptance which continues today.[1] The earliest reference appears in the *Code of Hammurabi* (1792–1750 BC):

> It is a fundamental principle of the *Code of Hammurabi* that the presumption is always in favor of the innocence of the accused: the burden of proof is thrown upon the accuser . . . not merely is the burden of proof upon the accuser, but in all primitive society the entire burden of accusation or indictment falls upon him. In this respect the legal procedure of Babylonia seems to have been that of the early nations.[2]

The implications of making an accusation were severe. The onus being on the accuser, if the accusation was for a capital offense, and the accuser could not prove their accusation, they were killed.[3]

These practices are evidenced in the law and practice of ancient Greece. For instance, the Greek orator Demosthenes (352 BC) said that "for no man comes under that designation [murderer] until he has been convicted and found guilty." He reflected on the connection between this and the morality of punishment, concluding that punishment could only be inflicted upon those proven guilty, "for then conscience permits us to inflict punishment according to knowledge, but not before . . . it is equally irreligious to let slip the guilty and to cast out the innocent before trial."[4] Aristotle expressed the view that "every one of us would rather acquit a guilty man as innocent than condemn an innocent man as guilty."[5]

There is evidence that these practices were embraced by Roman law.[6] A constitution of Emperor Antonin (AD 212) stated that "he who wishes to bring an accusation must have the evidence."[7] Two witnesses were required to prove the truth of an allegation. The principle that it was better that a guilty person go free than that an innocent person be convicted, which could draw upon biblical references for support,[8] was recognized.[9] Opprobrium (including criminal sanction) attached to a person who made accusations, but was not able to prove them. A subsequent constitution of Emperors Gratian, Valentinian and Theodose (AD 382) reiterated that accusers were required to provide evidence to support the truth of their assertions.[10] A subsequent constitution of Emperors Honorius and Theodose (AD 423) again reiterated that a person accused of a crime should not be assumed guilty, in order to protect the innocent.[11]

There is evidence that these doctrines were picked up in canon law, through the doctrine *non statim qui accusatur reus est, sed qui convincitur criminosus* (it is not the accusation, but the conviction, that makes the criminal).[12] Pennington claims the first expression in law of a presumption of innocence was in the *jus commune* in the early thirteenth century. However, at this point it was a *limited* right, dependent on the whim of the prince or judge. It was later, in the early fourteenth century, that the presumption of innocence became an absolute right. This change came from acceptance that the source of the right was biblical, hence binding the monarch or judge, arising from natural law, as opposed to a right derived from positive civil law.[13] Pennington states that the first articulation of the presumption as an *absolute* right came from a canon lawyer Monachus, as part of the *jus commune* in the early fourteenth century.[14] This would explain Bracton's recitation of the principle, heavily influenced as he was by Roman legal principle.[15] Quintard-Morenas notes that this meant that a defendant would not be denied communion whilst allegations had been made, but not proven, against them, and a priest accused, but not convicted, of adultery could continue to give sacraments.[16] Pennington cites a late 1300s Italian case where the presumption is used,[17] and in the works of Italian scholars of the early seventeenth century.[18] At a time when criminal proceedings typically comprised two private individuals, rather than the state, penalties applied to an accuser who was not able to prove their assertions.[19] The legal reforms of Henry II in the late twelfth century, including a new centralized system for the prosecution of crime and introduction of juries, reduced such risks for accusers,[20] although the irrational proof system, to which we will turn next, remained until the thirteenth century.

Some different views emerge as to when notions of the presumption of innocence first appeared in English law. Logic might suggest that in an era of trial by ordeal,[21] trial by oath and trial by battle (which can be compendiously described as trial by ordeal),[22] the presumption would have little place.[23] Many historians, including Pollock and Maitland, suggest that in this era a presumption of *guilt* applied.[24] The era of trial by ordeal is typically taken to be between three and four centuries,[25] largely ending shortly after the Lateran Council decree of 1215, although trial by battle continued on past this period. However, this suggestion of a "presumption of guilt" in earlier times is worthy of further investigation. And if it is found to be the case, the question arises as to how and why the law moved to the diametrically opposed position of presumption of innocence.

Many historical references seem to support a suggestion that during the era of the ordeal, and even earlier, English law recognized a presumption of guilt, in at least some circumstances.[26] It is evident in the writing of Bracton[27] and Stephen.[28] For example, in his scholarly article, Ireland speaks of those either caught in the act of committing a crime, or in possession of the proceeds of crime, as subject to a "violent presumption" as to guilt.[29] Presumptions of guilt were related to circumstances in which a victim of a crime, or their families, were legally justified in using force against the (presumed) offender, for example "other examples of legitimate slaying are also to be found in the law, such as that of a foreigner who strays from the track without audible warning, for he is presumed to be a thief."[30] Ireland writes of a 1222 case against John of Herwinton, an accused who was "convicted on the presumption of guilt which his seisin of the stolen goods generated."[31]

Further evidence that trial by ordeal was accompanied by a presumption of guilt appears in this passage by McAuley:

> Quite apart from frowning on the fact that this form of trial could be triggered by the existence of public suspicion, and thus did not require the presence of an accuser, leading canonists believed that the rule that the defendant was obliged to purge himself by a formal declaration of innocence ran counter to the fundamental principle of medieval canon law that the burden of proof rested on the prosecution, and that affirmative proof was necessary to convict in criminal cases. For good measure, there was concern that the purgatory oath violated the principle that a defendant should not normally be required to prove a negative—in this context, that he was not guilty of the crime of which he was suspected.[32]

In writing of the ordeal, Bigelow also refers to the presumption of guilt inherent in the process:

> If the proceeding was a criminal one, and the defendant was prosecuted by presentment on behalf of the public . . . the burden of proof again rested upon the defendant. The presentment, if properly raised, raised a presumption of the guilt of the accused, and this presumption must be repelled to save him from conviction. And the same was true in the case of appeals, when the defendant was taken in possession of stolen goods, or of the bloody instrument with which a homicide had been committed. Such facts made a presumption of guilt, and the court declared that the defendant must exculpate himself as best he could.[33] . . . The ordeal had answered the place of trial by a petit jury in modern times; being trial upon a traverse of the accusation of the public voice or of the finding of the jury . . . by these statutes, and by the

> ancient law of England, as well, accused persons, against whom a presumption of guilt had been raised by a presentment or by an accusation of the public voice, had the constitutional right of a further trial, a traverse of the presumption. But when at length the ordeal came to be considered as abolished . . . the judges were in straits to know what should be done with the prisoner . . . could he now be compelled to submit to some other mode of trial? If he could not be directly compelled . . . must he on refusal be pronounced guilty, as would have been the result of his refusal of the ordeal?[34]

The reality of a presumption of guilt is also evidenced by the fact that even an accused who successfully negotiated trial by ordeal might still be treated as suspected of wrongdoing, resulting in them having to abjure the realm, be sent to prison, or make pledges to others.[35] Historical considerations, such as the fact that there was no standing army at the time, no system of organized policing, and the fact that the sovereign was responsible for maintaining public peace, have been used to justify the past acceptance of presumption of guilt.[36]

However, these methods of determination of legal disputes had all but ended by the early thirteenth century,[37] replaced by a system of jury trial. Even in the early days of jury trial some remnant of presumption of guilt remained. "In its early days trial by jury met with some opposition in criminal cases long after it was well established and popular in civil cases. The primary reason for this was that there was no presumption of innocence, which was a concept as yet still unknown. The defendant had to prove his innocence."[38] However, some move towards a presumption of innocence is evident. Leading historian Van Caenegem[39] distinguishes the early Middle Ages (sixth to twelfth centuries) as one generally imposing a presumption of guilt,[40] as opposed to the later Middle Ages (twelfth to fifteenth centuries), by which time a presumption of innocence was generally applied.[41] Pollock and Maitland describe the procedure adopted in the thirteenth century. They state that

> when the parties stand opposite to each other, it then behoves the plaintiff to state his case by his own mouth or that of his pleader . . . it is not enough that the plaintiff should tell his tale: he must offer to prove its truth . . . no-one is entitled to an answer if he offers nothing but his bare assertion, his nude parole . . . the appellor alleges, and can be called upon to prove, fresh "suit"[42] . . . [the defendant] can object that no suit at all has been produced . . . in such cases the defendant protests that he need not answer the nude parole (simplex dictum) of the plaintiff. If . . . a suit has been produced . . . [it] can be examined . . . the court will give audience to the suitors one by one and try to discover whether they really know anything about the facts. If they break down under examination, if they know nothing, if they disagree, "the suit is null" and the plaintiff fails.[43]

James Thayer, in his classic article, states that "In Bracton, say in 1260, we find it in the most general form—*de quolibet homine presumitur quod sit bonus homo donec probetur in contrarium* [and] in a great and famous continental work on Presumptions by Menochius, three centuries later, we have the simple phrase *Illa presumption qua dicimus quemlibet presume innocentem.*"[44]

Earlier I noted that when Bracton wrote of the ordeal, he spoke of a presumption of guilt. Thus, Bracton saw within his lifetime a substantial change to English criminal procedure. These sentiments are mirrored in the works of Britton from the thirteenth century.[45]

Having said that, it must also be acknowledged that courts such as the Court of High Commission and Court of Star Chamber, as well as ecclesiastical courts, continued to use inquisitorial methods notwithstanding the Lateran Council's edict on trial by ordeal. If an accused failed to take an oath in these courts, they could be considered guilty, or imprisoned for contempt. If they remained silent, they could be jailed for life.[46] In effect, then, they were denied a presumption of innocence.[47]

There are numerous references to England's acceptance of the presumption of innocence in popular culture sources from the seventeenth and eighteenth centuries.[48] Many scholars commented on the related notion of it being "better" that many guilty people go free than that an innocent person be condemned.[49] Morano says this conception "incorporated the notion that the accused is presumed innocent."[50]

There are a range of views as to when the presumption became enshrined in English law. In terms of legal sources, evidence of the presumption of innocence appears in a 1293 decision of the Court of Common Pleas.[51] There is scant evidence of its use in the fourteenth to sixteenth centuries.[52] Accepting that in general legal records of this time are relatively scant and incomplete,[53] this is, at first blush, perplexing. If abolition of the ordeal and embrace of jury trial occurred in the early thirteenth century, one might have expected references to the presumption of innocence during that period. However, it should also be borne in mind that when jury trial was originally introduced, the role of jurors was to act as witnesses, with personal knowledge of the events.[54] A decision-making process relying on jurors with personal knowledge of events may not have needed presumptions regarding evidence.[55]

However, as the role of jurors changed over the years, and as the system adapted to the use of independent witnesses, as opposed to expecting jurors to act as witnesses,[56] there was a need to develop and refine rules for determining whether an accused was innocent or guilty, who should bear the onus of proof, and how much evidence should be required.[57] The timing of this evolution of the role of the jury is interesting. Whitman for instance notes that "historians have observed that jurors began to hear witness testimony in court by the fifteenth century, and especially by the sixteenth."[58] Evidence of a stricter distinction between witnesses and jurors appears in the seventeenth century,[59] and the requirement that jurors be drawn from the immediate place in which the disputed events occurred ended in 1705.[60] This requirement was redundant when jurors were not required, or expected, to have personal knowledge of the disputed events. These changes in the role of the jury would create the need for development of rules of evidence, including greater emphasis on the presumption of innocence. Holdsworth observes:

> It was during the course of the sixteenth and seventeenth centuries that the jury definitely assumed its modern functions as the judge of facts on the evidence produced to it in court. It follows, therefore, that the rules which regulate the admissibility of evidence, and exclude certain kinds of it, are a comparatively late development. In fact, their accurate definition, and the limitation on the sphere of their applicability, were the work of the eighteenth and nineteenth centuries.[61]

This, together with the relative dearth of complete materials recording English cases in the fourteenth to sixteenth centuries, might explain the relative lack of authoritative case reference to notions of presumption of innocence, though it appears to have been an accepted legal principle, and that authoritative references to it in the case law mainly commence in the eighteenth century.[62]

A 1624 speech in the House of Commons reminded listeners of the "ancient rule, every man is presumed to be innocent, till he be proved otherwise."[63] There is reference to it in 1657 in Massachusetts,[64] taken as evidence of its existence in English common law. Another scholar has claimed that the criminal trial of 1700 did not recognize a presumption of innocence,[65] and places acceptance of the presumption near the end of the eighteenth century.[66] English magistrate Henry Fielding noted in 1752 that "by the law of England all Persons were presumed innocent, till found guilty by their Country."[67] The introduction of legal representation for the defense by the mid-eighteenth century may also have played an important role in recognition of the principle.[68] English case law in the eighteenth century referred to the presumption of innocence,[69] and it was well established by the 19th.[70]

The other important point to note, as Lacey has eloquently described, is that the nature of the criminal trial itself was substantially evolving. It was moving from a system of "character responsibility" to a system of "capacity responsibility." She notes that during Blackstone's time in the mid-eighteenth century, character responsibility was extremely important. Juries formed opinions of an individual accused based on their reputation and previous conduct. That practice in turn seems to reflect Aristotlian ideas about a person being of inherently good or bad character.[71] They used such information to determine the likelihood that the accused committed this particular crime. This ties in with presumptions. Lacey describes:

> The idea that being a certain kind of person—or bearing a certain sort of status—itself grounds criminal responsibility. In this sense criminality might be seen as inhering in a type or group rather than in an individual. Within the logic of status offenses, a group membership or a given status is, presumptively or absolutely, criminal: we know criminals from the company they keep, or from the kind of person that they are.[72]

The criminal law evolved away from a system of character responsibility, whereby an accused was judged on their status or past conduct, towards a system of individual capacity responsibility, where a person's culpability for particular alleged conduct was considered. Changes in society fed this change, including the increased mobility of people, and the changed conception of juries as those having personal knowledge of the alleged events and the alleged wrongdoer, towards a more general community representativeness model. It may further be observed that criminal law has continued to evolve since that time, towards recognition of harm reduction as being a worthy goal of criminal law, where the moral culpability of an individual alleged is considered of less importance. And in most recent times, the criminal law has morphed again to emphasize risk minimization, evidenced by the rise and rise of preventive detention mechanisms in the criminal law, seeking to minimize the risk of future wrongdoing, rather than focus on past alleged wrongdoing.

Lacey thus puts acceptance and use of the presumption of innocence principle as part of English criminal law later than other scholars. She says the mid-eighteenth century trial was still based on the character responsibility model, the trial "being a chance for the defendant to explain himself or herself: the process was based not on a presumption of innocence, but rather on the assumption that the defendant was guilty . . . the key question was the defendant's reputation as a member of the law-abiding community."[73]

SYNOPSIS

If a study of legal history is a game of joining the dots, how may the above dots be joined? Firstly, we know that, notwithstanding prior practices in the *Code of Hammurabi*, and Greek and Roman times where presumption of innocence was used, for several centuries the English common law used a process of determining guilt (trial by ordeal) whereby a person who was accused was presumed to be guilty, unless the result of the ordeal indicated otherwise, and even then they would likely be subject to an unpleasant result such as abjuration of the realm, reflecting underlying suspicions of guilt, notwithstanding the result of the ordeal.

Numerous historians noted above have made this point. We also know that this system was, by and large, abolished in the early thirteenth century, and replaced by a system of jury trial. (In saying this, it must be conceded that inquisitorial procedures, including presumptions of guilt when an accused failed to respond to questions, continued until the mid-seventeenth century in some English courts.) At some point, the precise time at which is clearly contested by scholars, the common law legal system moved substantially away from its past practice of presumption of guilt, and embraced a presumption of innocence in favor of the accused.

The natural question to be asked is why the English common law swung from a presumption of guilt to the presumption of innocence. Now if the presumption of guilt fell out of the common law in the thirteenth century, roughly at the same time as the institution of jury replaced ordeals as the primary way to determine whether an accused was innocent or guilty, the natural conclusion might be that it was the change in decision maker which (eventually) precipitated the change in presumption. Specifically, was a presumption of guilt acceptable to a society when the ultimate decision as to guilt or innocence was made by God through the ordeal process, but became unacceptable when the decision making was transferred to mortals in courts? Are the two phenomena, the move from a presumption of guilt to a presumption of innocence, and a move from an irrational proof process to a system of rational proof, related? They occurred at roughly similar time, though the timing is not exact. Or was it mere coincidence, not cause and effect, that they occurred at a roughly similar time in English legal history?

Notions of Moral Comfort

At this point it is salient to refer to the work of James Whitman on English criminal procedure history. Whitman focuses on notions of reasonable doubt, in other words the standard of proof which is required in criminal cases, and the history by which that standard is reached. Now, opinions will differ regarding the extent of the relation between the presumption of innocence and notions of beyond reasonable doubt. Some say that the notion of beyond reasonable doubt is the "resultant" of the presumption of innocence, and its true origin.[74] Others might say that the two are logically distinct. The fact that one side of a dispute has an evidentiary burden to overcome (i.e., to overcome a presumption of innocence) does not *necessarily* imply the standard at which that burden must be overcome. It should also be acknowledged that some who support the presumption of innocence strongly criticize the reasonable doubt standard as being subjective.[75] However, obviously questions of the standard of proof are *at least connected* with notions of who bears the onus of proof, and any starting presumption as to guilt or innocence, in a way that might be of interest and use in the current context.

In a thought-provoking work Whitman discusses the history of "reasonable doubt" in common law and civil law systems.[76] His primary thesis is that the concept developed not, as is commonly thought, as a means of protecting an accused, but rather as a means of protecting those judging the accused, the judge and the jurors. He uses the biblical phrase from Matthew *Judge not lest ye be judged* to demonstrate the fear and anxiety with which those charged with determining an accused's fate approached their task. Specifically, they gravely feared mistakenly convicting an accused of a crime, where in those days someone convicted would often face the death penalty. They were concerned that they would suffer personal damnation if they made such an error. Christian moral theology at the time also suggested that, when in doubt, the safer option was to "do nothing."

Joseph Hall's 1654 *Cases of Conscience, Practically Resolved* noted:

> It is an evident and undeniable law of God which must be the rule of all Judges; the innocent and the righteous slay thou not (*Exod: 23:27*). This is a Law neither to be avoided, nor dispensed with. Accusations and false witnesses cannot make a man other than innocent; they may make him to seem so; in so much as those that know not the cause exactly, may perhaps be misled to condemne him in their judgments. But to the Judge, whose eyes were witnesses of the parties innocence, all the evidence in the world cannot make him other than guiltless; so as that Judge shall be guilty of blood, in slaying the innocent, and righteous.
>
> Secondly, the law of judging according to allegations and proofs is a good general direction in the common course of proceedings; but there are cases wherein this law must vaile to a higher, which is the law of Conscience. Woe be to that man who shall tye himselfe so close to the letter of the law, as to make shipwrack of conscience; and that bird in his bosom will tell him, that if upon what ever pretences, he shall wittingly condemne an innocent, he is no better than a murtherer.
>
> Let no man now tell me, that it is the law that condemnes the man, and not the Judge; This excuse will not serve before the Tribunall of heaven; The law hath no tongue; It is the judge that is lex loquens: If he then shall pronounce that sentence which his owne heart tells him is unjust and cruell, what is he but an officious minister of injustice? But, indeed, what law ever said, Thou shalt kill that man whom thou knowest innocent, if false witnesse will sweare him guilty? This is but a false glosse set upon a true text, to countenance a man in being an instrument of evil.[77]

The work of noted legal luminary of the time Sir Matthew Hale tends to support this view. In his *History of the Pleas of the Crown* he states *tutius semper est errare, in acquietando, quam in puniendo, ex parte misericordiae, quam ex parte justitiae* (it is always safer to err in acquitting, than punishing; on the part of mercy, than the part of justice); *tutius erratur ex parte mitiori* (it is always safer to err on the milder side, the issue of mercy); and *quod dubitas ne feceris* (where you are doubtful, never act). This theory might also explain the so-called "pious perjurers," jurors who refuse to convict despite the existence of strong evidence that the accused was in fact guilty, as well as other escape devices such as the benefit of clergy, and pardons.[78]

Whitman's essential thesis is that this background explains the development of the concept of "reasonable doubt" in relation to criminal matters, which he puts at approximately 1785.[79] Some scholars place it earlier, although a different phrase, such as "satisfied conscience," might have been used, and earlier standards may have been even higher than beyond reasonable doubt.[80] The standard of proof may have evolved from one of absolute certainty to one of moral certainty by the late eighteenth century.[81] While there is United States Supreme Court authority to support the idea that beyond reasonable doubt means moral certainty,[82] more recent decisions have cast doubt on the utility of continuing to use the moral certainty concept, on the basis it may be interpreted as requiring evidence that falls short of meeting the beyond reasonable doubt standard.[83]

Now, while Whitman's work was revelatory, the question is whether what it teaches us can be expanded. Whitman was focused on the historical development of the beyond reasonable doubt standard. His work does not focus on questions regarding the presumption of innocence. There are surprisingly (given the links between the identity of the person required to prove the accusation and the level at which they must prove it) very few references to the presumption of innocence in his work. However, it is suggested here that the same rationale that he uses to justify and explain the reasonable doubt standard can be applied to justify and explain adoption of the presumption of innocence many years earlier than when he says the reasonable doubt standard was adopted. In saying so, it is acknowledged that the question of who bears the onus of proof in a criminal case is different from the question of the level of proof required. An answer to one does not necessarily mandate the answer to the other. Indeed, as Langbein notes, notions of presumption of innocence predate notions of beyond reasonable doubt by centuries.[84] However, the concepts are clearly related, and what influenced one may well have influenced the other.

Specifically, it makes intuitive sense that during a period when the ultimate power to determine innocence or guilt had been transferred away from God and to mortal figures (judges and juries), these figures would be very concerned with making a mistake in decision making. They believed that the punishment for making an error, by condemning an innocent person to punishment (probably death), was eternal damnation. They were God-fearing. The moral responsibility of judging another weighed very heavily upon them. When jurors approached the task of jury service with this mind-set, a starting presumption that an accused was innocent would be entirely defensible, understandable and reasonable. It would coincide with Christian moral theology of the time that, when in doubt, a decision maker should do nothing.

In this context, it is considered reasonable to suggest that it was the introduction of the jury system, and its reposing of power to convict and condemn in mortals, that triggered the movement towards presumption of innocence in English law. This suggestion appears in the work of Beattie. After concluding that the presumption of innocence only became well established in English law in the early 1820s, he notes that

> [i]t was only then that the characteristics of the modern jury trial were beginning to emerge, and only in the nineteenth century that they took firm shape: it was then that juries came to be selected specifically for each case, that the prosecution and defense were normally managed by lawyers, that the judge invariably summed up and instructed the jury to retire and deliberate over the evidence in a frame of mind that required that they be persuaded of the prisoner's guilt beyond a reasonable doubt before convicting him. Little of that practice and few of the assumptions that underlie it are to be found in English jury trials before the nineteenth century.[85]

How else does one explain legal luminary Bracton's explanation of a presumption of guilt as applied to the ordeal, with his later evident expression of the presumption of innocence, said to be in 1260? As indicated, Whitman used a similar argument, but confined his to explaining and justifying adoption of the reasonable doubt standard, which was only adopted many years after most historians have documented acceptance of presumption of innocence. Other authors have explicitly linked the introduction of jury trial in England with abandonment of the past presumption of guilt.[86]

It is partly supported by the fact that on the European continent, which eschewed jury trial in favor of the torture of defendants as a means of determining truth and obtaining confessions, a presumption of guilt continued to be applied,[87] at least for a time. Writing of the continental situation, Pennington cites an anonymous letter written by a French jurst in 1270 as containing the first explicit formulation of a presumption of innocence. That letter in turn cited a decretal of Pope Innocent III, *Dudum,* apparently sent to the provost of Milan in 1207. Innocent told the provost that a cleric who carried a papal mandate including a benefice did not have to prove themselves worthy, because "he may be presumed worthy unless the contrary may be shown."[88]

Now, this "fit" between introduction of jury trial and the presumption of innocence is not as neat as we would like. It cannot be said that the end of most ordeals by the early thirteenth century led to an immediate abandonment of a presumption of guilt, and embrace of the reverse. It cannot be said that the introduction of the jury system led immediately to abandonment of a presumption of guilt, and embrace of the reverse. Change was much more gradual, and non-linear, than that. This was partly because the jury as initially conceived evolved substantially in its role. Understandably, the historical evidence is patchy, and as indicated above, there is broad disagreement among scholars as to precisely when it was that the English common law accepted notions of presumption of innocence. However, clearly there is a reference to use of the doctrine in a 1293 Court of Common Pleas case and in the work of Bracton in 1260. We understand that in the thirteenth century, juries were still making decisions based on personal knowledge which, together with a general lack of written historical materials from the period, might explain the dearth of reference to the concept of presumption of innocence during the fourteenth to sixteenth centuries.

We have a reference to it in parliamentary records of the early seventeeth century as being the "ancient rule," and the 1705 decision of *Regina v Best* where there is a reference to it. So it is considered reasonable to surmise that adoption of the jury system led *eventually* to the acceptance in English common law of the notion of presumption of innocence, a doctrine that had been applied in more ancient Roman and Greek times, and that it was adopted primarily because of the moral anxiety that judges and jurors felt about the act of judging another, and most especially, wrongfully convicting an innocent person, and the consequences that might attach to such a mistake. This anxiety obviously did not exist when judgments were being made by God through the ordeal. This anxiety about judging would have been strengthened (perhaps crystallized) when jurors were no longer making decisions about things of which they had personal knowledge, and when they were reliant on witnesses to bring evidence of what happened to them. This created uncertainty over the precise truth, a situation in which a presumption might be utilized. This had occurred by the sixteenth century. So it is suggested there is a cause and effect relationship between abandonment of the ordeal in English law and recognition of a presumption of innocence, even if the link is not as historically clear-cut in terms of timing as we might wish.

It may further be observed that this gradual acceptance in the common law of the presumption of innocence, and due process more generally, may well have sharpened citizens' appreciation of the egregiousness of some of the procedures being utilized in the Courts of Star Chamber and High Commission, including conclusions of guilt based on silence, which led to their eventual abolition in the mid-seventeenth century. Popular outcry about the injustice involved is commonly cited as the reason for the abolition of those courts.[89]

Hoffman traces the rise of the presumption of innocence with loss of faith in the oath. While individuals feared the oath, and believed that the consequences of lying in court was eternal damnation, there was no need for a doctrine of presumption of innocence. When faith in the oath began to wane, so did confidence in the ability of courts to determine truth, and "it is that loss of confidence in the oath that may have become the kernel at the core of the modern myth of factual innocence"[90] (a phrase he uses as a proxy for the presumption of innocence).

The other important development, as canvassed in the work of Lacey, was the gradual evolution in the criminal law from concepts of "character responsibility" to notions of "capacity responsibility." The law moved from a presumption that a person was a wrongdoer based on their community reputation and past conduct. Now, again there is not a precise linear relationship. It cannot be claimed that the presumption of innocence was adopted at the precise time that the criminal law moved from character responsibility to capacity responsibility. What can be said is that adoption of a presumption of innocence is congruent with a change in attitude in the criminal law that took place, away from character assessments in general terms, and towards consideration of specific culpability in relation to a particular allegation of wrongdoing.

Given the extent to which legislatures in the jurisdictions chosen have now departed from the presumption of innocence, as will be discussed at length in subsequent chapters, it might be lamented that as a society we have lost to some extent the moral anxiety associated with judging the guilt or innocence of one another. If it was the moral fear of the repercussions of wrongfully convicting a person that in effect gave us the presumption of innocence in the common law, it seems reasonable to conclude that the reduction in that moral fear has opened the door to legislatures acting to undermine it in common law jurisdictions, as they have. If it had not, there would be popular resentment and hostility towards legislation imposing reverse onus provisions undermining the presumption of innocence, rather than the general community attitude of apathy, assuming that most members of society are even aware of such intrusions on fundamental rights, perhaps not concerned with such erosions of basic civil liberties until the day it is applied to them, or someone close to them. Still today, however, the presumption of innocence can be justified based on our assessment that the cost of wrongly imprisoning the innocent is considered to outweigh the cost of the guilty going free, in terms of the law's moral force.[91]

Other Rationales for the Presumption of Innocence

Apart from the moral anxiety that decision makers felt, and feel, about making decisions (and, especially, wrong decisions), other rationales for the presumption of innocence may be observed.

Firstly, we understand the great stigma that society attaches to someone convicted of a crime.[92] The person will suffer punishment, including the possibility of a jail term. In some cases, this jail term might be lengthy. Any process by which a person's liberty and freedom could be taken away from them should be given serious respect.[93] A person should not decide to take away another's liberties and freedoms lightly. In extreme cases, a guilty verdict in some jurisdictions around the world can lead to administration of the death penalty. Many of those convicted of a crime will face life-long consequences of their conviction, including denial of the right to vote (particularly in the United States)[94] and denial of participation in other aspects of democratic governance, such as jury trial.[95] At a practical level, a person's ability to gain meaningful employment, or to embark on their chosen career, may be severely hampered. The person may be restricted in their ability to travel to parts of the world. The fact of their conviction may have adverse consequences for their relationship with family and friends. In short, the act of convicting a person is likely to have serious short- and long-term consequences for the person convicted. In that light, it is sensible for those charged with determining whether or not a person is guilty of a crime to approach their task with extreme caution. A presumption that the person is innocent, and is entitled to the benefit of the doubt, makes sense in that context.

Secondly, we understand the significant resource disparity between the government that accuses a person of wrongdoing, and a person accused of wrongdoing.[96] The government will have significant financial resources at its disposal in terms of running a case, including the ability to pay to obtain expert evidence regarding matters in dispute, to fund necessary searches in relation to evidence, and to retain expert counsel to argue their case in court. The government will also be a repeat player in the context of criminal prosecution. The counsel it uses to prosecute crimes will likely be experienced, having run trials in the past, and be better counsel for that experience. Junior counsel will have the benefit of being able to access more senior counsel and tap into their experience. As repeat players, they are much more likely to be aware of the rules of engagement, know how the rules work, be familiar with court process and procedure, rules of evidence and, in some cases, the relevant background of the judge hearing the case. They have significant powers of investigation at their disposal, including the use of warrants to obtain evidence and issue of subpoenas to would-be witnesses. The state can turn all of this superior knowledge and experience to its advantage.

On the other side of the case is the accused. The accused is often not experienced in the criminal justice system. They may or may not have access to legal representation, and will have to find funds to pay for it, unless provided by the government. There is very limited public funding available for criminal defense, and in some jurisdictions, funding may not be available to a particular accused, or only available in relation to more serious criminal allegations. In some cases, due to a heavy workload a government-appointed lawyer may have less time to prepare for a criminal process than the prosecutor does. The accused is likely to be unfamiliar with the rules of engagement and the "rules of the game."

They may not be familiar with court process and procedure and rules of evidence. They may find it difficult to gather evidence that would be favorable to their case. All of this can greatly compromise their ability to mount an effective defense.

This great resource disparity that is typical in a criminal case may also justify the placing of the burden of proof on the state, to prove their allegations beyond reasonable doubt, and in response to a starting presumption of innocence. The presumption would serve, at least to some extent, to ameliorate the great resource imbalance that would otherwise exist, loading the dice in favor of the prosecution and leading to a risk of incorrect convictions.

Talking of the power of the state in criminal cases, we should also acknowledge the fallibility of some of its actors in this space. Prosecutors make mistakes; on occasion they might, innocently or in some cases deliberately, suppress evidence unfavorable to their case in order to secure convictions. The police too are human and fallible. On occasion they may manipulate evidence to "fit" their preferred hypothesis. They may develop a kind of "tunnel vision," where they prematurely conclude that a particular person is guilty, and subconsciously or otherwise reach out for, or solicit, evidence that fits their vision, and discard evidence that does not fit.[97] The United States Supreme Court has noted that laboratories which produced forensic evidence used in trials were often administered by law enforcement authorities.[98] The Court noted the findings of a research report[99] suggesting that forensic scientists "sometimes face pressure to sacrifice appropriate methodology for the sake of expediency [and] may feel pressure—or have an incentive—to alter the evidence in a manner favorable to the prosecution."[100] Similar problems have been identified by Australian researchers.[101]

Others ground the presumption of innocence in notions of respect for the individual's autonomy and dignity.[102] On this argument, a liberal society[103] pays appropriate respect to its members by not deciding that a person is a wrongdoer deserving of society's condemnation and opprobrium unless there is very strong evidence that they, in fact, are.[104] Some have noted that the presumption of innocence reflects who we are as a society.[105] A presumption that an individual is good may also have religious overtones, reflecting the idea that an individual, as a person created by God, is good, at least in their original state.[106]

The role of the presumption of innocence in the protection of essential public confidence in the justice system was elaborated upon at some length by Sachs J of the South African Constitutional Court in the following terms:

> The starting point of any balancing inquiry where constitutional rights are concerned must be that the public interest in ensuring that innocent people are not convicted and subjected to ignominy and heavy sen-

> tences, massively outweighs the public interest in ensuring that a particular criminal is brought to book . . . hence the presumption of innocence, which serves not only to protect a particular individual on trial, but to maintain public confidence in the enduring integrity and security of our legal system. Reference to the prevalence and severity of a certain crime therefore does not add anything new or special to the balancing exercise. The perniciousness of the offense is one of the givens, against which the presumption of innocence is pitted from the beginning, not a new element to be put into the scales as part of a justificatory balancing exercise. If this were not so, the ubiquity and ugliness argument could be used in relation to murder, rape, carjacking, housebreaking, drug smuggling, corruption . . . the list is unfortunately endless, and nothing would be left of the presumption of innocence, save, perhaps, for its relic status as a doughty defender of rights in the most trivial of cases.[107]

Members of the United States Supreme Court expressed similar sentiments in *In Re Winship*. There Brennan J for the Court noted:

> It is also important in our free society that every individual going about his ordinary affairs have confidence that his government cannot adjudge the guilty of a criminal offense without convincing a proper factfinder of his guilt with utmost certainty . . . it is critical that the moral force of the criminal law not be diluted by a standard of proof that leaves people in doubt whether innocent men are being condemned.[108]

Farmer also reflected on the importance of criminal law in the broader political milieu of society: "It is seen as vital in the protection of social institutions and values, but its overuse, or the discriminatory application of the law to certain sectors of society, can bring the legitimacy not only of the law but also of the other political institutions of the state into question."[109]

It is considered important to bear in mind the rationale for the presumption of innocence because it can assist in the resolution of marginal cases. We will explore such cases in later chapters. However, one example at this point might suffice. Difficult issues arise involving reverse onus provisions, requiring an accused to make out a defense in order to avoid conviction, or presuming that an element of an offense has been met, unless the defendant can prove otherwise. Courts have split in determining whether such provisions are constitutionally/legally valid or not. However, at least some justices, in seeking to determine whether or not such provisions are valid, resort to at least some of the rationales for the presumption of innocence. So for example in *Patterson v New York*[110] Powell Brennan and Marshall JJ stated that the presumption of innocence doctrine required the state to prove beyond reasonable doubt (at least) every factor that substantially affected punishment and stigma.[111] It was indicated above that the stigma attached to a conviction helps to justify the presumption of innocence, as does the grave punishment which often follows conviction.

Links with Other Rights

It should also be acknowledged that the presumption of innocence links with other fundamental due process rights, as shown by human rights instruments which include the presumption of innocence in or near lists of attributes of a fair trial.[112] Specifically, the presumption of innocence is very closely linked with the right to silence. If an inference of guilt could be drawn from a person's silence at trial, this would undermine their presumption of innocence. Similarly, a reverse onus provision, which effectively compels an accused to speak on pain of punishment, undermines a person's presumption of innocence (as well as their right to silence), as will be discussed in more detail in subsequent chapters. Similarly, provisions which require that criminal charges be heard as soon as possible are linked with a presumption of innocence.[113] Because we presume that an individual is good, the fact that they have an allegation of wrongdoing against them is a serious matter, to be cleared up as soon as possible. The person may have been denied bail and may be in prison while their guilt or innocence is determined. Societal values weigh strongly against keeping a person in custody against their will, when we presume they are innocent of that of which they are accused.

Black and Douglas JJ in *Turner v United States* reflected on the links between the presumption of innocence and other due process rights in the following terms:

> [E]ach of the weapons given by the Bill of Rights to the criminal accused to defend his innocence—the right to counsel, the right to confront the witnesses against him and to subpoena witnesses in his favour, the privilege against self-incrimination—is nullified to the extent that the government, to secure a conviction, does not have to introduce any evidence to support essential allegations of the indictment it has brought. It would be a senseless and stupid thing for the Constitution to take all these precautions to protect the accused from governmental abuses if the government could by some sleight-of-hand trick with presumptions make nullities of those precautions.[114]

Meaning of the Presumption

It should also be acknowledged that the presumption can be interpreted in many different ways. For instance, Laudan distinguishes between material innocence (the defendant in a trial is materially innocent; they did not commit the crime), and probatory innocence (defendant is considered notionally innocent if the case against them does not meet the criminal standard of proof).[115] He says that the presumption of innocence should really be seen as probatory innocence, rather than material innocence. The jury must believe that the accused's guilt has not been proved, and nothing can be deduced from the fact the accused was charged, and sits in the court room accused by the state of crime. He says that material innocence in the sense described above is "at best gratuitous."[116] Similarly de Jong and van Lent assert that

> [t]he presumption of innocence is not to be equated with a factual presumption and is therefore not inconsistent with the factual suspicions that usually trigger the commencement of criminal proceedings. The presumption of innocence does not force upon the authorities an actual presumption that the suspect is innocent and therefore does not conflict with the presumption of guilt with which the criminal process commences . . . the term presumption of innocence misleadingly suggests that it is primarily concerned with actual innocence as a counterpart of actual culpability; rather, however, it is concerned with the idea of a "not yet established" culpability.[117]

Leading evidence scholar Sir Rupert Cross puts it this way: "When it is said that an accused person is presumed to be innocent, all that is meant is that the prosecution is obliged to prove the case against [the accused] beyond reasonable doubt."[118]

Now, it should be borne in mind that this is applied differently in the jurisdictions we will shortly discuss. In the United Kingdom the practice, adopted in Canada and Australia, is that the accused is presumed innocent unless and until the existence of each element of the offense is shown, together with the non-existence of any defense, excuse or justification raised by the accused.[119] The burden of persuasion always remains on the prosecution in relation to things to be proven (elements) or disproven (defense, etc.) (insanity aside). The accused may have a burden of *production* (only) in relation to particular defenses. We should contrast this position with that in the United States. Obviously, criminal law in the United States is a state matter, and a variety of practices abound. However, some states do cast the burden of *persuasion* on an accused with respect to a defense.[120]

The constitutional ability of legislatures to do this has been the subject of intense debate on the Supreme Court. For instance, a state imposed upon an individual accused the (persuasive) burden of proving a defense of self-defense in relation to a murder charge. Murder had been defined by that state as deliberately causing the death of another with prior calculation or design. A bare majority of the Supreme Court rejected a constitutional challenge to the scheme,[121] on the basis that states were free to cast a matter as a defense, and place the onus on the accused to prove it on the preponderance of the evidence. The dissentients said that the existence of facts supporting self-defense were relevant to both the defense the state had framed, as well as to the elements of the offense. It would be extremely rare that someone who was acting in self-defense had acted "with prior calculation or design." They found it constitutionally invalid to require the accused to prove self-defense, given it overlapped elements of the offense, and they were worried this would confuse a jury into thinking that it could be satisfied that at least one of the elements of the offense need not be proven by the prosecution at the level of beyond reasonable doubt. This case raises a difficult question—the extent to which legislatures are free to define, and redefine, offenses and defenses at will, and to transfer something that was traditionally a component of an offense into a defense. This will be the subject of greater examination in chapter 4. We will see that this is a grave risk to the preservation of the presumption of innocence principle across the countries studied. Some solutions to that problem will be suggested in that chapter.

CONCLUSION

In conclusion, the presumption of innocence is a principle of ancient vintage. The importance of starting with a presumption that one accused of wrongdoing is innocent, and the resultant onus of proof on accusers, can be traced back thousands of years. It was not used in England while trial by ordeal held sway in medieval times, whereby effectively a presumption of guilt applied. However, as the jury system became established, and the composition of juries adapted, a presumption of innocence was eventually recognized. However, this was a very gradual process. It was not evident immediately at the time when trial by ordeal ended, or jury trial introduced. Its recognition took centuries, and historical scholars continue to debate the most accurate estimate of the time at which it can be said that the presumption of innocence became established.

It seems easier to pinpoint recognition of a related doctrine, the concept of proof beyond reasonable doubt, in the late eighteenth century. Whitman's thesis was that that concept was explicable in terms of "moral comfort." When juries became personally responsible for judging the innocence or guilt of another, rather than it being left to divine intervention or a judge, the moral gravity of this process weighed heavily upon them. I have argued here that the presumption of innocence is best theorized in the same way—as a reflection of the moral seriousness we properly feel about judging another, and our default position of "doing nothing" in the face of doubt. I have suggested that we must recall this theoretical basis of presumption of innocence—anxiety about judging another in the presence of doubt—today. We seem to have lost this anxiety, as subsequent chapters will show. We need to return to it. There are other important theoretical rationales for the presumption of innocence, including the stigma associated with guilt, the resource disparity between state and individual, the risk of error, the respect for an individual's autonomy and dignity, the essential importance of retaining public confidence in legal institutions, and links with other due process rights that we also recognize as being important.

Thus, the presumption of innocence is of ancient vintage, whose importance has been proven over centuries. It can be theorized in many important ways. These arguments must be recalled when, in chapters 2 and 3 of this book, I outline the extent to which the presumption of innocence has been limited and marginalized in case law in the jurisdictions studied. Specifically, as we will see, legislatures have undermined the presumption by redefining offenses and defenses in unusual, nontraditional ways, and by reverse onus provisions. If courts recall the importance of the presumption of innocence, and in particular the kind of "moral comfort" doctrine that underpins it, they may have a different view of the extent to which they will permit effective departures from the presumption through the use of such mechanisms.

NOTES

1. Article 11(1) *Universal Declaration of Human Rights* (1947); Article 14(2) *International Covenant on Civil and Political Rights* (1951); Article 26 of the *American Declaration of the Rights and Duties of Man*; Article 6(2) of the *European Convention on Human Rights*; Article 8(2) *American Convention on Human Rights*; Article 7(1) *African Charter on Human and People's Rights*; s11(d) *Canadian Charter of Rights and Freedoms* (1982); s25(c) *New Zealand Bill of Rights Act* (1990); and implicit in the Fifth and Fourteenth Amendments to the United States *Constitution* (1789). In *Coffin v United States* 156 US 432, 455 (1895), White J for the Court said that "this presumption is to be found in every code of law which has reason, and religion, and humanity, for a foundation."

2. Allen Godbey, "The Place of the Code of Hammurabi," *The Monist* 15 (1905): 210; Robert Harper, *The Code of Hammurabi: King of Babylon* (Chicago University Press, Chicago, 1904), 11.

3. Robert Harper, *The Code of Hammurabi: King of Babylon* (Chicago University Press, Chicago, 1904), 11.

4. Demosthenes *Against Meidias, Androtion, Aristocrates, Timocrates, Aristogeiton* (J H Vince trans, Harvard University Press, 1935), 229–231. I am indebted to the article by Francois Quintard-Morenas, "The Presumption of Innocence in the French and Anglo-American Legal Traditions," *American Journal of Comparative Law* 58 (2010): 107, in providing me with these references to Greek and Roman law.

5. 2 Aristotle, *Problems* bk. 29.13, 144–145 (W S Hett trans, Harvard University Press, Cambridge, 1937).

6. John Langbein, *The Origins of Adversary Criminal Trial* (Oxford University Press, Oxford, 2003) 262.

7. *Code Just*. 2.1.4 (Antonin 212). In *Coffin v United States* 156 US 432, 454 (1895), White J for the Court noted that the principle of presumption of innocence "pervaded" Roman law, citing Code L, IV, T. XX, I 1, 25 for the proposition that "let all accusers understand that they are not to prefer charges unless they can be proven by proper witnesses or by conclusive documents, or by circumstantial evidence which amounts to indubitable proof and is clearer than day."

8. *Genesis* 18:23–32, where God spoke to the fact he would not destroy the city of Sodom if ten "righteous" people lived there.

9. *Digest of Justinian*, Book 48, Title 19, Clause 5 where Emperor Trajan states that a person ought not "to be condemned on suspicion, for it was preferable that the crime of a guilty man should go unpunished than an innocent man be condemned." Theodor Mommsen, Paul Krueger and Alan Watson eds, *The Digest of Justinian Vol IV* (University of Pennsylvania Press, Pennsylvania, 1985); Alexander Volokh, "n Guilty Men," *University of Pennsylvania Law Review* 146 (1997): 173.

10. *Code Just.* 4.19.25 (Gratian, Valentinian and Theodose 382): "let all accusers understand that they are not to prefer charges unless they can be proven by proper witnesses or by conclusive documents, or by circumstantial evidence which amounts to an indubitable proof and is clearer than day."

11. *Code Theod.* 9.1.19. In the early United States decision of *Coffin v United States* 156 US 432, 455 (1895), White J states: "Ammianus Marcellinus relates an ancient anecdote of Emperor Julian which illustrates the enforcement of this [presumption of innocence] principle in Roman law. Numerius, the Governor of Narbonenis, was on trial before the emperor and, contrary to the usage in criminal cases, the trial was public. Numerius contented himself with denying his guilt, and there was not sufficient proof against him. His adversary, Dephidius, 'a passionate man,' seeing that the failure of the accusation was inevitable, exclaimed 'Oh, illustrious Caesar! If it is sufficient to deny [one's own guilt] what hereafter will become of the guilty?' to which Julian replied, 'If it suffices to [do no more than] accuse, what will become of the innocent?'" (Rerum Gestarum, 1.b. 18, c.1).

12. Richard Fraher, *Ut Nullus Describatur Reus Prius Quam Convincatur': Presumption of Innocence in Medieval Canon Law?* Proceedings of the Sixth International Congress of Medieval Canon Law (1985) 493 (cited in Francois Quintard-Morenas, "The Presumption of Innocence in the French and Anglo–American Legal Traditions," *American Journal of Comparative Law* 58 [2010]: 113–114); *Decretum Gratiani de Presumptionibus*, L. II, T. XXIII, c 14, AD 1198 (cited by White J in *Coffin v United States* 156 US 432, 455 [1895]).

13. Kenneth Pennington, "Innocent Until Proven Guilty: The Origins of Legal Maxim," *The Jurist* 63 (2003): 114.

14. Kenneth Pennington, "Innocent Until Proven Guilty: The Origins of Legal Maxim," *Jurist* 63 (2003): 115. Monachus cited Innocent III's decretal *Dudum* (X 2.23.16) for the presumption of innocence, *item quilbet presumutur innocens nisi probetur nocens*. This was part of Monachus' thesis that no person could be found guilty without having been provided with the opportunity of a trial, and due process. He traced this to God's judgment of Adam from biblical times (Genesis 3: 9–12). Pennington interprets this to mean that "God could not condemn Adam without a trial because even God must presume that Adam was innocent until proven guilty."

15. Henry de Bracton, *De Legibus et Consuetudinibus Angliae* (1268), 193: "de quolibet homine praesumitur quod sit bonus donec probetur in contrarium," translated from Samuel E Thorne ed, *Bracton on the Laws and Customs of England Vol III* (Harvard University Press, Cambridge, 1977), 91, noted in Andrew Stumer, *The Presumption of Innocence: Evidential and Human Rights Perspectives* (Hart Publishing, Oxford, 2010), 2.

16. Francois Quintard-Morenas, "The Presumption of Innocence in the French and Anglo-American Legal Traditions," *American Journal of Comparative Law* 58 (2010): 114.

17. The case was brought against two Jewish men alleging they had had sexual relations with two Christian women under false pretences. The judge (Johannes de Pogiali) found the allegations had not been proven. In so doing, he concluded that "it was better to leave a crime unpunished than to condemn an innocent person," cited in Kenneth Pennington, "Innocent Until Proven Guilty: The Origins of Legal Maxim," *The Jurist* 63 (2003): 117–118.

18. Prosperus Farinacci, *Praxis et Theoricae Criminalis Libri duo in Quinque Titulos Distributi* (Frankfurt, 1606) Liber I, tit. I, quaestio XI, 141, num 9 and 143–144, num 15; Frederick von Spee, *Cautio Criminalis seu De processibus contra sagas liber* (Rinthelii, 1631) Dubium XXXIX 262–263: "I assume that no one can be condemned unless his guilt is certain: an innocent person ought not be killed. Everyone is presumed inno-

cent, who is not known to be guilty," both sources quoted in Kenneth Pennington, "Innocent Until Proven Guilty: The Origins of Legal Maxim," *The Jurist* 63 (2003): 121–122.

19. Raoul Van Caenegem, *Legal History: A European Perspective* (Cambridge University Press, Cambridge, 1991), 1.

20. Raoul Van Caenegem, *Legal History: A European Perspective* (Cambridge University Press, Cambridge, 1991), 50.

21. Ordeals including requiring the accused to carry a hot iron for a specified distance, walking over hot coals for a specified distance, requiring them to obtain an item from a cauldron of boiling water, placing the bound accused in a tub of cold water and seeing whether they sank or floated, and requiring them to eat a particular item of food, or the ordeal of the cross, requiring parties to the dispute to hold their arms up. Trisha Olson, "Of Enchantment: The Passing of the Ordeals and the Rise of the Jury Trial," *Syracuse Law Review* 50 (2000): 117–118.

22. Trisha Olson, "Of Enchantment: The Passing of the Ordeals and the Rise of the Jury Trial," *Syracuse Law Review* 50 (2000): 118.

23. Morris Hoffman, "The Myth of Factual Innocence," *Chi-Kent Law Review* 82 (2007): 677: "the myth of innocence [which that scholar approximates to the presumption of innocence] was not necessary, or even conceivable, in [ancient] systems because God told us . . . what was true and was false . . . and who was guilty, and who was innocent . . . a truth–finding system that gives witnesses, including the accused, the choice between telling the truth and suffering eternal damnation can have a high level of confidence in its accuracy, and needs no myth of factual innocence" (682); Andrew Stumer, *The Presumption of Innocence: Evidential and Human Rights Perspectives* (Hart Publishing, Oxford, 2010), 2 ("early medieval law had little use for the definitive proof of guilt since the procedure of trial by ordeal left the final declaration of the defendant's guilt to the infallible decision of God. However with the abolition of trial by ordeal . . . lawyers needed to develop principles and procedures to ensure the accuracy of fact finding"); cf James Thayer, "The Presumption of Innocence in Criminal Cases," *Yale Law Journal* 6 (1897): 189, says that the presumption of innocence (*presumitur pro neganti* or *presumitur pro reo*) "always operated for the accused."

24. Frederick Pollock and Frederic Maitland, *The History of English Law II* (Little, Brown and Company, Boston, 1895), 600–601: "a great deal of the jurisprudence of the wise has consisted in rules about the allotment of the proof. Their wisdom has consisted in ability to answer the question—these being the allegations of the parties, which of them must go to the proof and to what proof must he go? It is in the answer to this question that a nascent rationalism can make itself felt. The general rule seems to have been that the defendant must prove." The defendant would "prove" their innocence by "passing" the ordeal.

25. This is often placed as being between the ninth and thirteenth centuries. Peter Leeson, "Ordeals," *Journal of Law and Economics* 55 (2012): 693: "for 400 years the most sophisticated persons in Europe decided difficult criminal cases by asking the defendant to thrust his arm in a cauldron of boiling water and fish out a ring. If his arm was unharmed, he was exonerated. If not, he was convicted. Alternatively, a priest dunked the defendant in a pool. Sinking proved his innocence. Floating proved his guilt."

26. On numerous occasions in Robert Bartlett, *Trial by Fire and Water: The Medieval Judicial Ordeal* (Oxford University Press, USA, 1986), passages appear to the effect that the accused was required to "clear themselves" through the ordeal process (19, 96 and 125), and there is a reference to an admonition of the Council of Rheims in 1157 that an accused person might wish to "prove their innocence" by resort to the ordeal (53). Notions of a presumption of guilt are reinforced when Bartlett notes that even those who passed the ordeal were often still subject to sanction as if they were guilty (68–69). Leading historian Raoul Van Caenegem, *Legal History: A European Perspective* (Cambridge University Press, Cambridge, 1991), writing of the sixth to twelfth centuries in Western medieval law (obviously, including England), stated that "the burden of

proof usually fell on the accused; it was he who underwent the unilateral ordeal or swore the purgatory oath proclaiming his own innocence."

27. "From rumor suspicion arises and from rumor and suspicion a strong presumption, which must stand until the man indicted has purged himself of such suspicion, since it admits of proof to the contrary, that is purgation": 2 *On the Laws and Customs of England* (Samuel E Thorne trans and ed, Harvard University Press, Cambridge, 1968), 403.

28. James Fitzjames Stephen, *A General View of the Criminal Law of England* (Macmillan and Co, London, 1863) 194–195: "the jury expected from [the prisoner] a clear explanation of the case against him; and if he could not give it they convicted him."

29. R W Ireland, "The Presumption of Guilt in the History of English Criminal Procedure," *Journal of Legal History* 7 (1986): 243 (citing *Praesumptio violenta*—Bracton Fo. 137).

30. R W Ireland, "The Presumption of Guilt in the History of English Criminal Procedure," *Journal of Legal History* 7 (1986): 244.

31. R W Ireland, "The Presumption of Guilt in the History of English Criminal Procedure," *Journal of Legal History* 7 (1986): 246; Roger Groot, "The Jury of Presentment Before 1215," *American Journal of Legal History* 26 (1982): 6, who noted that when the presenting jury added that the accused was "suspected," in effect they were presumed guilty, subject to the results of the ordeal.

32. Finbarr McAuley, "Canon Law and the End of the Ordeal," *Oxford Journal of Legal Studies* 26(3) (2006): 489; see also Kurt Saunders, "Race and Representation in Jury Service Selection," *Duquesne Law Review* 36 (1997): 51, "trials by ordeal, with their presumption of guilt," and Roger Groot, "The Jury of Presentment Before 1215," *American Journal of Legal History* 26 (1982): 2, "in virtually all medieval litigation judgment precedent proof. Generally the issue was joined when the movant's complaint was met with defendant's denial. Once the issue was joined, a 'medial judgment' was entered awarding proof to one of the parties, usually the defendant"; M N Howard et al, *Phipson on Evidence* (Sweet and Maxwell, London, 1990), 91, "[i]n early times the law appears to have presumed guilt, not innocence"; William Laufer, "The Rhetoric of Innocence," *Washington Law Review* 70 (1995): 331, in discussing evolution of jury trial in England, refers to the fact that "modern standards emerged and burdens of production and persuasion shifted from the accused to the accuser" and notes that "the requirement that an accused demonstrate factual innocence became inapposite following the abolition of ordeal and other ancient modes of trial" (334); Hermine Meyer, "Constitutionality of Pre-Trial Detention," *Georgetown Law Journal* 60 (1972): 1148, "only one party could prove. In criminal cases this was always the defendant"; James Fitzjames Stephen, *A History of the Criminal Law of England* (Macmillan, London, 1883), 246, "inasmuch as the appeal was considered to raise a presumption of his guilt he was to be tried by the country as if he had been indicted," "the body of the country are the accusers. Their accusation is practically equivalent to a conviction" (252).

33. Melville Madison Bigelow, *History of Procedure in England From the Norman Conquest* (Rothman Reprints, New Jersey, 1987), 292.

34. Melville Madison Bigelow, *History of Procedure in England From the Norman Conquest* (Rothman Reprints, New Jersey, 1987), 324.

35. Melville Madison Bigelow, *History of Procedure in England from the Norman Conquest* (Rothman Reprints, New Jersey, 1987), 330; James Fitzjames Stephen, *A History of the Criminal Law of England* (Macmillan, London, 1883), 251–252; James Thayer, *Preliminary Treatise on Evidence at the Common Law* (Little Brown and Company, Boston, 1898), 38; Raoul Van Caenegem, *The Birth of the English Common Law* (Cambridge University Press, 1988), 70.

36. James Fitzjames Stephen, *A History of the Criminal Law of England* (Macmillan, London, 1883), 354.

37. The Fourth Lateran Council (1215) Canon 18 condemned use of the judicial ordeal. Four years later, King Henry III issued a directive to his judges to find an alternative method of dispute resolution, given the Church had forbidden judgments

of fire and water. James Whitman, *The Origins of Reasonable Doubt* (Yale University Press, Connecticut, 2008), 126–127.

38. John Hostettler, *The Criminal Jury Old and New: Jury Power from Early Times to the Present Day* (Waterside Press, Hampshire, 2004), 23.

39. Raoul Van Caenegem, *Legal History: A European Perspective* (Cambridge University Press, Cambridge, 1991).

40. 73.

41. 82: "the system of proofs from the later Middle Ages is fundamentally different from that of the preceding period . . . the burden of proof falls henceforth on the plaintiff. One no longer asks the accused to purge himself, but rather asks the plaintiff to produce his evidence."

42. Frederick Pollock and Frederic Maitland, *The History of English Law II* (Little Brown and Co, Boston, 1895), 602–603.

43. Frederick Pollock and Frederic Maitland, *The History of English Law II* (Little Brown and Co, Boston, 1895), 607; Frederic Maitland, *The Constitutional History of England* (Cambridge University Press, Cambridge, 1968) 130.

44. James Thayer, "The Presumption of Innocence in Criminal Cases," *Yale Law Journal* 6 (1897): 190; see also William of Ockham (1285–1349), *Dialogue* (1476) ("quia sicut unusquisque presumitur bonus nisi probetur contrarium").

45. Francis Nichols, *Britton—An English Translation and Notes* (Byrne and Co, Washington, DC, 1901), 26–27: "if the jurors are in doubt of the matter and not certain," they must acquit the accused. Morano's reading of the thirteenth century works leads to a similar conclusion: "this emphasis upon the solemnity of the jurors' duty during the thirteenth century indicates that the burden of persuasion applied in criminal cases closely approximated absolute certainty—jurors were to acquit if they had any doubts": Anthony Morano, "A Reexamination of the Development of the Reasonable Doubt Rule," 55 *Boston University Law Review* 55 (1975): 511.

46. Gregory O'Reilly, "England Limits the Right to Silence and Moves Towards an Inquisitorial System of Justice," *Journal of Criminal Law and Criminology* 85(2) (1994): 411.

47. This was noted by lawyer and member of parliament James Morice, *A Brief Treatise of Oathes Exacted by Ordinaries and Ecclesiastical Judges, to Answere Generallie to all such Articles or Interrogatories, as Pleaseth Them to Propound. And of their Forced and Constrained Oathes Ex Officio, Wherein is Proved That the Same are Unlawful* (Richard Schilders ed, 1600), 194–196. The Court of Star Chamber and Court of High Commission were abolished in 1641.

48. Sir Peter Pett, *The Happy Future State of England* (1688), 382 ("that presumption of the Civil Laws, both in our own, and all other Kingdoms . . . to wit, that every one is presumed to be good, until the contrary is proved by some outward Action"); George Herbert, *Outlandish Proverbs* (University of Illinois Reprint, 1640) ("all are presumed good, until they are found in a fault"); *The Universal Museum; or the Entertaining Repository, for Gentlemen and Ladies, Containing No Only a Number of Original Compositions, in Prose and Verse, But Also a Great Variety of Curious Pieces, Both Entertaining, Moral and Political* (1765), 149, "why then, sir, are we to condemn a minister by anticipation? By our law every man is presumed to be innocent, until the contrary appears"; 1 *The Lawyer's and Magistrate's Magazine: In Which is Included an Account of Every Important Proceeding in the Courts at Westminster* (1792), 405–406, "while I revere the law of my country, which presumes every man to be innocent till proved guilty." Again, assistance derived from Francois Quintard-Morenas, "The Presumption of Innocence in the French and Anglo-American Legal Traditions," *American Journal of Comparative Law* 58 (2010): 107, in relation to these historical references is gratefully acknowledged.

49. For example, Sir William Blackstone in 4 *Commentaries on the Laws of England 1765–1769* (Clarendon Press, Oxford, 1768) 358 (eighteenth century): "it is better that ten guilty persons should escape than that one innocent person should suffer"; Sir Matthew Hale: "it is better than five guilty persons should escape unpunished than that one innocent person should die" (seventeenth century); and Fortescue: "truly I

would rather that twenty guilty men should escape through pity than that one just man should be unjustly condemned" (fifteenth century); James Thayer, "The Presumption of Innocence in Criminal Cases," *Yale Law Journal* 6 (1897): 187; and, in the context of witchcraft trials, Richard Bernard's *Guide to Grand Jurors in Cases of Witchcraft* (London, 1627), who stated that unless the "witchcraft be very cleere [it was better] to [acquit] than upon oath to [go to full trial] and so thrust an intricate case upon a jury of simple men [who often proceeded] upon relations of meere presumptions, and these sometimes very weak ones too, to take away men's lives" (cited in Barbara Shapiro, *Beyond Reasonable Doubt and Probable Cause* [University of California Press, Berkeley, 1991] 52). James Fitzjames Stephen says that the common law's fixation on such principles, in association with the presumption of innocence, are explained by the "extreme severity of the old criminal law, and even more to the capriciousness of its severity and the elements of chance . . . introduced into its administration": *A History of the Criminal Law of England* (Macmillan, London, 1883) 439.

50. Anthony Morano, "A Reexamination of the Development of the Reasonable Doubt Rule," *Boston University Law Review* 55 (1975): 509. Similarly, in discussing the fact that presumption of innocence was accepted earlier than the beyond reasonable doubt standard, Langbein cites Fortescue, Coke and Blackstone on the "better x guilty persons go free rather than one innocent person be condemned" principle: John Langbein, *The Origins of Adversary Criminal Trial* (Oxford University Press, New York, 2002) 262.

51. "Felony is never fastened on any person before he is by judgment convicted as guilty of the deed": 2 *Year Books of the Reign of King Edward The First Years XXI and XXII* 56–57 (Alfred J Horwood ed, Longman and Co, London, 1873).

52. In *Coffin v United States* 156 US 432 (1895), White J for the Court cited the 1198 Decretum as containing the presumption of innocence. He noted there was conjecture as to when the doctrine found its way into the common law, and there was a view that there was no express reference to it in the common law until 1802. White J said whether or not that statement was true was of no moment, because "if the principle had not found formal expression in the common law writers at an earlier date, yet the practice which flowed from it has existed in the common law from the earliest time" (455).

53. George Fisher, "The Jury's Rise as Lie Detector," *Yale Law Journal* 107 (1998): 602–603.

54. Frederick Pollock and Frederic Maitland, *The History of English Law* 2 (Little, Brown and Co, Boston, 1895) 619; Frederic Maitland, *The Constitutional History of England* (Cambridge University Press, Cambridge, 1968) 122–131; Melville Madison Bigelow, *History of Procedure in England from the Norman Conquest* (Rothman Reprints, New Jersey, 1987) 335–336; James Fitzjames Stephen, *A History of the Criminal Law of England* (Macmillan, London, 1883) 259.

55. This point is also made by Barbara Shapiro in *Beyond Reasonable Doubt and Probable Cause* (University of California Press, Berkeley, 1991) 48: "like petty juries, grand juries originally required no clearly articulated evidentiary standards, for it was assumed that they would have personal knowledge of the events and persons involved"; Thomas Andrew Green, *Verdict According to Conscience: Perspectives on the English Criminal Trial Jury 1200–1800* (University of Chicago Press, Illinois, 1985) 16.

56. Frederick Pollock and Frederick Maitland, *The History of English Law* 2 (Little Brown and Co, Boston, 1895) 655.

57. Barbara Shapiro, "'To a Moral Certainty': Theories of Knowledge and Anglo-American Juries 1600–1850," *Hastings Law Journal* 38 (1986): 156; Barbara Shapiro, *Probability and Certainty in Seventeenth-Century England* (Princeton University Press, New Jersey, 1983) 183: "a sophisticated and consistent treatment of the law of evidence could not develop until the jury had ceased to be witnesses as well as judges of matters of fact."

58. James Whitman, *The Origins of Reasonable Doubt* (Yale University Press, Connecticut, 2010) 152, citing Thomas Green, *Verdict According to Conscience: Verdicts on the*

English Criminal Trial Jury 1200–1800 (University of Chicago Press, Illinois, 1985). Green compares the medieval jury, who were expected to have personal knowledge of events, with juries of the mid-sixteenth century, with much greater use of witnesses (who were not members of the jury) (108–110). John Langbein, "The Criminal Trial Before the Lawyers," *University of Chicago Law Review* 45(2) (1978): 274–275, notes jury practice in England in the period 1675–1735 where single juries dealt with large numbers of cases, evidencing the move away from the requirement that jurors have personal knowledge of the events at issue; John Hostettler, *The Criminal Jury Old and New: Jury Power from Early Times to the Present Day* (Waterside Press, Hampshire, 2004) 40: "by the fourteenth century witnesses from outside the ranks of the jury began to make their appearance in criminal cases although it was not until 1468 that Fortescue was the first judge and jurist to refer to witnesses giving evidence"; Frederick Maitland in *The Constitutional History of England* (Cambridge University Press, Cambridge, 1968) writes of the period at the time when Henry VII's reign ended (1509) that the jury system had "under[gone], without losing its identity, the great change which turned the body of neighbour witnesses into judges of the evidence given by other witnesses." James Fitzjames Stephen, *A History of the Criminal Law of England* (Macmillan, London, 1883), 265, states that the fundamental principles of trial by jury, including that jurors are no longer witnesses, were settled by the mid-fifteenth century.

59. James Bradley Thayer refers to a 1670 judgment of Vaughan CJ to the effect that "a witness swears to but what he hath heard or seen; generally or more largely to what hath fallen under his sense. But a juryman swears to what he can infer and conclude from the testimony of such witnesses by the act and force of his understanding to be the fact inquired after": *A Preliminary Treatise on Evidence at the Common Law* (Little Brown and Co, Boston, 1896) 167. Theodore Waltman concludes that by the mid-seventeenth century precautions were taken to avoid jurors making decisions based on personal knowledge: "Origins of the Legal Doctrine of Reasonable Doubt," *Journal of the History of Ideas* 20 (1959): 309; William Laufer, "The Rhetoric of Innocence," *Washington Law Review* 70 (1995): 349: "by the middle 1600s jurors were factfinders and evaluators, judging the credibility of testimony and evidence against standards of proof that had emerged from religious and philosophical sources"; Anthony Morano, "A Reexamination of the Development of the Reasonable Doubt Rule," *Boston University Law Review* 55 (1975): 511: "it was firmly established in the seventeenth century that the jury's verdict was to be based primarily upon evidence presented in court."

60. William Holdsworth, *A History of English Law* 1 (Little, Brown and Co, Boston, 1956), 332.

61. William Holdsworth, *A History of English Law* 9 (Little, Brown and Co, Boston, 1956), 127.

62. J M Beattie, *Crime and the Courts in England 1660–1800* (Princeton University Press, New Jersey, 1986), 341, suggests that until well into the eighteenth century "the prosecution was required to provide evidence that the prisoner was guilty of the charge laid. But if any assumption was made in court about the prisoner himself, it was not that he was innocent until the case against him was proved beyond a reasonable doubt, but that if he were innocent he ought to be able to demonstrate it for the jury by the quality and character of his reply to the prosecutor's evidence."

63. *House of Commons Journal* Volume 1 1547–1629 (1802).

64. *Records of Mass*, iii, 434–435 (1657), cited in James Thayer, *A Preliminary Treatise on Evidence at the Common Law* (Little Brown and Co, Boston, 1898) 552.

65. J M Beattie, "Scales of Justice: Defense Counsel and the English Criminal Trial in the Eighteenth and Nineteenth Centuries," *Law and History Review* 9 (1991): 223, speaking of a form of trial in 1700 that "did not presume the innocence of defendants, but rather that the best indication of innocence was provided by the defendant's immediate and unrehearsed responses to the evidence as it was presented."

66. "The presumption of innocence was not a rule of the criminal courts in Blackstone's day: it was not a notion that sprang readily to the lips of judges when they summed up for and instructed trial juries . . . a more positive presumption in favour of

the accused . . . was explicitly formulated in its modern form before the end of the century" (formulated by defense counsel): J M Beattie, "Scales of Justice: Defence Counsel and the English Criminal Trial in the Eighteenth and Nineteenth Centuries," *Law and History Review* 9 (1991): 248–249.

67. *The Covent-Garden Journal and a Plan of the Universal Register-Office* 84 (Bertrand A Goldgar ed, Oxford University Press, 1988 [1752]), 85; see also Thomas Branch, *Principia Legis and Aequitatis* 92 ("quisquis praesumitur bonus") (J and W T Clarke, London, 1753).

68. John Hostettler, *The Criminal Jury Old and New: Jury Power from Early Times to the Present Day* (Waterside Press, Hampshire, 2004) 87; J M Beattie, "Scales of Justice: Defence Counsel and the English Criminal Trial in the Eighteenth and Nineteenth Centuries," *Law and History Review* 9(2) (1991): 248–249; John Langbein, *The Origins of Adversary Criminal Trial* (Oxford University Press, Oxford, 2003) 258; Allyson May, *The Bar and the Old Bailey 1750–1850* (University of North Carolina Press, Chapel Hill, 2003).

69. *Regina v Best* (1705) 87 ER 941, 942 (QB) ("every man is presumed innocent until the contrary appears"); *Bird v Bird* (1753) 161 ER 78, 79: "the law presumes, on the contrary, every body to be innocent, till they are proved guilty" (Sir George Lee); and the trial judge's summing up in *Norburg's Case* (14 January 1784) in *The Proceedings of the Old Bailey* 1674–1834, 150: "[T]he laws of England is different [from other countries], and, presuming every man to be innocent until his guilt is established, it allows his guilt to be established only by evidence directly connected with the charge brought against him. . . . [T]here must be the strongest conviction in your minds that he was guilty of this offense and if there be any reasonable doubt remaining in your mind, you will give him the benefit of that doubt."

70. *Wargent v Hollings* (1832) 162 ER 1436; *N v N* (1852) 164 ER 1264; *Spill v Maule* (1869) LR 4 Ex 232, 237 (Cockburn CJ). Allyson May, *The Bar and Old Bailey 1750–1850* (University of North Carolina Press, Chapel Hill, 2003), states that the concept of the presumption of innocence was developed in the eighteenth century (233–235). Smith writes of mid-eighteenth century British statutes which imposed a presumption of guilt on those in possession of stolen goods; this suggests that the common law had embraced a presumption of innocence by this time: Bruce Smith, "The Presumption of Guilt and the English Law of Theft, 1750–1850," *Law and History Review* 23 (2005): 154–156. Similarly, J M Beattie, *Crime and the Courts in England 1660–1800* (Princeton University Press, New Jersey, 1986): "the dogma that a prisoner is to be regarded as innocent until he is proven guilty so pervades modern Anglo-American law that it is reasonable to assume that such a presumption of innocence has always been the rule at common law. In fact, the notion in its modern form arose as an active principle only toward the end of the period we are concerned with as one aspect of a complex change in the character of criminal trials. The idea that men ought actively to be regarded as innocent before being tried was being expressed in the 1780s and by 1820 it could be confidently asserted."

71. "The Nichomachean Ethics" in Richard McKeon ed, *The Basic Works of Aristotle* (Random House, New York, 1941): "every person choosed to develop good and bad character through autonomous actions. Once a person chooses their character, he or she is not free to simply undo the choice": 972–973.

72. Nicola Lacey, *In Search of Criminal Responsibility: Ideas, Interests and Institutions* (Oxford University Press, New York, 2016) 40.

73. Nicola Lacey, *In Search of Criminal Responsibility: Ideas, Interests and Institutions* (Oxford University Press, New York, 2016) 116–117.

74. *Coffin v United States* 156 US 432, 460 (1895); in *In Re Winship* 397 US 358, 363 (1970), Brennan J for the Court stated that the beyond reasonable doubt standard "provides concrete substance for the presumption of innocence"; in *Taylor v Kentucky* 436 US 478 (1978), Powell J, for Burger CJ Brennan Stewart White Marshall and Blackmun JJ, Brennan J concurring, stated the two principles were "logically similar" and that the presumption of innocence was an "implied corollary" to the beyond reason-

able doubt standard (485). In *Clark v Arizona* 548 US 735 (2006), Souter J, for Roberts CJ Scalia Thomas Alito and Breyer JJ, noted the link in the following way: "the force of the presumption of innocence is measured by the force of the showing needed to overcome it, which is proof beyond a reasonable doubt that a defendant's state of mind was in fact what the charge states" (766).

75. Larry Laudan, "The Presumption of Innocence: Material or Probatory?" *Legal Theory* 11 (2005): 352: "outside the law, standards of proof are never couched in terms of the subjective confidence of investigators . . . outside the law, rational confidence in a conjecture follows on its proof; it does not precede it . . . current practice in the United States and [elsewhere] leaves reasonable doubt either wholly undefined or defined so vaguely as to be entirely unhelpful . . . the system offers the juror no neutral or objective standard of proof . . . the intensity of the [juror's] subjective confidence in guilt determines [the outcome]."

76. James Whitman, *The Origins of Reasonable Doubt* (Yale University Press, Connecticut, 2008).

77. Case VI.

78. John Hostettler *The Criminal Jury Old and New: Jury Power from Early Times to the Present Day* (Waterside Press, Hampshire, 2004) 30; Robert Palmer, "Conscience and the Law: The English Criminal Jury," *Michigan Law Review* 84 (1986): 792; J B Weinstein, "Jury Nullification: The Contours of the Controversy," *Journal of Law and Contemporary Problems* 43 (1980): 56; Thomas Green, *Verdict According to Conscience: Perspectives on the English Criminal Jury Trial 1200–1800* (University of Chicago Press, Illinois, 1985) 34; Jack Weinstein, "Considering Jury Nullification: When May and Should a Jury Reject the Law to Do Justice?" *American Criminal Law Review* 30 (1993): 239; John Hostettler, *The Criminal Jury Old and New: Jury Power from Early Times to the Present Day* (Waterside Press, Hampshire, 2004) 97–99.

79. James Whitman, *The Origins of Reasonable Doubt* (Yale University Press, Connecticut, 2008) 4; Rupert Cross states that the beyond reasonable doubt rule was "firmly established" in the second half of the nineteenth century: *The Golden Thread of the English Criminal Law: The Burden of Proof* (Cambridge University Press, New York, 1976) 4.

80. Lord Coke, *The Third Part of the Institutes of the Laws of England* 29, 137, 210 (E and R Brooke, London, 1797), cited in Anthony Morano, "A Reexamination of the Development of the Reasonable Doubt Rule," *Boston University Law Review* 55 (1975): 512, where he concludes that Coke "stated that the defendant was adequately protected because the prosecution's evidence had to be so persuasive that there could be no defense against it"; for discussion of satisfied conscience, see Barbara Shapiro, *Beyond Reasonable Doubt and Probable Cause* (University of California Press, Berkeley, 1991) 13–18.

81. Anthony Morano, "A Reexamination of the Development of the Reasonable Doubt Rule," *Boston University Law Review* 55 (1975): 513. Morano cites the trial associated with the Boston Massacre (1770), where one justice (Justice Oliver) used the phrase "reasonable doubt" in jury directions: 518; Steve Sheppard, "The Metamorphoses of Reasonable Doubt: How Changes in the Burden of Proof Have Weakened the Presumption of Innocence," *Notre Dame Law Review* 78 (2003): 1165, 1180–1183; Thomas Starkie, *A Practical Treatise of the Law of Evidence and Digest of Proofs in Civil and Criminal Proceedings* (T and J W Johnson, Philadelphia, 1824): "what circumstances will amount to proof can never be [a] matter of general definition; the legal test is the sufficiency of the evidence to satisfy the conscience and understanding of the jury . . . it is sufficient if they produce moral certainty to the exclusion of every reasonable doubt."

82. *Wilson v United States* 232 US 563, 570 (1914).

83. *Clarence Victor v Nebraska; Alfred Arthur Sandoval v California* 511 US 1, 14–16 (1994) (O'Connor J, for Rehnquist CT Stevens Scalia Kennedy Thomas and Ginsburg JJ).

84. John Langbein, *The Origins of Adversary Criminal Trial* (Oxford University Press, Oxford, 2003) 261–262.

85. J M Beattie, *Crime and the Courts in England 1660–1800* (Princeton University Press, New Jersey, 1986) 341.

86. R W Ireland, "The Presumption of Guilt in the History of English Criminal Procedure," *Journal of Legal History* 7 (1986): 243, "if jury trial is rendering the old presumption redundant by the fourteenth century we should remember that in cases prosecuted by the appeal of felony the option of trial by combat remained with the defendant. It will not surprise us then to learn that the issue of the *violenta praesumptio* retains its significance in these cases."

87. Kenneth Pennington, *The Prince and the Law 1200–1600: Sovereignty and Rights in the Western Legal Tradition* (University of California Press, Berkeley, 1993) 43.

88. Kenneth Pennington, *The Prince and the Law 1200–1600: Sovereignty and Rights in the Western Legal Tradition* (University of California Press, Berkeley, 1993) 157. Pennington notes that it is doubtful that Innocent III intended to establish the presumption of innocence as a general legal principle, but it was used by legal scholars from the thirteenth to nineteenth centuries to justify it.

89. *Brown v Walker* 161 US 591, 597 (1896).

90. Morris Hoffman, "The Myth of Factual Innocence," *Chi-Kent Law Review* 82 (2007): 683.

91. Andrew Ashworth, "Four Threats to the Presumption of Innocence," *International Journal of Evidence and Proof* 10 (2006): 249.

92. *In Re Winship* 397 US 358, 363 (1970) (Brennan J, for the Court); *R v Oakes* [1986] 1 S.C.R 103, 120 (Dickson CJ, for Chouinard Lamer Wilson and Le Dain JJ).

93. Richard Lippke, *Taming the Presumption of Innocence* (Oxford University Press, London, 2016) 106; and historically, James Fitzjames Stephen, *A History of the Criminal Law of England* (Macmillan, London, 1883) 354: "society in the present day is so much stronger than the individual, and is capable of inflicting so very much more harm on the individual than the individual as a rule can inflict upon society, that it can afford to be generous."

94. Data from the Sentencing Project indicates that existing United States laws deny the right to vote to approximately six million individuals due to their criminal record, with about 45 percent of such individuals having completed their sentence: *Felony Disenfranchisement Laws in the United States* (the Sentencing Project); *The Impact of Felony Disenfranchisement Laws in the United States* (the Sentencing Project); Alec Ewald, "Civil Death: The Ideological Paradox of Criminal Disenfranchisement Laws in the United States," *Wisconsin Law Review* (2002): 145; Anthony Gray, "Securing Felons' Voting Rights in America," *Berkeley Journal of African-American Law and Policy* 16 (2014): 1. Constitutional challenges to felon disenfranchisement laws have been unsuccessful: *Richardson v Ramirez* 418 US 24 (1974).

95. Thirty-one American states permanently preclude an ex-felon from participating in jury service: James Binnall, "EG 1900 . . . The Number They Gave Me When They Revoked My Citizenship: Perverse Consequences of Ex-Felon Civic Exile," *Willamette Law Review* 44 (2008): 667, 669–670.

96. Andrew Stumer, *The Presumption of Innocence: Evidential and Human Rights Perspectives* (Hart Publishing, Oxford, 2010) 34.

97. Kent Roach, "Wrongful Convictions in Canada," *University of Cincinnati Law Review* 80 (2012): 1465, 1502–1508; Richard Lippke, *Taming the Presumption of Innocence* (Oxford University Press, London, 2016) 111.

98. *Melendez-Diaz v Massachusetts* 557 US 305 (2009).

99. National Research Council of the National Academies, *Strengthening Forensic Science in the United States: A Path Forward* (2009) 183–184.

100. *Melendez-Diaz v Massachusetts* 557 US 305, 318–319 (2009) (Scalia J, for Stevens Souter Thomas and Ginsburg JJ).

101. "Many of the substantial problems with forensic science and medicine seem to be methodological, statistical or linked to subtle forms of contamination. Whether we

can expect lay individuals to follow critiques in these areas, or fully appreciate how they might undermine the probative value of incriminating opinion evidence, is open to doubt . . . where such evidence is not challenged, we can confidently assume that juries will generally have few, if any, ideas about the evidentiary limitations or magnitudes of risks. In many situations, liberal admissibility standards will systematically advantage the state with little evidence of corresponding improvements in the accuracy of decisions": Gary Edmond and Andrew Roberts, "Procedural Fairness, the Criminal Trial and Forensic Science and Medicine," *Sydney Law Review* 33 (2011): 370.

102. Laurence Tribe, "Trial by Mathematics: Precision and Ritual in the Legal Process," *Harvard Law Review* 84 (1971): 1329, 1370–1374: "a rule which requires the prosecution to prove the guilt of an accused in the course of an ordinary judicial proceeding . . . ensures that the prosecution must treat the accused as an innocent person whose rights as a human being must be respected"; *R v Oakes* [1986] 1 S.C.R 103, 119: "the presumption of innocence protects the fundamental liberty and human dignity of any and every person accused by the state of criminal conduct" (Dickson CJ, for five members of the Court); Markus Dubber, "Towards a Constitutional Law of Crime and Punishment," *Hastings Law Journal* 55 (2004): 509.

103. Ian Dennis, "The *Human Rights Act* and the Law of Criminal Evidence: Ten Years On," *Sydney Law Review* 33 (2011): 354.

104. Victor Tadros, "The Ideal of the Presumption of Innocence," *Criminal Law and Philosophy* 8 (2014): 458; Andrew Ashworth and Lucia Zedner, "Defending the Criminal Law: Reflections on the Changing Character of Crime, Procedure and Sanctions," *Criminal Law and Philosophy* 2 (2008): 22; Hamish Stewart, "The Right to Be Presumed Innocent," *Criminal Law and Philosophy* 8 (2014): 408–410.

105. Sherman Clark, "The Juror, the Citizen and the Human Being: The Presumption of Innocence and the Burden of Judgment," *Criminal Law and Philosophy* 8 (2014): 421, 429, noting that "how we judge is recognised as saying something important about who we are. And it does"; Andrew Ashworth, "Four Threats to the Presumption of Innocence," *International Journal of Evidence and Proof* 10 (2006): 249: "the presumption of innocence is a moral and political principle, based on a widely shared conception of how a free society (as distinct from an authoritarian society) should exercise the power to punish"; D A Nance, "Civility and the Burden of Proof," *Harvard Journal of Law and Public Policy* 17 (1994): 647; *R v Oakes* [1986] 1 S.C.R. 103, 120, noting that the presumption of innocence "is essential in a society committed to fairness and social justice" (Dickson CJ, for five members of the Court).

106. Joseph Cascarelli, "Presumption of Innocence and Natural Law: Machiavelli and Aquinas," *American Journal of Jurisprudence* 41 (1996): 229; Marvin Fox, *Interpreting Maimonides: Studies in Methodology, Metaphysics, and Moral Philosophy* (University of Chicago Press, Illinois, 1992) 190; obviously those with a Hobbesian or Machiavellian view of human nature would not accept this justification for a presumption of innocence.

107. *State v Coetzee* [1997] 2 LRC 593, 677–678.

108. 397 US 358, 364 (1970); and see Charles Nesson, "Reasonable Doubt and Permissive Inferences: The Value of Complexity," *Harvard Law Review* 92 (1979): 1195: "the strategy of the system is to seek the observers' acceptance of the jury as a surrogate decision maker, trusted because it is understood to be an impartial, responsible and representative body, operating in a fair and structured system and deciding according to an exceedingly strict standard of guilt"; Andrew Stumer, *The Presumption of Innocence: Evidential and Human Rights Perspectives* (Hart Publishing, Oxford, 2010) 38: "the presumption of innocence is essential to ensure that people do not lose confidence in the justice system."

109. Lindsay Farmer, *Making the Modern Criminal Law: Criminalization and Civil Order* (Oxford University Press, Oxford, 2016) 13.

110. 432 US 197 (1977).

111. 226.

112. For instance, s14(2) and s14(3) *International Covenant on Civil and Political Rights;* Articles 6(1) and (2) *European Convention on Human Rights;* Article 8(2) *American Convention on Human Rights;* s11 *Canadian Charter of Rights and Freedoms;* s25 *New Zealand Bill of Rights Act 1990.*

113. For example, S14(3)(c) *International Covenant on Civil and Political Rights; Sixth Amendment* to the United States *Constitution;* s11(b) *Canadian Charter of Rights and Freedoms;* s25(b) *New Zealand Bill of Rights Act 1990; Betterman v Montana* 136 S.Ct 1609, 1614 (2016): "the speedy trial clause implements that presumption [of innocence] by preventing undue and oppressive incarceration prior to trial, . . . minimizing anxiety and concern accompanying public accusation, and . . . limiting the possibilities that long delay will impair the ability of an accused to defend himself" (Ginsburg J, for a unanimous court) (internal quotation marks removed).

114. 396 US 398, 430 (1970).

115. Larry Laudan, "The Presumption of Innocence: Material or Probatory?" *Legal Theory* 11 (2005): 339.

116. 350.

117. Ferry de Jong and Leonie van Lent, "The Presumption of Innocence as a Counterfactual Principle," *Utrecht law Review* 12(1) (2016): 32.

118. *Cross on Evidence.*

119. Andrea Tuck-Jackson, "The Defence of Due Diligence and the Presumption of Innocence," *Criminal Law Quarterly* 33 (1991): 29.

120. Byron Sheldrick, "Shifting Burdens and Required Inferences: The Constitutionality of Reverse Onus Clauses," *University of Toronto Faculty of Law Review* 44(2) (1986): 189; an example is the legislation considered in *Patterson v New York* 432 US 197 (1977), where the Court validated a state law creating an "affirmative" defense of "extreme emotional disturbance" which the accused was required to show on the preponderance of the evidence. Refer to chapter 2 for further discussion of the case.

121. *Martin v Ohio* 480 US 228 (1987) (White J, for Rehnquist CJ Stevens O'Connor and Scalia JJ; Powell J, for Brennan Marshall and Blackmun JJ, dissenting).

TWO

United States Case Law

This chapter will summarize, discuss, and critique United States Supreme Court jurisprudence concerning the presumption of innocence. It is considered necessary to provide an account of the important case law in this field, before offering some critical comments regarding the existing state of United States jurisprudence in this area. Criticism must be informed by a sound understanding of the principles concerned, so it is logical to begin with a concise description of how those principles have evolved over the years. This will permit a critical comparison with other jurisdictions studied, to determine common strengths, pathologies in the existing jurisprudence, continuing problems and weaknesses, and specific ways in which the existing case law doctrine could be improved. Further, readers who are not from the United States may be quite unfamiliar with the United States case law.

In contrast to more modern constitutions and human rights instruments, the United States *Constitution* does not expressly refer to the presumption of innocence. However, the presumption has long been considered as being implicitly protected by the due process requirement of the *Fifth Amendment* to the United States *Constitution*, and the due process requirement is applicable to the states through the *Fifth* and *Fourteenth Amendments*.

OUTLINE OF CASES

The Court briefly discussed the presumption of innocence in *Cummins v Missouri*. Missouri state legislation required those wishing to hold public office, or to work in various occupations and callings, to make an oath of loyalty to the Missouri *Constitution*. A person who failed to do so would vacate their office and/or be unable to practice in particular fields. The

Court invalidated the legislation on retrospectivity and bill of attainder grounds, but also found that the provisions offended the presumption of innocence. They described that principle as a "universally recognized principle of the common law [and] supposed to be fundamental and unchangeable."[1]

The Court validated legislation providing for the deportation of Chinese individuals out of the United States without typical due process protections.[2] For instance, one section provided that Chinese individuals arrested under the act would be judged to be unlawfully within the United States, unless they could show by affirmative proof to the satisfaction of the court that they had a lawful right to remain. In validating the legislation, the majority stated that it was within the power of a legislature to make provision for rules of evidence in their courts. The dissentients pointed out various ways in which the legislation did not accord individuals due process protections, including imposing a burden of proof on the individual to prove particular matters, on pain of punishment if they did not do so.

Soon after, the Court validated court directions to a jury that where an accused had in his possession property belonging to the deceased victim shortly after the victim's apparent murder, an inference could be made that the possession was "guilty possession."[3] Although this was only prima facie evidence, the Supreme Court found it could be of controlling weight unless explained by the circumstances or otherwise accounted for in a way consistent with the accused's innocence. Similarly, the Supreme Court found that "destruction, suppression or fabrication" of evidence "undoubtedly [gave] rise to a presumption of guilt" for the jury to consider.[4]

A presumption that a person in possession of materials typically used to play an illegal gambling game was guilty of a gaming offense was validated in *Adams v New York*.[5] The Court found it was unlikely that an innocent person would have possession of such material, given their distinctiveness. Further, the material was often found in large quantities, making innocent possession even more unlikely. The Court noted that innocent individuals would have no trouble explaining their innocence, and that the presumption was prima facie evidence only, the accused being given an opportunity to rebut the inference.

The first Supreme Court decision to consider the presumption of innocence in detail was *Coffin v United States*.[6] There it was said that the trial judge has mistakenly refused to instruct the jury on the concept of presumption of innocence, their comments being confined in that context to notions of beyond reasonable doubt. In overturning the guilty verdict due to the inadequate jury directions, White J for the Court noted the presumption of innocence was "axiomatic and elementary, and its enforcement lies at the foundation of the administration of our criminal law."[7] The judgment refers to the placement of the presumption of innocence in Roman law, and acknowledged the role of canon law in its preservation and spread.[8] It suggested that even if express reference to it in the common law was originally sparse, it was an established practice in common law "from the earliest time."[9] White J concluded the presumption "is to be found in every code of law which has reason, and religion, and humanity, for a foundation."[10] He drew some express links between notions of presumption of innocence, stating that the "true origin" of the beyond reasonable doubt standard was the presumption of innocence.[11]

A reverse onus provision considered in the relatively rare context of a civil case occurred in *Mobile, Jackson and Kansas City Railroad Company v Turnipseed, Administrator*.[12] There the Court rejected a constitutional challenge to legislation that cast a reverse onus of proof on a railway company in cases where a person had been injured by a rail carriage, and negligence was alleged. The Court noted the general competence of legislatures to enact rules of evidence, including those permitting proof of one fact to constitute prima facie evidence of another. This is the first case in which the concept of rational connection appears in this context. There the court said that a due process challenge to a legislative presumption would be unsuccessful where "there shall be some rational connection between the fact proved and the ultimate fact presumed, and . . . the inference of one fact from proof of another shall not be so unreasonable as to be a purely arbitrary mandate."[13] The Court insisted also that any presumption not effectively prevent a party from presenting their evidence as to the main fact/s in dispute. Here, it was not an unreasonable inference that a derailment of railway cars was caused by the railroad's negligence.[14]

In a later case applying the rational connection test, the Court found a legislature could not, consistent with due process, declare an individual to be guilty, or presume an individual to be guilty, of a crime.[15]

The Court considered a permissive inference in *Bailey v State of Alabama*.[16] There an offense comprised four elements, including intent.[17] Given the practical difficulties involved in proving intent, an amendment provided that a refusal to perform the service, or to refund the money received, without just cause was prima facie evidence of the required intent to injure or defraud. The Court found there was no evidence as to the accused's intent, and that apart from the amendment, they would not have been convicted of the offense.[18] It was no answer to constitutional concern to say that the jury may not accept the presumption as creating sufficient evidence to convict; the point was that the jury may do so.[19] While legislatures had general power to prescribe rules of evidence, this was subject to constitutional requirements. The Court would not permit constitutional prohibitions to be circumvented via sleight of hand by the legislation drafter.[20] Similarly, a legislature could not be permitted to do indirectly what it was precluded from doing directly.[21]

The Supreme Court validated citizenship legislation containing a presumption.[22] An applicant for citizenship had to demonstrate intention to reside permanently within the United States. After a particular applicant obtained US citizenship, he moved permanently to South Africa. The legislation provided that this was prima facie evidence of a lack of intention on the applicant's part to become a United States citizen. The Court validated the provision, on the basis it was a rebuttable presumption, and that the legislature was merely providing for a rule of evidence, as opposed to legislating upon a substantive right. The Court stated that the applicant was free to lead evidence contrary to the presumption, and noted that "these are matters of which he possesses full, if not special, knowledge."[23] There was a reasonable basis for the presumption.[24]

The Supreme Court emphasized that statutory presumptions could not be arbitrary or effectively operate to deny a person accused of wrongdoing a fair opportunity to rebut it.[25] A statutory presumption had to be reasonable and not irrebuttable. It reconfirmed that legislative fiat could not replace the role of the judicial arm of government in fact finding.[26] For these reasons, legislation which presumed that every insolvency of a bank was fraudulent, and the company president and directors imprisoned, unless they could show that the business was fairly administered, did not meet due process standards. The accused could not effectively counter the presumption since the legislation did not prescribe particular elements of an offense, rather relying on vague, generalized concepts. The accused's indictment did not specify particular allegations of wrongdoing, making it difficult for the accused to effectively mount a defense.[27]

The Court during this era considered the possibility that statutory presumptions could, in effect, abrogate the accused's privilege against self-incrimination. For example, a statute created an offense of concealing opium, knowing it had been unlawfully imported. A statutory presumption stated that a person in possession of such substance was deemed to be aware of its unlawful importation, unless they showed otherwise. In validating the presumption, the Court said that it left the accused free to testify or not to testify. It did not affect constitutionality that the accused might be the only one with practical knowledge as to the matter. The Court also reiterated here that, "Every accused person . . . enters upon his trial clothed with the presumption of innocence. But that presumption may be overcome, not only by direct proof, but, in many cases, when the facts standing alone are not enough, by the additional weight of a countervailing legislative presumption."[28] The Court seemed to suggest that presumptions were more likely to be valid when they involved personal matters of knowledge: "It is consistent with all the constitutional protections of accused men to throw on them the burden of proving facts peculiarly within their knowledge and hidden from discovery by the Government."[29]

The Court considered the matter again in *Morrison v California*.[30] The offense alleged a conspiracy to own certain land when one of the owners was an alien, and thus not generally legally permitted to own the land at the time. The legislation cast the onus on an individual to prove they were a United States citizen, rather than the state to prove they were an alien. In *Morrison* the Court suggested some new limits on the use of statutory presumptions. It said that the state must have been required to prove sufficient so that it was just for the defendant to meet the case made against them.[31] It would be necessary that the balance of convenience or opportunities for knowledge supported the transfer of the burden, and such a transfer would not cause the accused hardship or oppression.[32] The Court found that with respect to a statutory presumption, constitutional limits included that the fact proven must at least be a "warning signal" as to the thing inferred, according to the teachings of experience.[33] The thing proven would have to have at least a "sinister significance,"[34] or there must a "manifest disparity in convenience of proof and opportunity for knowledge."[35] The Court also considered the subject matter to which the presumption related. In this case it related to questions of citizenship. The Court found that because citizenship was a privilege rather than a common right, it was fair to call on someone claiming to be a citizen to prove it.[36]

The presumption of innocence was considered again in *Tot v United States*.[37] There the challenged federal legislation made it an offense for a convicted person or a fugitive from justice to receive any firearm or ammunition which had been transported in interstate or overseas commerce. The provision expressly contained a presumption that possession of such firearm or ammunition was transported in violation of the act, and that such transportation occurred after the date at which the act became effective. The act was written in such a way to try to make it constitutional, relying on Congress's commerce clause, and so as not to make the law retrospective in operation, which would likely also have drawn constitutional challenge.

The Court invalidated the provision.[38] In so doing, it found that a statutory presumption would not be valid if there was no rational connection between the fact proved and the ultimate fact presumed.[39] If there was no such connection, if it did not relate to "circumstances of life as we know them," the inference from one to the other would be arbitrary.[40] A legislature could not validly create such a rule. Applying such tests, neither presumption in the challenged legislation could be upheld. There was no reasonable ground for a presumption that a given firearm or ammunition was derived from interstate or overseas, or that such transportation occurred after the date at which the legislation commenced.[41]

The Court also addressed an argument that a presumption was valid as to an issue where it was more convenient for the accused to present evidence on the matter; in other words, that they had the better means of knowledge of the matter. Earlier in *Luria* the Court had referred to this as being apparently relevant. The Court here clarified that this was not an alternative basis for the acceptance of presumptions in innocence; it was better seen as a corollary of the primary rule around rational connection.[42] Specifically, imposition of an onus of proof on an accused (through a presumption against them) could not be justified solely on the basis that the accused had the better means of knowing the truth as to that matter. While it may be true that the accused had the better means of knowing the truth of a matter, the presumption would still need to be shown to be a permissible one. It would also need to be shown that in fact, they did have the better means of accessing evidence on the matter, and that requiring them to produce such evidence would not subject them to hardship or unfairness.[43]

The Court considered the specific question of intent and statutory presumptions in *Morissette v United States*.[44] The accused was charged with stealing after he ventured onto government property to retrieve spent bomb castings from government property on which individuals hunted game. The specific charge was knowingly stealing and converting government property. The accused's defense was that he did not have the required intent, believing he was entitled to retrieve the casings because they did not belong to anyone. The trial judge stated to the jury that this was no defense. He told them that the question regarding intent was whether "the accused intended to take the property." The accused appealed his conviction on due process grounds.

The Court referred to the "ancient requirement of a culpable state of mind" in relation to criminal behavior.[45] It was "as universal and persistent in mature systems of law as belief in the freedom of the human will."[46] The Court referred to Blackstone's statement that to constitute a crime there must be a "vicious will."[47] The Court noted that traditionally, criminal behavior was constructed from an "evil-meaning mind with an evil-doing hand."[48] State statutes that omitted the intention requirement for criminal offenses did not signify disapproval or departure from the traditional intent requirement. The idea that wrongdoing must be conscious was deeply embedded in the criminal law.[49] The Court also acknowledged that increasingly legislatures had introduced regulatory structures, particularly around industry, in order to protect the public. Often, defined wrongdoing here involved neglect, and intent was in some ways academic, because the focus was on preventing the harm, rather than punishing the wrongdoer.[50]

The Court acknowledged it had never attempted to construct a dividing line between crimes that required a mental element, and those that did not.[51] However, in relation to the current offense of stealing, the criminal law had traditionally insisted upon proof of intent, and the offense charged here should be read as if to include an intent requirement.[52] The legislature was assumed to have been aware of, and embraced, all of the legal tradition surrounding the construct of particular offenses; specifically here, that stealing required intent.[53]

Here, on the basis that intention was in fact an element of the crime charged, its existence or otherwise had to be submitted to, and found by, a jury. It was not acceptable for the trial judge to presume it, or to instruct the jury to presume it, from the mere fact the accused took the property.[54] The trial judge presented the presumption as being a conclusive one, which the jury was not at liberty to ignore. This took from the jury a live issue which they should have deliberated upon, and reached their own conclusions. Even if the judge's directions were viewed as non-conclusive, and the jury took into account the presumption as one fact, it assisted in the prejudgment of a live issue. It might have the effect in the jury's mind of tipping the balance in favor of conviction, when otherwise they favored acquittal. Either way, the accused's right to presumption of innocence was compromised.[55]

The Court took a similar attitude to the absence of an express reference to intent in antitrust provisions the subject of challenge in *United States v United States Gypsum Co et al.*[56] There the jury was instructed that if they found as a fact that competitors were exchanging information and that this had had the effect of raising prices, they should presume as a matter of law that this result was intended. The Court rejected such an approach. As it had done in *Morissette,* it reflected on the importance of mens rea as a principle underpinning the American system of criminal justice.[57] Intention was generally an indispensable element in a criminal offense. Thus, they interpreted the antitrust provisions to require proof of intent, and found that this was an issue that had to be found by the fact finder, and should not be the subject of an irrebuttable presumption. A permissive inference of such intent could be drawn from the swapping of information and effect on prices, but had to be left to the fact finder for ultimate resolution.[58]

In *Speiser v Randall*[59] the Supreme Court considered the validity of California property tax provisions. These provisions permitted an exemption from taxes to veterans, but on the condition that they specify that they did not advocate the overthrow of the government. A particular claimant sought the exemption but refused to make the requested specification. He was denied the exemption. He argued that such state behavior contravened his right to presumption of innocence, as well as infringing his *First Amendment* expression rights.

Whilst this was a non-criminal context, the Court upheld the importance of presumption of innocence. They reiterated its importance in cases involving "transcending values," in many cases an individual's liberty, but including other fundamental values, such as freedom of speech, implicated in this case. The Court was concerned with the possible chilling effect on conduct of reverse onus provisions in the current context:

> The man who knows that he must bring forth proof and persuade another of the lawfulness of his conduct necessarily must steer far wider of the unlawful zone than if the State must bear these burdens. This is especially to be feared when the complexity of the proofs and the generality of the standards applied . . . provide but shifting sands on which the litigant must maintain his position. How can a claimant whose declaration is rejected possibly sustain the burden of proving the negative of these complex factual elements?[60]

So in this case, one of the reasons why the reverse onus provision was struck out was the practical difficulty for the accused involved in proving a complex matter in the negative.

In *United States v Gainey*[61] the Court considered the validity of provisions deeming elements of an offense to have been committed, unless the accused showed to the contrary. The accused had been charged with offenses involving (a) possession, custody or control of an unregistered still and distilling apparatus, and (b) carrying on the business of a distiller without having paid the required bond. Statutory provisions permitted a jury to infer guilt of the offenses from the fact of a defendant's unexplained presence at the site of the illegal still. The Court noted that prosecutors had in the past found it very difficult practically to prove that a particular accused has participated in unlawful still activity. Further, lower courts had split on the weight to be given to unexplained presence at an illegal still, in relation to possible criminal offense.

In this light, a majority of the Court found that Congress was entitled to enact the statutory presumption. It passed the "rational connection" test. The majority noted that the application of this test was highly empirical, and typically Congress would be in the better position to make this kind of assessment, rather than the courts.[62] However, the majority noted that the presumption was rational, finding that manufacturers of illegal liquor were notorious for their skill in finding unexpected places to ply their trade, and "the folklore teaches . . . that strangers to the illegal business rarely penetrate the curtain of secrecy."[63] Nor did the provision impinge on judicial power. The judge retained substantial discretion, as did the jury; the presumption was permissive, not mandatory or conclusive. It was one circumstance, among many, to be considered.[64]

Strong dissents were written by Black and Douglas JJ. Black J noted that statutes creating presumptions needed to be considered on an individual basis, rather than as a collective. There would be most concern with such a presumption in the case of a criminal trial.[65] Black J said that even if a presumption is rational, it could not be used to convict a person of a crime if it meant that the accused's constitutional rights had been sacrificed.[66] Here, while presence at an illegal still was relevant to the question of whether the accused had committed the crimes of which they had been charged, it was not sufficient, in the absence of supporting evidence, to permit a finding that the accused had committed the crimes charged at the level of beyond reasonable doubt.[67] He dismissed use of a reverse onus provision with respect to an element of a crime as a "boon to prosecutors and an incongruous snare for defendants."[68] Black J also noted separation of powers issues with the legislation, finding that it was the role of courts, not legislatures, to resolve facts.[69] Black and Douglas JJ found that the reverse onus provision in substance interfered with the accused's right to remain silent at their trial, and not to have adverse inferences drawn from their decision to do so. In effect, the provision presuming existence of an element of a crime against the accused compelled them to testify.[70]

Somewhat similar legislation was held to be invalid in *United States v Romano et al.*[71] There the accused were convicted of possession, custody and control of an illegal still (first charge), illegal production of distilled spirits (second charge), and conspiracy to produce (third charge). The challenged provisions stated that the presence of the accused at the site of an illegal still was sufficient evidence to authorize conviction, unless the accused explained such presence to the jury's satisfaction. These provisions were read word for word to the jury. The challenge was to a conviction on the first charge.

All members of the Court found that the accused's conviction on the first charge should be overturned. The Court found that there was sufficient evidence that the accused was guilty of the first charge. However, it was troubled by the fact that the jury was instructed that presence at the still was deemed by the legislation to be sufficient evidence that the offense of possession, custody and control had been committed. Obviously no one could say for sure, but it was possible that a jury might have accorded the presumption substantial weight.

Applying the rational connection test, the Court found that it was constitutionally unacceptable to infer commission of the offense of possession, custody and control from mere presence. It found that presence likely indicated that the accused played a part in the illegal business; however, it was silent as to the accused's precise role. Specifically, the Court found it carried "no legitimate, rational or reasonable inference that [the accused] was engaged in one of the specialized functions connected with possession."[72] The fact of presence was probative evidence on the charge of possession, custody and control, but its connection with the offense was too tenuous to support the making of the presumption that the legislation deemed. In no other case had mere presence been sufficient to support a possession charge.

The rational connection test was considered further in *Leary v United States*.[73] There the accused was charged with knowingly, with intent to defraud the government, importing into the United States marijuana contrary to law, or facilitating transportation, concealment or sale of such marijuana after being imported or brought in, knowing it to have been illegally imported. The offense provision stated that where an accused was shown to have marijuana in their possession, such possession shall be deemed sufficient to authorize conviction, unless the accused explained such possession to the jury's satisfaction. In other words, the presumption could be used to help prove requirements of illegal importation, and knowledge of such fact.

The main joint reasons explained that under the rational connection test, it had to be said with substantial assurance that the presumed fact was more likely than not to flow from the fact proven.[74] Here, the law did not meet the rational connection test. Evidence suggested that a substantial quantity of marijuana in circulation in the United States had been grown locally. As a result, the fact of possession could not be rationally connected with the fact that the particular drug had been imported. Further, even if the drug had been imported, that fact could not be used to show rationally that the possessor knew of its importation.[75] The main joint reasons also considered that the argument that it was not unreasonable to cast a burden on an accused where they were likely to have the better means of knowing the truth of a particular matter had been rejected in *Tot*.[76] In a concurrent judgment, justices again raised separation of powers concerns with reverse onus provisions.[77]

Presumptions in the context of drug offenses were also considered in *Turner v United States*.[78] There the accused was charged with receiving, concealing and facilitating transportation of heroin knowing that it had been unlawfully imported. A similar offense was alleged in relation to cocaine ("receiving offenses"). There were also allegations that the accused had purchased, possessed, dispensed and distributed heroin contrary to laws requiring packages to be stamped, in relation to both the heroin and cocaine ("stamp offenses"). One statutory presumption stated that possession of the drug was deemed sufficient evidence of the commission of the receiving offenses, unless the accused explained the possession to the jury's satisfaction. Another stated that the absence of tax paid stamps on a package was prima facie evidence of commission of the stamp offenses.

The majority judgment noted that different tests had been suggested in relation to application of the rational connection test—that of the more-likely-than-not standard, and the reasonable doubt test. It did not express a preference for either test,[79] but proceeded to apply the more-likely-than-not test.[80]

A majority of the Court upheld the conviction with respect to the heroin receiving offense, but overturned the conviction with respect to the cocaine receiving offense. This was due to the existence of evidence that little to no heroin was produced locally in the United States, whereas there was evidence that substantial quantities of cocaine were produced locally.[81] It was not more-likely-than-not that a person in possession of cocaine would know it had been illegally imported. As a result, logically a person in possession of heroin would have known that it had been imported, in a way that a person in possession of cocaine would not have known.[82]

These facts affected the decision on the stamp offenses as well. Given that all heroin in the United States would have been illegally imported at some stage, a person in possession of heroin would not have obtained it from a stamped package. As a result, the conviction for the stamp offense in relation to the heroin was valid.[83] However, it was different for the cocaine. This drug was legally manufactured in the United States. There was evidence that cocaine was stolen from legal channels. As a result, there was a reasonable possibility that Turner stole it, or obtained it from someone who obtained it in a stamped package. As a result, that conviction could not stand.[84]

Black J, with whom Douglas J joined, wrote a stirring dissent. He commenced with an observation that there were few Supreme Court decisions that did more to undercut the due process safeguards in the United States *Bill of Rights* than the majority opinion. He noted that the prosecution did not lead evidence on two of the three elements of some of the offenses with which the accused had been charged (illegal importation, and knowing illegal importation):

> Apparently the court feels that the government can be relieved of the constitutional burden of proving the essential elements of its case by a mere congressional declaration that certain evidence shall be deemed sufficient to convict. Such an idea seems to me to be totally at variance with what the *Constitution* requires. Congress can undoubtedly create crimes and define their elements, but it cannot under our *Constitution* even partially remove from the prosecution the burden of proving at trial each of the elements it has defined. The fundamental right of the defendant to be presumed innocent is swept away to precisely the extent judges and juries rely upon the statutory presumptions of guilt . . . and each of the weapons given by the Bill of Rights to the criminal accused to defend [their] innocence . . . is nullified to the extent that the Government to secure a conviction does not have to introduce any evidence to support essential allegations of the indictment. It would be a senseless and stupid thing for the *Constitution* to take all these precautions to protect the accused from governmental abuses if the Government could by some sleight-of-hand trick with presumptions make nullities of those precautions. Such a result would completely frustrate the purpose of the Founders to establish a system of criminal justice in which the accused . . . would be able to protect [themselves] from wrongful charges by a big and powerful government. It is little less than fantastic even to imagine that those who wrote our *Constitution* and the Bill of Rights intended to have a government that could create crimes of several separate and independent parts and then relieve the government of proving a portion of them.[85]

Black and Douglas JJ repeated their assertions made in *Gainey* regarding other constitutional problems with statutory presumptions in relation to elements of crimes, in particular the fact that they effectively interfered with the accused's privilege against self-incrimination, requiring them to present evidence in order to avoid prosecution.[86] They indicated separation of powers problems with statutory presumptions, finding that they interfered with an accused's right to have a jury determine whether or not the proven facts were sufficient to demonstrate, beyond reasonable doubt, that an offense had been committed.[87] Black and Douglas JJ also noted that the evidence relied upon by the majority to justify the presumptions in relation to the heroin offenses had not been led at the trial of the accused. The accused had been denied the opportunity to test the veracity of such evidence through the typical process of cross-examination.[88]

The next case, *In Re Winship*,[89] is largely a re-assertion of the importance to the criminal justice system of the presumption of innocence, in the context of legislation applicable to juveniles that permitted convictions based on a preponderance of the evidence. There the Court, in invalidating that provision, referred to the beyond reasonable doubt standard as being "virtually unanimously adhered to" in the common law world,[90] reflecting a "profound judgment about the way in which law should be enforced and justice administered."[91] It was constitutionally required due to its inextricable links with the presumption of innocence. That presumption was reasserted as a "bedrock axiomatic and elementary principle" laying at the foundation of criminal justice.[92] The Court reflected on the very strong interests involved in the criminal trial, and the justification for placing a strong burden on the state to prove the truth of criminal allegations, references to which appeared in chapter 1. The Court reasserted that it was imperative that the moral force of the law not be undermined by use of a standard of proof which left members of the public unsure as to whether a given person was in fact guilty of a crime with which they had been charged, and reconfirmed the essentiality of public confidence in the outcome of criminal justice deliberations.[93]

Then the Supreme Court considered an offense of possession of United States Treasury checks stolen from the mail system, knowing that such mail had been stolen.[94] The trial judge instructed the jury that it would be justified in inferring, from unexplained possession of checks not made out to the holder of the checks, that the holder of the checks knew they had been stolen. This instruction was challenged on due process grounds. A majority of the Court dismissed the challenge.

The majority acknowledged there was ambiguity in past case law on the standard of proof applicable to the rational connection test. Specifically, whether the thing being inferred from the proven fact had to flow from the proven fact at the level of beyond reasonable doubt, or whether a more-likely-than-not standard was sufficient. The majority dismissed this debate as relating to "language and focus" rather than substance.[95] The Court said it was clear that if the thing presumed met both the beyond reasonable doubt and more-likely-than-not standard, due process had been satisfied.

They stated that for centuries courts had instructed juries that guilt could be inferred from unexplained possession of stolen goods. Common sense and experience suggested that someone in possession of checks made out to others was highly likely to be aware the checks were stolen. The Court was satisfied the fact of possession of checks made out to others, in the absence of an explanation by the accused as to how they innocently came into possession of the checks, proved at the beyond reasonable doubt standard that the accused committed the crime with which they had been charged. The majority rejected the suggestion that the trial judge's statements to the jury infringed the accused's privilege against self-incrimination. The mere amassing of evidence against an accused did not infringe the privilege. The trial judge told the jury that the accused was within his rights not to testify.

Strong dissents were written by Douglas, Brennan and Marshall JJ. Douglas J called use of presumptions and inferences to prove defined elements of crimes "treacherous," because it allowed accused individuals to be convicted although the prosecution had not proven at least one defined element of a crime at the beyond reasonable doubt standard. He found that this implicated the integrity of the judicial system, and "subtly diluted" the protections of the *Bill of Rights*.

Again, Douglas J raised concerns that the use of presumptions interfered with the principle of separation of powers, concluding that "Congress is as unwarranted in telling courts what evidence is enough to convict an accused as we would be to tell Congress what criminal laws should be enacted." He focused on the fact that, as framed, the offense specifically related to property known to have been stolen from the mail system. Even if unexplained possession of stolen property could be rationally connected with an offense of knowing possession of stolen property, this presumption went further. Here, it was inferred from possession of stolen property that the holder knew from whence the property had been stolen. Douglas J found this presumption was untenable, even if a standard below beyond reasonable doubt could be utilized.[96] Similarly, Brennan and Marshall JJ would have invalidated the accused's conviction, because the effect of the trial judge's directions to the jury raised the possibility than the accused could be convicted "even though the actual evidence bearing on knowledge may have been insufficient to establish guilt beyond a reasonable doubt."[97] They reiterated the requirement from *In Re Winship* that it was incumbent upon the prosecution to prove the existence of each element of a defined crime beyond reasonable doubt.[98]

Next the Court considered the provocation defense in the context of unlawful killing.[99] State law recognized offenses of murder and manslaughter. Intention was an element of both offenses. Malice aforethought was an element of the murder offense. The act provided that if an unlawful killing occurred in the heat of passion or sudden provocation, malice aforethought would not be established. In such a case the individual would be convicted of manslaughter only. Under the act, the defendant was required to make out the existence of heat of passion/provocation, on the preponderance of the evidence standard. All members of the Court found the provision was contrary to the due process requirement of the *Fifth Amendment*, and unconstitutional.

The Court took a substantive view of the requirement of presumption of innocence in the criminal law. It stated that criminal law was substantively concerned with the degree of an accused's criminal culpability.[100] In that context, the law traditionally placed great importance on whether a person accused of wrongful killing had acted in the heat of passion. They said it was often the single most important factor in determining the extent of culpability.[101] The consequences of a conviction for murder, as opposed to manslaughter, were vastly different.

The Court found that unless a substantive view was taken of what *Winship* required in terms of the presumption of innocence, the state could effectively undermine the substantive interests sought to be protected by *Winship*. It could redefine elements of crimes as factors only relevant to punishment, for example.[102] In order to prevent the state from undermining the interests protected by *Winship*, a substantive view was required. The Court seemed to be suggesting that matters relating, in substance, to an alleged offender's culpability would need to be proven at the beyond reasonable doubt level by the state, regardless of what the statute said, in order to preserve the teaching of *Winship*. And that the question of heat of passion/provocation was one of those matters bearing on culpability. The Court was also mindful of the consequences of a wrongful conviction in a case such as this. If an individual was actually convicted of murder, because they could not show the defense at the preponderance of the evidence level, they would receive a very serious punishment. The Court also noted that the defendant's burden of proof was at the preponderance of the evidence level, rather than a mere burden of production. The Court said that the due process clause required even more exacting standards in such cases.[103]

Legislation operating on a somewhat similar factual scenario was also challenged in *Patterson v New York*,[104] but on that occasion the challenge was not successful. Patterson had been charged with second degree murder relating to his ex-wife's friend. The elements of the offense included causing the death of another, and intending to do so. The prosecution bore the onus as to these elements. New York law provided for an affirmative defense of "extreme emotional disturbance," casting the onus of proof onto the defendant in relation to it, at the preponderance of the evidence level. That defense was a partial one; if successfully raised, it would reduce the offense to manslaughter.

Five justices dismissed the due process challenge.[105] The majority noted that, subject to the requirements of due process, states had substantial latitude in terms of legislating with respect to evidentiary burdens in cases. Here New York had legislated the "extreme emotional disturbance" defense, which was in terms significantly expanded from the traditional common law doctrine of provocation.

The majority noted that the prosecution bore the onus of proof at the level of beyond reasonable doubt with respect to each element of the offense, as defined by the New York legislature.[106] Lack of "severe emotional disturbance" was not included as an element of the crime with which the accused had been charged, distinguishing this case from the statutory scenario in *Mullaney*. There, malice (in other words, lack of provocation) was an express element of the crime with which the accused had been charged.[107]

The majority noted that the presumption of innocence had historically been partly justified on the basis it was better for the guilty to go free than an innocent person be condemned. The Court noted that the concern about the risk that an innocent person be wrongly condemned was "not without limits."[108] Specifically, due process did not mean that "every conceivable step be taken, at whatever cost, to eliminate the possibility of convicting an innocent person."[109] The majority pointedly rejected the suggestion that the prosecution was required to disprove at the level of beyond reasonable doubt the existence of every fact giving rise to any affirmative defense relating to the accused's culpability.[110] Due process required only that the prosecution prove all of the stated elements of the offense as defined by the legislature beyond reasonable doubt; it did not mandate an onus or standard of proof in relation to legislated affirmative defenses.

The majority was mindful that this formalistic approach could lead to opportunistic behavior by legislators:

> This view may seem to permit state legislatures to reallocate burdens of proof by labelling as affirmative defenses at least some elements of the crimes now defined in their statutes. But there are obviously constitutional limits beyond which the States may not go in this regard. It is not within the province of a legislature to declare an individual guilty or presumptively guilty of a crime . . . the legislature cannot validly command that the finding of an indictment, or mere proof of the identity of the accused, should create a presumption of the existence of all the facts essential to guilt. (quotation marks omitted)[111]

The dissenters attacked what they saw as the formalism inherent in the majority view.[112] They found the majority view basically allowed legislatures too broad a discretion in terms of how they framed their criminal offenses. Comparing the results in *Mullaney* and this case, the dissentients pointed out that essentially a very similar argument was run in the two cases, yet in one case the Court found the legislation offensive to due process, and in the other it was held valid.[113] For the dissentients, this showed the unacceptable formalism of the majority position: "The test the Court today establishes allows a legislature to shift, virtually at will, the burden of persuasion with respect to any factor in a criminal case, so long as it is careful not to mention the nonexistence of that factor in the statutory language that defines the crime."[114] The dissentients rejected the majority's concession as to the possible risks of legislative abuse in this area, and specifically that there were "obviously . . . limits beyond which the states may not go" in terms of defining elements of criminal behavior. The dissentients countered that such "obvious limits" were not evident in the majority reasoning, and nor did the majority provide a conceptual framework for distinguishing alterations in the burden of proof which were consistent with due process, and those which were not.[115]

Applying a substantive approach to the question of what a defendant could properly be asked to show and what it was that the prosecutor had to prove, the dissentients noted that the presence or absence of heat of passion/provocation traditionally made a substantial difference in terms of the punishment, and resulting stigma, to which someone convicted would be subject.[116] They used as their conceptual framework in determining burden of proof matters that "the Due Process clause requires that the prosecutor must bear the burden of persuasion beyond a reasonable doubt only if the factor at issue makes a substantial difference in punishment and stigma."[117] They said that in applying this test, the historical record would be important. If, historically, a factor made such a difference, this suggested that due process would require the prosecution to prove it (or its absence), at the beyond reasonable doubt level.[118] The dissentients also noted the crucial distinction between burdens of production and burdens of persuasion, finding that the state could legitimately transfer the former to an accused.[119]

A trial judge's directions to a jury that a person is generally presumed to intend the ordinary consequences of their actions was successfully challenged on due process grounds.[120] The accused had been charged with deliberate homicide. He admitted the killing, but claimed he did not do so knowingly, so was guilty only of a lesser charge. The Supreme Court found the direction offended the presumption of innocence. The jury was not instructed that this presumption was permissible, rather than mandatory. Reasonable juror members may have interpreted the trial judge's directions to refer to a mandatory presumption, i.e., one that must be made. In addition or alternative, they could have interpreted the presumption as being irrebuttable by the accused. In the further alternative, they may have interpreted it as being rebuttable, but only where the defendant met a preponderance of the evidence standard. Any of these interpretations resulted in a constitutionally improper allocation of the burden of proof on the accused.

The Court returned to the "rational connection" principle in *County Court of Ulster County, New York v Allen.*[121] The case considered a challenge to the constitutionality of a New York drugs provision which permitted a presumption to be made that a firearm found a vehicle was in the "possession" of all those occupying the vehicle. The accused had been charged with illegal possession of firearms found in a vehicle which they occupied. By a majority of 5–4, the Supreme Court rejected a constitutional challenge to the legislation.[122]

The majority said that inferences and presumptions were a staple characteristic of the adversarial system.[123] In assessing the validity of a particular presumption or inference, it was not necessary that it be accurate in every possible case.[124] A presumption or inference would be invalid if it undermined the fact finder's responsibility to find the ultimate facts in dispute beyond a reasonable doubt, based on evidence.[125] In determining whether or not an inference or presumption did this, the strength of the connection between the basic and elemental facts was important, as well as the extent to which the presumption or inference curbed the fact finder's freedom to assess the evidence.[126] An assessment of the constitutionality or otherwise of such provisions would typically be on a case-by-case basis, given the particular situation and the particular way in which the judge described the device to the jury, rather than by applying a blanket rule.[127]

Specifically, the majority distinguished between permissive inferences and mandatory presumptions. Permissive inferences allowed the jury to retain ultimate responsibility for finding facts, and did not shift the burden of proof onto the accused. Such inferences were likely to be constitutionally valid, unless there was "no rational way" that the fact inferred could in fact be drawn from the proven fact.[128]

A mandatory presumption was more likely to be vulnerable to constitutional challenge. Effectively, it did shift the evidentiary burden onto the accused.[129] It may be found to be unconstitutional, even if there is other evidence implicating the accused,[130] because the Court can never know the extent to which the jury relied on the mandatory presumption in determining that an accused was guilty.

The Court seemed to suggest a different standard for assessing permissive inferences, as opposed to mandatory presumptions. A permissive standard would be valid if the thing which could be inferred was "rational" given the proven facts, and/or more likely than not to be the case.[131] In contrast, with a mandatory presumption, where it was the entire basis for the state's case, the state would need to show the thing presumed was rationally connected to the fact proven at the level of beyond reasonable doubt.[132] If there were other evidence of guilt as well, the state would only need to show the thing presumed was rationally connected to the fact proven on the more-likely-than-not standard.[133]

Applying these standards to the permissive inference here, the trial judge's directions were valid. There was evidence that the firearms were sticking out of the purse of one of the occupants of the vehicle, because they were too large to be contained entirely within it. As a result, it was very likely they were visible to other occupants of the vehicle. It was rational to infer their awareness of the firearms, and there was a rational connection between occupancy of the vehicle and knowledge of the firearms. It was more-likely-than-not that they were aware of the firearms.[134]

The dissenters agreed with application of the more-likely-than-not standard, but found that a person occupying a vehicle was not more likely than not to be aware that another occupant was carrying a gun, given common sense and ordinary experience of those in cars.[135] It was unknown how much reliance jurors placed on the inference.[136] The dissenters rejected the majority's use of the simple "rationality" test for permitting a permissive inference, as opposed to the more-likely-than-not standard.[137] And an otherwise unconstitutional inference or presumption could not be validated just because there was other evidence on the record suggestive of an accused's guilt.[138]

Mandatory presumptions were struck out by the Supreme Court in *Carella v California* in relation to theft offenses.[139] The accused was charged with theft offenses arising from the non-return of a rental vehicle. One statutory provision stated that a person shall be presumed to have embezzled a rental vehicle if it was not returned within five days of the expiration of the agreement. Another stated that intent to commit theft by fraud was presumed by failure to return the vehicle within 20 days of demand. All members of the Court found the provisions were constitutionally invalid, due to their infringement of due process rights.

The Court found that the presumptions were cast by the trial judge in mandatory terms. This precluded the jury from independently assessing whether or not all elements of the offense had been made out on the facts.[140] Elsewhere, the Court has debated (and divided) on whether the *Fifth Amendment* requires the Court to express to the jury the accused's right to presumption of innocence in all cases.[141]

The presumption of innocence principle in the context of sentencing enhancement factors was considered in *Apprendi v New Jersey*.[142] That case involved a charge of possession of a firearm for an unlawful purpose, and unlawful possession of a bomb. The statute provided "sentencing enhancement factors," including commission of the offense with a purpose to intimidate because of race. The lower court found by a preponderance of the evidence that the accused had committed the offense with that purpose in mind. A majority of the Supreme Court found that this reflected the lack of due process. Given that the fact was explicitly relevant to the sentence that the offense could attract, a majority of the

Court found that the fact had to be proven at the standard of beyond reasonable doubt.

The majority noted that the institution of jury trial had long been thought to require that the truth of every allegation made against the accused had to be put and considered by the jury. English common law did not recognize a distinction between elements of an offense and "sentencing enhancement factors."[143] A prosecution was submitted to a jury once all facts and circumstances relating to the offense were made available to them. The majority cited Hale's *Pleas of the Crown* to the effect that the longstanding practice was that if a statute attached a higher level of punishment to a crime committed under particular circumstances, the prosecutor was required to specifically allege, and prove, that it was committed under those circumstances.[144]

The majority referred to earlier Supreme Court decisions which had emphasized the punishment and stigma aspects of a finding of guilt, as a basis for justifying a strong presumption of innocence doctrine. The majority noted that a finding that a sentencing enhancement factor existed had a significant bearing on the accused's likely punishment and resulting stigma.[145] As a result, it was imperative that the defendant's presumption of innocence be retained at a time when a court was considering whether or not the sentencing enhancement factor was established on the facts, or not. This led the majority to conclude that "other than the fact of a prior conviction, any fact that increases the penalty for a crime beyond the prescribed statutory maximum must be submitted to a jury, and proved beyond a reasonable doubt."[146] Concurring, Scalia and Thomas JJ found that in substance, the definition of a crime included every element which was a basis for imposing or increasing punishment.[147]

In dissent, O'Connor (for Rehnquist CJ Kennedy and Breyer JJ) found that the legislature had broad discretion in how it framed particular offenses.[148] This was entitled to due deference. Although, as acknowledged in *Patterson*, there were limits beyond which the legislature could not go, the Court had to tread warily in altering the legislature's decision as to what comprised elements of an offense. Here, the legislature's decision that the racial motivation for activity was not a matter that the jury had to be convinced of beyond reasonable doubt was entitled to respect. The validity of such legislative judgments should be considered carefully on a case-by-case basis, not subject to the new test provided by the majority.[149]

Having summarized the major developments in the American case law regarding the presumption of innocence, I now record my reflections on some of the major developments and doctrines in this area, and where I perceive there to be some gaps and deficiencies in the case law as it currently stands. These observations will be utilized in chapter 3 as part of the critical comparison across the chosen jurisdictions regarding presumption of innocence doctrine. My analysis and critique will be framed with the background that the presumption of innocence is a fundamental due process right, with lengthy historical recognition, and playing a pivotal role in the criminal justice system, linked closely with other fundamental due process rights, and with the reputation of the legal system as a whole. It is also with the recognition that on occasion, prosecutors find it difficult to prove the truth of their suspicions of criminal behavior at the level of beyond reasonable doubt, and that in general, some things, for instance notions of intent, are traditionally very difficult to prove. In this environment, it is not surprising that legislators have turned to the use of presumptions and inferences in an effort to "grease the wheels" of the prosecution process. And, of course, we all want to live in a safer society, and we all want those guilty of crime to be brought to justice. However, this must be balanced against the risks of improper convictions, the very great interests at stake in a criminal trial, and the essentiality that the public retain confidence in the judicial arm of government. I also bear in mind that there are many different types of presumptions and inferences in legislation and case law, and care must be taken in making generalized observations given that the Court has generally preferred to take a case-by-case approach to constitutionality on such matters. For ease of reference, I will refer below to legislation which presumes an element of an offense against an accused as a "reverse onus" provision. I will distinguish between permissive, mandatory and irrebuttable presumptions later in this discussion.

REFLECTIONS ON THE UNITED STATES CASE LAW

Suggestions that Reverse Onus Provisions Are Acceptable Where It Is "Easy" for the Accused to Overcome a Reverse Onus Provision

There appears in some of the case law and literature in this area the notion that, in considering whether a reverse onus provision is constitutionally valid, the ease or otherwise with which an accused might overcome the burden is relevant. So, for example, in validating a presumption that a person in possession of material used in an illegal game knowingly possessed it contrary to legislation, the Court in *Adams* noted that "innocent persons would have no trouble in explaining the possession of these tickets."[150] The Court in validating a presumption against an accused in *Luria* noted that it related to "matters of which [the defendant] possesses full . . . knowledge."[151] In *Casey* five justices agreed that "it is consistent with all the constitutional protections of [the accused] to throw on them the burden of proving facts peculiarly within their knowledge and hidden from discovery by the government."[152] In *Tot* the Court did not overrule this principle, but found it was a "corollary" of the main test of "rational connection."[153] This factor was apparently utilized again in *Speiser v Randall*, but in the reverse way—in invalidating a reverse onus provision, the Court commented on the practical difficulties that imposition of the burden of proof imposed on the accused.[154] And finally in *Leary v United States*, six justices said that the earlier finding in *Tot* had "implicitly abandoned" the comparative convenience doctrine.[155] Use of the comparative convenience doctrine has enjoyed some academic support.[156]

The comparative convenience doctrine is not supported here. It is hard to argue that the fact something is relatively easy for an accused to do justifies departure from constitutional principle. It might be easy for an accused to answer a question put to them by police or by the prosecutor, but this does not mean that their *Fifth Amendment* privilege against self-incrimination disappears. Nor should it. In history, where many centuries ago we decided that allegations against an accused needed to be proven by the allegor, no distinction was made between occasions where it was "easy" for an accused to answer allegations made, and where it was not. Nothing has changed to now justify such a distinction. The rationales for insisting on the presumption—the risk of wrongful convictions, the imbalance in resources in favor of the state, notions that individuals are generally good, unless proven otherwise—none of these disappear in cases where it is easy for an accused to provide some evidence suggestive of their innocence. And where is the line drawn? When does it become sufficiently "easy" for an accused to provide evidence of innocence that the law should insist that they do so, on pain of conviction?

Such a suggestion seems to appeal to a Benthamite utilitarianism. Not surprisingly, Bentham was not a strong advocate of the presumption of innocence, declaring it to be "contrary to fact," concluding that the accused is not in fact treated as if he were innocent and, in any event, "it would be absurd to deal with him as if he were."[157] Its approach seems odd to a *Constitution* infused with notions of social contract theory and the concept of the inalienability of fundamental human rights.

It is not recommended that the comparative convenience doctrine be seen as a corollary to the rational connection doctrine. The two are essential unrelated. The question of who can more conveniently prove a particular matter is entirely unrelated to the question of whether one thing can be inferred from proof of another.

Rational Connection and Standard of Proof

As indicated, the Supreme Court has developed the principle of "rational connection" with respect to presumptions. It is sufficient if the thing presumed is rationally connected with the fact proven. There are several concerns with this test. Firstly, it calls for a particular kind of evidence regarding common affairs, as to the likelihood that one thing is logically linked to another. For instance, how likely is it that a person in possession of stolen property knows that it is stolen? How likely is it that a person in possession of drugs is aware of the source of the drugs? Now, while individuals might be able to hazard an educated guess about such matters, it is questionable at the least to hang the fact of an individual's conviction or otherwise on the basis of this kind of evidence, where the presumption helps to prove the existence of one or more of the elements of the crime with which the accused has been charged. Reasonable minds may well differ on questions of whether a particular fact can or should be inferred from the existence of other facts. On occasion, expert evidence may be led about such a matter; however, the cases demonstrate that this does not always occur. And even so, such evidence can only be based on general probabilities of the connection, not that there exists such a connection on the particular facts before the Court. An accused may be denied an opportunity to test such evidence through a process of cross-examination. Given that such matters are often a matter of empirical evidence, courts may (and have)[158] simply defer to Congress's assessment that such connection exists, presuming that the presumption is valid, contrary to the interests of the accused. And, of course, to say that such a connection commonly exists, is not to say that such connection does in fact exist in the present case.

There is also the question of the standard of proof to be applied in relation to the rational connection requirement. In a criminal case where such a presumption is utilized, must the thing inferred be proven by the fact proved at the level of beyond reasonable doubt, or is preponderance of the evidence, or some other test, to be applied? Now it should be recalled that the first case in which the rational connection test was espoused was the *Mobile* decision, a civil case. In such a context, where the civil standard of proof applied, a rational connection test involving presuming a fact where it is more likely than not to flow from a proven fact is entirely justifiable and unremarkable.[159] The problem is that the test was subsequently applied in a criminal context, obviously involving a beyond reasonable doubt standard. Yet the Court was slow, and remains slow, to insist that the beyond reasonable standard applies in respect of the proven link between the thing proved and the thing sought to be presumed from it.

It was accepted in *Leary v United States* (in the criminal context) that "substantial assurance that the presumed fact is more likely than not to flow from the proved fact on which it is made to depend" was required.[160] The Court in *Turner v United States* noted that both the beyond reasonable doubt and more-likely-than-not standards had been applied to presumptions, before applying the latter test.[161] It tried to paper over the differences between the tests in *Barnes v United States*, calling them "variations in language and focus rather than to differences in substance."[162]

Serious issue is taken with a suggestion that a variation between the criminal standard of proof and the civil standard of proof is a mere "variation in language and focus" rather than a substantive difference. Acceptance of this explains the dissent of Brennan and Marshall JJ in *Barnes*. They invalidated the presumption used in that case because it may have resulted in an accused being convicted when their guilt had not been proven beyond reasonable doubt.[163] There is substantial academic support for the suggestion that the statutory presumption of a fact from proven facts must have a sufficient connection proven at the beyond reasonable doubt level.[164] Most of the literature would suggest that in fact a substantial gulf exists between the two standards. Some scholars suggest that beyond reasonable doubt is at the 99 percent confidence level.[165] One survey of judges showed different interpretations of what the standard required in terms of probability, with most quantifying it at around 87–93 percent.[166] The civil standard of proof is normally quantified at a probability of 51 percent,[167] suggesting that there is in fact a significant disparity between the criminal and civil standards of proof. Some scholars have even suggested that proof of the "rational connection" beyond reasonable doubt still does not meet constitutional requirements.[168]

When the law in other jurisdictions is discussed in chapter 3, we will learn that the test espoused in the Canadian case law, which has been adopted in some of the United Kingdom decisions, is that a statutory presumption is contrary to the presumption of innocence principle, and invalid unless saved by proportionality analysis in those jurisdictions, where the law permits an accused to be convicted of a crime despite the existence of reasonable doubt as to their guilt of the offense with which they have been charged. This test and approach are supported in those jurisdictions, and also has lessons for the American approach.

It will be obvious to readers that the application of a "rational connection" test, coupled with acceptance of satisfaction of the thing presumed from the thing proven at the level of "more likely than not," will clearly offend the rule espoused in the Canadian case law. It will clearly permit an accused to be convicted despite the existence of reasonable doubt as to whether at least one of the elements of the crime with which the accused has been charged has been proven at the level of beyond reasonable doubt.[169] There is also the concern, which others have expressed, that the use of a statutory presumption skews the jury's deliberations on matters of guilt. Ashford and Risinger point out that jurors are often not aware of the precise meaning of beyond reasonable doubt. Where the law permits a presumption to be used that an element of the crime has been committed, once another fact is proven, Ashford and Risinger suggest this sways the jury away from considering whether the prosecution has proven each and every element of the subject crime at the level of beyond reasonable doubt, to the question of whether the accused has raised reasonable doubt.[170]

Any suggestion of a differential approach to permissive as opposed to mandatory presumptions is also problematic. Most fundamentally, we cannot know how much emphasis a jury actually did place on the presumption in their deliberations. Much can turn on the way in which the presumption was explained by the relevant judge. Jurors may not appreciate fine distinctions between mandatory and permissive inferences, in the way that a lawyer would.[171] Others have pointed out the great influence that an enacted presumption might have on decision makers who are relatively inexperienced in their task. Ironically, just as the presumption of innocence and beyond reasonable doubt standard were designed to provide jurors with moral comfort about their decision, so too a statutory presumption against the accused can provide jurors with moral comfort about their decision to convict.

Substantive versus Procedural View of Elements of a Crime

The traditional view has been that the *Bill of Rights* is concerned with fair procedures, rather than the substantive content of the criminal law. This view holds that it is within the competence of (primarily) state legislatures to frame their criminal law as they wish. This includes defining elements of a crime as they see fit, framing defenses in the language they choose, and making determinations as to the extent to which defenses are available to a defendant in particular circumstances. A classic legal positivist view would be that the *Constitution* says nothing about what the substance of the criminal law should be, and that the Court should not second guess the content of the legislature's criminal law.[172] A state would be free to craft offense provisions, including elements, precisely how it wished. It would be free to craft defenses and excuses precisely how it wished, or not have them at all. Mens rea would not be a constitutionally required element of any offense.[173] This theory, probably best illustrated in the *Patterson* decision, has been criticized.[174] A state would also have the broad power to legislate with respect to rules of evidence, including burden and standard of proof. In saying this, it should be acknowledged that at least some of the *Bill of Rights is* concerned with substance. The *Eighth Amendment* prohibition on cruel and unusual punishments is directed to the substance of a law. A requirement that just terms be paid for involuntary confiscation of property is also directed to the substance of a law.

In contrast to a legal positivist position, a substantive view may also be taken as to the criminal law. According to that view, the Court is within judicial remit in reviewing the substance of a criminal law, and due process is not merely concerned with procedure.[175] The difficulty with this position is that there are no clear bright lines as to what the scope of that inquiry should be.[176] By what criteria would the Court decide that the content of a criminal law was, in substance, satisfactory constitutionally?[177] Some suggestions have been made, including that the criminal law only applies where there is some element of mens rea involved in the alleged wrongful activity, that the behavior must traditionally have been regarded as warranting punishment, or that the alleged behavior traditionally attracts stigma; or in other words, that the conduct is regarded as being sufficiently (morally) blameworthy.[178] The American Law Institute generally takes this position.[179] Oliver Wendel Holmes did as well.[180] It draws philosophical support from scholars such as Blackstone, and his insistence upon a "vicious will" as a necessary (substantive) element to any criminal law,[181] and the classic criminal law maxim of *actus non facit reum, nisi mens sit rea.*[182] Related to that is the suggestion that justification for review is derived from the *Eighth Amendment,* and it is when the punishment is cruel and unusual, having regard to the elements of the relevant offense as defined by the legislature, that the Court should intervene on the legislature's framing of an offense in a particular way.[183] Some have argued that concepts of voluntariness and/or willed acts provide limits.[184] There has been a suggestion that purely passive behavior, not involving an act, for example failing to register, could not be the basis of criminal sanction.[185] Mere status cannot be the basis of criminal sanction.[186]

Others, in seeking to distinguish the "true" criminal law from regulatory offense–type schemes, which typically do not require proven intent as a basis of liability, insist that it is the degree of punishment at stake. Specifically, because those who commit "true" criminal offenses are liable to imprisonment, some insist that such offenses must comprise an element of "sufficient" moral blameworthiness.[187]

It might assist to be specific. From the cases, issues have arisen where legislatures have created criminal offenses which do not contain intention as an element. I have earlier noted that intention is often a difficult thing for a prosecutor to prove, so it is well understandable that a legislature may omit this requirement. The common law of crime would traditionally require proof of intent, at least with respect to the vast majority of offenses. It is also acknowledged that criminal law more recently has been populated with regulatory-type offenses designed to curb socially dangerous behavior. Typically, these regulatory-type offenses do not require intent for their commission.

How should the Supreme Court respond to a legislature enacting a criminal law that omits intention as a requirement of an offense? A legal positivist would say that the Court should enforce the legislation on its terms. A scholar concerned with the substance of the criminal law might say that such a law as framed is invalid, so that intention would need to be read into the provision or, perhaps, the provision is declared to be unconstitutional.

This issue has played out in some of the Supreme Court decisions dealing with the presumption of innocence. I argue that in *Mullaney* the

Court seemed to suggest a substantive view, finding that matters relating to culpability had to be proven by the prosecutor. They could not be presumed away. However, shortly thereafter, a sharply divided Court in *Patterson v New York* seemed to back away from this approach, the bare majority adopting a more positivistic line that the legislature was free to frame its offenses as it wished, subject to some "obvious limits" that it did not care to quantify.[188] Cases like *Morissette v United States* and *United States v United States Gypsum Co et al* can also be read as being somewhat equivalent to *Mullaney* in their willingness to look beyond the positive terms of the offense statute, in those cases effectively reading a requirement of intention into the statute where none existed on its face. I will explore in more detail in chapter 4, after having explored comparative provisions in other nations in chapter 3, the extent to which a substantive or procedural view should be taken on the question of how a legislature is constrained, if at all, in how it defines criminal activity.

Public Confidence in the Judiciary

It is trite to observe that the retention of public confidence in the judiciary is absolutely fundamental to its ability to continue to perform its functions. Specifically in the criminal law context, ordinary citizens must be generally confident that the legal system gets it "right"—in particular that trials do not result in innocent people being found guilty, as well as that guilty people are generally not acquitted. As indicated in chapter 1, the essentiality of public confidence in the administration of the judicial power in part explains and justifies application of the presumption of innocence principle in American courts.[189]

Clearly, society's confidence in the correctness of a legal outcome in a criminal trial could well be compromised if the jury was required to apply irrebuttable presumptions drafted in general terms, without the specific case at hand in mind. Real doubt would exist as to whether the presumption was appropriate given the particular factual scenario. This is critical when the presumption is being used to convict a person. So there seems little argument that irrebuttable presumptions, those which a jury must apply without exception, should be held to be contrary to due process requirements.

Another type of presumption is the mandatory presumption; in other words, one the jury must make once the prosecutor has proven other facts, but subject to the accused providing evidence to the contrary, usually in the case law at the preponderance of the evidence standard, about which more is said below. The mandatory presumption is a more arguable situation. Part of the difficulty is that juror deliberations are secret in nature. No one knows how much weight the jury places on the mandatory presumption.[190] As alluded to above, in some cases the Court has permitted a mandatory presumption to be applied where there is a rational connection between the thing proven and the thing inferred, when that connection has merely been proven at the more-likely-than-not standard. It was suggested that in such cases, the prosecution would need to prove the existence of the connection between the thing proven and the thing inferred, at the beyond reasonable doubt standard.[191]

Where a mandatory but not irrebuttable presumption is involved, the further question is what the accused must do by way of response, when the mandatory presumption is enlivened against them to prima facie prove the existence of one or more of the elements of the crime with which they have been charged. It is suggested here that in such cases, the accused must only be required to satisfy a burden of *production*, i.e., to produce enough evidence such as would create the existence of reasonable doubt. If this is the rule, an accused could not be convicted of a crime although there was reasonable doubt as to whether they committed it. The prosecution would have had to have proven the existence of all of the elements of the crime (either directly, or through presumptions), at the level of beyond reasonable doubt, and the defense would have had an opportunity to raise the existence of reasonable doubt.

I would not permit a more onerous burden on the accused to meet a burden of *persuasion*, i.e., to prove by a preponderance of the evidence that at least one of the elements of the crime (i.e., one proven through the presumption) has not been committed.[192] Any imposition of a burden of persuasion on the accused raises the spectre of a person being convicted of a crime although there is reasonable doubt as to their guilt. As indicated, as well as being catastrophic for the accused, this gravely undermines the moral basis of, and public confidence in, the judicial arm of government. This possibility arises because the accused may be able to raise some evidence that the thing mandatorily presumed against them is not in fact the case, but perhaps cannot do so on the preponderance of the evidence. The only sensible way in which an accused should be called to overcome a mandatory presumption made against them in relation to a crime is to satisfy a burden of *production* in relation to it, not a burden of *persuasion*. I thus respectfully disagree with the position of the majority in *County Court of Ulster County*, indicating that use of mandatory presumption only attracted the beyond reasonable doubt requirement where the presumption was the *only* basis for the finding of guilt of a particular offense, and that where that was not the case, the more-likely-than-not standard would suffice.[193] And I agree with the dissenting view that in such cases a preponderance of the evidence requirement on the accused is not constitutionally satisfactory,[194] and with their observation that the position of the majority, that of permitting a more-likely-than-not standard applied to the statutory presumption provided there was other evidence, is not a satisfactory solution.[195] As Powell J says, for Brennan Stewart and Marshall JJ, given the secret nature of jury deliberations, no one can say for sure how much weight jurors placed on the statutory presumption. They could have dismissed the other evidence, and relied solely on the presumption. In this way, the "solution" of the majority is wanting.

Regarding a permissible inference, a jury is entitled to accept this invitation from the legislature to draw an inference from a proven fact to another fact, one directly pertaining to the offense of which the accused is charged. However, again the jury must be informed that it should not draw this inference unless it is satisfied, at the level of beyond reasonable doubt, that it is appropriate to infer the one from the other.

The question of public confidence in the judicial process also relates to discussion under the previous sub-heading on fundamental questions of the nature of crime and the criminal law. Some argue that imposition of criminal penalties on persons who have not been shown to have committed actions that the community regards as sufficiently "morally blameworthy" to attract such sanctions undermines public confidence:

> To subject defendants entirely free from moral blameworthiness to the possibility of prison sentences is considered revolting to the community sense of justice; and no law which violates this fundamental instinct can long endure . . . the moral obloquy and the social disgrace incident to criminal conviction are whips which lend effective power to the administration of criminal law. When the law begins to permit convictions for serious offenses of men who are morally innocent and free from fault . . . its restraining power becomes undermined.[196]

Separation of Powers

Clearly a feature of the United States *Constitution* is the strict separation of powers between the legislative, executive and judicial arms of government, each with well-defined powers and responsibilities, reflecting the Montesquiean idea of checks and balances among arms of government.

Understandably, concern has been raised that irrebuttable presumptions, and perhaps mandatory presumptions, represent such an interference with the role of the fact finding jury as to amount to a breach of separation of powers principles. There is little doubt that a legislative direction to a jury to find an individual or organization guilty, or (what might be the same thing) to require them to apply an irrebuttable presumption of guilt against an accused, would so gravely interfere with the jury's constitutionally protected role in the system of government as to amount to a clear breach of separation of powers principles.[197]

Again, a mandatory presumption presents more of a grey area here. Certainly, the way in which the mandatory presumption is explained to the jury is critical. If it is expressed to them in a way that suggests that they must apply the presumption, this would seem to be offensive to due process. The more difficult possibility arises when a jury may interpret the mandatory presumption as being something that they must apply, or accord it "disproportionate" weight, though it is accepted that decisions regarding weighting of the evidence are properly for the jury. We cannot know what use the jury makes of the presumption, and the weight they place on it. However, we all know that jury members might be heavily influenced by the prosecutor or the judge in terms of the weight they accord the statutory presumption.

At least some judges have been alert to the separation of powers implications. For instance, in relation to a provision whereby possession at an illegal still "shall be deemed sufficient evidence to authorize conviction," one of the reasons Black J found the law to be contrary to due process was that it encroached on the functions of courts in resolving facts.[198] So in a situation where we cannot know the weight that a jury places on the statutory presumption, we can perhaps only note the *possible* separation of powers implications of a statutory presumption, and require special care from the trial judge in explaining what would be a proper, and what would be an improper, use of the statutory presumption. Specifically, at the very least, the jury should be reminded that the statutory presumption is not intended to, and constitutionally is forbidden from, usurping its fundamental fact finding role in the criminal trial, and that the statutory presumption is merely one piece of evidence, to be considered amongst all of the evidence, in reaching their conclusion on disputed matters of fact.

Relatedly, it should be noted that the United States Supreme Court found, when assessing the validity of the establishment of a Sentencing Commission charged with providing sentencing guidelines to courts, that the only way the guidelines could be found constitutional was to read them down in such a way that they were discretionary, rather than mandatory.[199] This was how the Court dealt with the arguments that the scheme was offensive to the separation of powers principle. By analogous logic here, it might be argued that statutory presumptions should be read down as being merely discretionary in nature, rather than mandatory. Even so, some would argue that such permissive inferences are contrary to constitutional due process.[200]

Privilege Against Self-Incrimination

As was noted in chapter 1, one of the fundamental features of the presumption of innocence is its close links with other constitutional rights and freedoms. Specifically here, the use of a statutory presumption of guilt can interfere with the *Fifth Amendment* privilege against self-incrimination. It is hard to say that an accused has a "right to silence" when they know that, if they remain silent, the jury can use a statutory presumption of guilt to convict them. A pyrrhic right indeed. As a result, the Supreme Court decision in *Yee Hem* that a reverse onus provision did not offend the *Fifth Amendment* because it "leaves the accused entirely free to testify or not as he chooses"[201] cannot be accepted as correct. The Court elsewhere in its constitutional jurisprudence recognizes that coercion may be practical, as well as theoretical.[202] Presuming a fact against an accused in practice coerces their testimony. As the Supreme Court noted in *Wilson v United States*:

> It is not every one who can safely venture on the witness stand though entirely innocent of the charge against him. Excessive timidity, nervousness when facing others and attempting to explain transactions of a suspicious character, and offenses charged against him, will often confuse and embarrass him to such a degree as to increase rather than remove prejudices against him . . . counsel is forbidden by the statute . . . to make any statement which would create or tend to create a presumption against the defendant from his failure to testify.[203]

Again, the implications of the use of statutory presumptions on an accused's privilege against self-incrimination have been noted by dissenting justices in a range of the case law.[204] I can only express my agreement with their sentiments. It was alluded to above that juries are sometimes influenced by presumptions in a disproportionate way, given the large quantity of evidence they are often asked to consider. Their inquiry may stray from a consideration of whether the prosecution has established each element of the offense charged beyond reasonable doubt, to a consideration of whether the accused has raised doubt sufficient to displace the adverse presumption being utilized against them. Of course, no one can say for sure how much influence a presumption has had in a given case. In this light, presumptions can have a particularly insidious effect on the accused's right to silence:

> When no evidence is produced by the defendant the jurors have little to look to in order to find reasonable doubts, and it is likely that they will find none. In this situation the legislative statement as to the weight of the basic fact has a profound practical influence on the decision making of the jury. By looking for reasonable doubts rather than for proof beyond a reasonable doubt, the jury is much more likely to draw inferences of guilt from the silence of the defendant.[205]

Practical Difficulties for the Defendant

We should also acknowledge the practical difficulties for the accused in terms of rebutting any presumption made against them. As was noted in chapter 1, one of the rationales for the presumption of innocence was to counteract the natural advantage enjoyed by the state in terms of resources, and ability to obtain evidence pertinent to matters in dispute, through various government agencies, use of subpoenas, etc. The state has access to a prosecutions team well versed in how the criminal law works. It was noted in chapter 1 that one justification for the presumption of innocence is to try to counter some of this power and resource imbalance, in favor of the accused.

This means that there is grave concern when the presumption of innocence is undermined by the use of statutory presumptions against them. Their relative resource deficiency might inhibit their ability to counteract the thing/s presumed against them. They may not be aware of the full detail of the case made against them, and the evidence to be used to make it out. They have serious difficulties obtaining evidence that would favor them, by not being able to afford to obtain such information, not knowing how to access it, etc. The prosecution may not be as forthcoming with evidence and witnesses to be used as might be hoped.[206]

CONCLUSION

This chapter has documented how, in important ways, the Supreme Court of the United States has accepted a diminution in the legal protection afforded by the *Fifth* and *Fourteenth Amendments* to the presumption of innocence. It has accepted reverse onus provisions on the basis that it is easier for an accused to prove a particular thing. It has accepted substitutions in what prosecutors must prove in order to obtain convictions, on the basis of "rational connection." It has allowed legislatures very broad power to define crimes in the way they wish, with few limitations. As a result of that, together with an accused's procedural and resource disadvantages, the protection afforded to the presumption of innocence has been undermined. Accused persons are being convicted although there is reasonable doubt as to their guilt. The moral authority of judicial decision is being compromised. The moral comfort that a strong application of the presumption of innocence principle would bring has disappeared as a result. And along the way, related rights, like the right to silence, are also effectively compromised. Some justices have recognized this trend, and argued cogently against it. However, they are usually in dissent, or if they do comprise a majority in the odd decision, the value of that decision as precedent has tended to be undermined by later decisions.

NOTES

1. 71 US 277, 328 (1867) (Feld J, for the Court). The Court cited Alexander Hamilton's description of the presumption of innocence as a "great principle of social security" (330), departure from which would "excite scruples in the honest and conscientious" (331).
2. *Fong Yue Ting v United States* 149 US 698 (1893).
3. *Wilson v United States* 162 US 613, 619 (1896) (Fuller CJ, for the Court).
4. 621 (Fuller CJ, for the Court).
5. 192 US 585 (1904).
6. 156 US 432 (1895).
7. 453.

8. 454–455.
9. 455.
10. 456.
11. 460; White J's statement that the presumption of innocence was a kind of evidence (460) was later overturned.
12. 219 US 35 (1910), followed in *Hawkins v Bleakly* 243 US 210 (1917).
13. 43 (Lurton J, for the Court); later, in applying the rational connection principle, the Supreme Court added that evidentiary presumptions were valid unless they were "merely arbitrary mandates . . . or discriminat[ory] . . . between different persons in substantially the same situation": *Lindsley v Natural Carbonic Gas Company* 220 US 61, 82 (1911) (Van Devanter J, for the Court).
14. 43. In contrast, the court in *Western and Atlantic Railroad v Henderson et al* 279 US 639 (1929) struck out a statutory presumption that a railroad was liable for injury or damage caused to individuals or property. The Court rejected the suggestion that the mere fact of collision between a railroad carriage and a vehicle was rationally connected to negligence of the railroad.
15. *McFarland, Supervisor of Public Accounts of Louisiana v American Sugar Refining Company* 241 US 79, 86 (1916) (Holmes J). There, in applying the rational connection test, the Court invalidated statutory presumptions that (a) a person engaged in sugar refining in the state who systematically paid less for sugar within the state than they paid elsewhere was involved in a monopoly or restraint of trade; and that (b) an individual whose refinery was closed within the state for at least one year was presumed to have closed it for antitrust purposes or other purposes contrary to the act. Both were rebuttable, but the Court found the presumptions did not reflect common experience.
16. 219 US 219 (1911).
17. These were: (a) written contract to which the accused was a party for the performance of an act or service, (b) intent on the accused's part when entering into the contract, to injure or defraud their employer, (c) accused obtains a financial benefit as a result of such contract, as intended, and (d) accused refuses, with like intent, without just cause, and without refunding such money, or paying for such property, to perform such act or service.
18. 234.
19. 235.
20. 239.
21. 244; specifically, because the state could not punish the servant as a criminal for failing to serve and not repaying, it must not be permitted to effectively achieve the same objective by use of a statutory presumption to assist a finding of criminal guilt.
22. *Luria v United States* 231 US 9 (1913).
23. 25 (Van Devanter J, for the Court). Similarly, a statutory presumption against the owner of a farm on which an illegal still operated was upheld. The statute required the accused to show he was unaware of the illegal still, located 300 yards from his home. This presumption was valid because distillation was not an ordinary farming activity, and was typically not silent or obscure such that the owner of the farm was likely to have been unaware of its presence. The farmer was offered the chance to explain, and had the means to do so: *Hawes v State of Georgia* 258 US 1 (1922).
24. 27.
25. *Manley v State of Georgia* 279 US 1 (1929).
26. 6 (Butler J, for the Court).
27. In contrast, in relation to an offense against a director of a bank for assenting to the bank accepting deposits at a time when it was insolvent, there was a statutory presumption from the fact of a bank's accepting a deposit when it was insolvent that the relevant director knew of such insolvency and consented to the deposit. A majority of the Supreme Court dismissed a due process challenge to this provision: *Ferry v Ramsey et al; Harris, Executor v Ramsey et al* 277 US 88 (1928).
28. *Yee Hem v United States* 268 US 178, 185 (1925) (Sutherland J, for the Court).

29. *Casey v United States* 276 US 413, 418 (1928) (Holmes J, for Hughes Van Devanter Sutherland and Stone JJ); see similarly *Rossi v United States* 289 US 89, 91 (1933) where one of the reasons the Court validated a reverse onus provision was that the allegations "could be readily disproved by the production of documents or other evidence probably within the defendant's possession or control" (McReynolds J, for the Court).
30. 291 US 82 (1934).
31. 88–89.
32. 89.
33. 90.
34. 90.
35. 91.
36. 89.
37. 319 US 463 (1943).
38. Roberts J delivered the opinion of the Court, with which Black and Douglas JJ concurred. Murphy J did not participate in the case.
39. Charles Nesson in "Reasonable Doubt and Permissive Inferences: The Value of Complexity," *Harvard Law Review* 92 (1979): 1192, is strongly critical of use of the rational connection test in *Tot* and subsequent cases, on the basis that "any structure which reduces criminal cases to a simplified assessment of what might be called the chances of guilt is fundamentally at odds with the concept of a reasonable doubt, and hence to be discouraged as a mode of determining the ultimate question of guilt or innocence." He criticizes the Supreme Court in *Tot* for failing to reconcile use of the rational connection test with the beyond reasonable doubt standard (1202).
40. 468.
41. 468.
42. 467.
43. 469–470.
44. 342 US 246 (1952).
45. 250 (Jackson J, for the Court).
46. 250.
47. 250.
48. 251.
49. 252.
50. 255–256.
51. 260.
52. 260–261.
53. 263.
54. 274.
55. 275.
56. 438 US 422 (1978).
57. 436–437 (Burger CJ, for the Court).
58. 445–446 (Burger CJ, for the Court).
59. 357 US 513 (1958).
60. 526 (Brennan J, for Frankfurter Burton Clark Harian and Whittaker JJ); Douglas J, with whom Black J agreed, concurred.
61. 380 US 63 (1965). Earlier, the Court had found that it could reasonably be presumed that a person operating the business of an illegal still did so with the intent of defrauding taxation authorities: *Bozza v United States* 330 US 160 (1947).
62. 67 (Stewart J, for Warren CJ Clark Harlan Brennan Stewart White and Goldberg JJ).
63. 67.
64. 68–70; again Charles Nesson in "Reasonable Doubt and Permissive Inferences: The Value of Complexity," *Harvard Law Review* 92 (1979): 1206, is critical: "the *Gainey* Court based its approval on a judgment that the permissive inference was rational, and then assumed that rationality was all that was required. The Court thus made no explicit attempt to harmonize the inference with the concept of reasonable doubt."

65. 78–79.
66. 80.
67. 82.
68. 83.
69. 88.
70. 74 (Douglas J) and 87 (Black J).
71. 382 US 136 (1965).
72. 141.
73. 395 US 6 (1969).
74. 36 (Harlan J, for Warren Douglas Brennan White and Marshall JJ).
75. 46–47 (Harlan J, for Warren Douglas Brennan White and Marshall JJ).
76. 45.
77. "Under our system of separation of powers, Congress is just as incompetent to instruct the judge and jury in an American court what evidence is enough for conviction as the courts are to tell the Congress what policies it must adopt in writing criminal laws. The congressional presumption . . . violates the constitutional right of a defendant to be tried by a jury in a court set up in accordance with the commands of the *Constitution*. It clearly deprives a defendant of his right not to be convicted and punished for a crime without due process of law" (55) (Black JJ).
78. 396 US 398 (1970).
79. 416 (White J, for Burger CJ Harlan Brennan and Stewart JJ).
80. 419.
81. 409–410.
82. Cf Charles Nesson, "Reasonable Doubt and Permissive Inferences: The Value of Complexity," *Harvard Law Review* 92 (1979): 1208, in relation to *Turner*: "it simply does not follow that because a fact is objectively true [e.g., that all heroin is imported], a person would 'doubtless' know it to be true," before concluding that "the concept of reasonable doubt is inconsistent with a procedure that permits an otherwise unassisted leap from aggregate likelihood to a conclusion of guilt in a specific case" (1208).
83. 421–422.
84. 423–424.
85. 429–431.
86. 430.
87. 431.
88. 433.
89. 397 US 358 (1970).
90. 361 (Brennan J, for five members of the Court).
91. 361–362.
92. 363.
93. 364.
94. *Barnes v United States* 412 US 837 (1973).
95. 843 (Powell J, for the Court).
96. "It would take a large degree of assumed omniscience to say with substantial assurance that this petitioner more likely than not knew from the realities of the underworld that this stolen property came from the mails" (852).
97. 853.
98. 854.
99. *Mullaney v Wilbur* 421 US 684 (1975).
100. 697–698 (Powell J, for the Court).
101. 696 (Powell J, for the Court).
102. 698.
103. 702.
104. 432 US 197 (1977).
105. White J, for Burger CJ Stewart Blackmun and Stevens JJ; Powell Brennan and Marshall JJ dissenting; Rehnquist J not participating.
106. 205.

107. 215–216.
108. 208.
109. 208.
110. 210.
111. 210.
112. The formalistic/procedural versus substantive approach to the presumption of innocence, perhaps exemplified most sharply in the decisions in *Mullaney* and *Patterson*, has been the subject of extensive academic work. I will consider such issues in more detail in chapter 4 of this book. See, for example, Scott Sundby, "The Reasonable Doubt Rule and the Meaning of Innocence," *Hastings Law Journal* 40 (1989): 457; John Calvin Jeffries Jr and Paul B Stephan III, "Defenses, Presumptions and Burden of Proof in the Criminal Law," *Yale Law Journal* 88 (1979): 1325; Mark Tushnet, "Constitutional Limitation of Substantive Criminal Law: An Examination of the Meaning of *Mullaney v Wilbur*," *Boston University Law Review* 55 (1975): 775.
113. 221–222.
114. 223.
115. 225.
116. 226.
117. 226; see, similarly, *Martin v Ohio* 480 US 228, 242–243 (1987) (Powell J, for Brennan Marshall and Blackmun JJ, dissenting); cf Ronald Jay Allen, "*Mullaney v Wilbur*, the Supreme Court, and the Substantive Criminal Law—An Examination of the Limits of Legislative Intervention," *Texas Law Review* 55 (1977): 281: "neither *Winship* nor *Wilbur* elaborates on the meaning of stigma . . . if stigmatization plays an independent role, then a more thorough explication of the meaning of stigmatization and its relevance in distinguishing degrees of culpability would seem to have been in order."
118. Interestingly, the dissentients concluded there was constitutionally nothing to prevent a legislature from abolishing the distinction between murder and manslaughter, treating all unjustifiable homicide as murder (228).
119. 230–231.
120. *Sandstrom v Montana* 442 US 510 (1979); to like effect *Connecticut v Johnson* 460 US 73 (1983).
121. 442 US 140 (1979).
122. Stevens J, for Burger CJ White Blackmun and Rehnquist JJ; Powell Brennan Stewart and Marshall JJ dissenting.
123. 156.
124. 156.
125. 156.
126. 156.
127. 163.
128. 157.
129. 159.
130. 160.
131. 157.
132. 167.
133. 167. The Court's distinction between mandatory and permissive presumptions has been subject to trenchant criticism. For example, Charles Collier argued that the strict distinction in theory between the two types of presumption is really illusory, since jurors may treat permissive presumptions as something akin to a mandatory presumption. He cites numerous psychological studies to the effect that within the parameters of a structured environment where a decision maker is subject to a higher authority, the decision maker may treat instructions from the authority as more binding than they actually are: "The Improper Use of Presumptions in Recent Criminal Law Adjudication," *Stanford Law Review* 38 (1986): 441–450; similarly, Leslie Harris, "Constitutional Limits on Criminal Presumptions as an Expression of Changing Concepts of Fundamental Fairness," *Journal of Criminal Law and Criminology* 77 (1986): 341: "it is still very hard to believe that jurors hear, much less are profoundly affected by,

the kinds of differences that *Sandstrom* makes crucial" (i.e., the mandatory/permissive distinction), and noting that "categorizing instructions as permissive or mandatory is not easy" (footnote 155); Shari Jacobson, "Mandatory and Permissive Presumptions in Criminal Cases: The Morass Created by *Allen*," *University of Miami Law Review* 42 (1988): 1032: "the theoretical distinction between permissive and mandatory presumptions . . . has resulted in much confusion and serves no practical purpose"; and Ronald Allen and Ethan Hastert, "From *Winship* to *Apprendi* to *Booker*: Constitutional Command or Constitutional Blunder?" *Stanford Law Review* 58 (2006): 206, "all presumptions . . . modify the jury's inferential process by enhancing [the importance of certain facts] . . . and thus modify the parties' relative burdens of persuasion."

134. 164–165.
135. 172.
136. 175–176.
137. 176.
138. 177.
139. 491 US 263 (1989).
140. 266.
141. *Paul Delo, Superintendent, Potosi Correctional Center, Petitioner v Frederick Lashley* 507 US 272 (1993), where Rehnquist CJ White O'Connor Scalia Kennedy and Thomas JJ said that a defendant was not automatically entitled to an instruction that they were entitled to a presumption of innocence (278), while Stevens and Blackmun JJ (dissenting) found that failure to do so was a constitutional error (285).
142. 530 US 466 (2000).
143. 478.
144. 480.
145. 484.
146. 490.
147. 501.
148. 524.
149. 524.
150. *Adams v New York* 192 US 585, 599 (1904) (Justice Day, for the Court).
151. *Luria v United States* 231 US 9, 25 (1913) (Van Devanter J, for the Court).
152. *Casey v United States* 276 US 413, 418 (1928) (Holmes J, for Hughes Van Devanter Sutherland and Stone JJ).
153. *Tot v United States* 319 US 463, 467 (1943) (Roberts J, for the Court).
154. 357 US 513, 526 (1958) (Brennan J, for Frankfurter Burton Harlan and Whittaker JJ).
155. 395 US 6, 45 (1969) (Harlan J, for Warren Douglas Brennan White and Marshall JJ).
156. For example, Harold Ashford and Michael Risinger, "Presumptions, Assumptions and Due Process in Criminal Cases: A Theoretical Overview," *Yale Law Journal* 79 (1969): 165, 180, who found that the question of comparative convenience should be viewed as a threshold question before determining whether a state interest prima facie justified the presumption.
157. Jeremy Bentham, *Principles of Judicial Procedure*, in John Bowring ed., *The Works of Jeremy Bentham* (Tait, Edinburgh, 1829) 169.
158. *United States v Gainey* 380 US 63, 67 (1965) (Stewart J, for Warren CJ Clark Harlan Brennan White and Goldberg JJ).
159. Allen Fuller and Robert Urich, "An Analysis of the Constitutionality of Statutory Presumptions That Lessen the Burden of the Prosecution," *University of Miami Law Review* 25 (1971): 433: "the rational connection test is totally unresponsive to the constitutional questions it seeks to resolve. As a test of civil presumptions it might suffice, but as a test of the validity of statutory criminal presumptive devices it is patently inadequate."
160. 395 US 6, 36 (1969) (Harlan J, for Warren CJ Douglas Brenna White and Marshall JJ).

161. *Turner v United States* 396 US 398, 416 and 419 (1970) (White J, for Burger CJ Harlan Brennan and Stewart JJ).
162. 412 US 837, 843 (1973) (Powell J, for Burger CJ Stewart White Blackmun and Rehnquist JJ).
163. 853.
164. Harold Ashford and Michael Risinger, "Presumptions, Assumptions and Due Process in Criminal Cases: A Theoretical Overview," *Yale Law Journal* 79 (1969): 183: "we submit that a standard of precision approaching 99 percent, and certainly greater than 90 percent, should be required before a presumption can be constitutionally sustained consistent with notions of due process." They add that "given the [more-likely-than-not] interpretation of rational connection . . . unless the Court is willing to inquire into the number of innocent defendants who can overcome a presumption or establish an affirmative defense, statutes may be upheld which wrongly convict up to half of the individuals convicted pursuant to them . . . This reasoning may explain the Court's suggestion in *Leary* that the standard of 'proof beyond a reasonable doubt' may require a correlation stronger than a mere rational connection . . . the major thrust of this article has been to urge that such a higher correlation is required by due process" (205); Charles Nesson, "Reasonable Doubt and Permissive Inferences: The Value of Complexity," *Harvard Law Review* 92 (1979): 1190: "for such permissive inferences one could well understand a requirement that the inference be strong enough to support a conclusion of guilt beyond a reasonable doubt. Indeed, any less rigorous evaluation would effectively enable the legislature to authorize convictions where guilt was not proved beyond reasonable doubt"; Charles Collier, "The Improper Use of Presumptions in Recent Criminal Law Adjudication," *Stanford Law Review* 38 (1986): 461 concluding that presumption doctrine needed to be re-oriented so that no accused could be convicted by proof of a fact at the more-likely-than-not standard only. Peter Bewley concludes that "the rational connection test, even as strengthened in *Leary*, can never adequately protect the defendant's right to have all elements of the prosecution's case proved beyond a reasonable doubt, and . . . statutory criminal presumptions of material elements of a crime themselves violate the reasonable doubt standard": "The Unconstitutionality of Statutory Criminal Presumptions," *Stanford Law Review* 22 (1970): 342; James Ranney, "Presumptions in Criminal Cases: A New Look at an Old Problem," *Montana Law Review* 41 (1980): 21: "the test last approved by a majority of the United States Supreme Court for assessing the constitutional validity of such presumptions, the so–called 'more likely than not' test, is conceded by virtually all commentators to be totally inadequate . . . the test bears no reasonable relation to the vital due process fairness considerations actually involved"; N Huntley Holland and Harvey Chamberlin, "Statutory Criminal Presumptions: Proof Beyond a Reason able Doubt?" *Valparaiso University Law Review* 7 (1973): 164: "a statutory criminal presumption meeting the 'more likely than not' standard sends a case to the jury where the evidence is insufficient to allow a rational juror to find guilt beyond a reasonable doubt. In such a case, the accused would normally be entitled to a directed verdict of acquittal"; Shari Jacobson, "Mandatory and Permissive Presumptions in Criminal Cases: The Morass Created by *Allen*," *University of Miami Law Review* 42 (1988): 1017. For a rare defense of the more-likely-than-not standard, see W Page Keeton, "Statutory Presumptions—Their Constitutionality and Legal Effect," *Texas Law Review* 10 (1932): 49.
165. Glanville Williams, "The Mathematics of Proof," *Criminal Law Review* (1979): 306: "if a juror is able to calculate that he is 99 percent sure, then he already has a doubt, in legal theory, and ought not to convict"; Jonathan Cohen, "The Logic of Proof," *Criminal Law Review* (1980): 102 (99 percent). Charles Nesson, "Reasonable Doubt and Permissive Inferences: The Value of Complexity," *Harvard Law Review* 92 (1979): 1193, stated that 96 percent confidence level may not be sufficient.
166. Rita James Simon and Linda Mahan, "Quantifying Burdens of Proof," *Law and Society Review* 5 (1971): 319.
167. *Davies v Taylor* [1974] AC 207, 219 (Lord Simon).

168. Robert Mosher, "Statutory Criminal Presumptions: Reconciling the Practical with the Sacrosanct," *UCLA Law Review* 18 (1971): 172: "even assuming that the Court has somehow moved to a 'beyond a reasonable doubt' test, problems . . . remain. A legislature is not capable of determining when one fact implies another fact beyond a reasonable doubt. All a legislature can do is compile statistics and state in general terms the likelihood of a correlation between two facts. A jury sits on one particular case and, while knowledge of these statistics may be helpful, the determination as to reasonable doubt depends on the specific facts of the particular case. In other words, the determination of guilt can only be made by a jury."

169. N Huntley Holland and Harvey Chamberlin, "Statutory Criminal Presumptions: Proof Beyond a Reasonable Doubt?" *Valparaiso University Law Review* 7 (1973): 147: "the statutory criminal presumption has become a popular device in criminal proceedings, often enabling the prosecutor to prove elements of an offense and get his case to the jury in circumstances where he might otherwise be unable to do so"; Peter Bewley, "The Unconstitutionality of Statutory Criminal Presumptions," *Stanford Law Review* 22 (1970): 349: "statutory criminal presumptions which have had to pass only the rational connection test are, when applied to a material element of a crime, unconstitutional denials of due process because they permit verdicts based upon evidence insufficient to support a finding beyond a reasonable doubt"; Shari Jacobson, "Mandatory and Permissive Presumptions in Criminal Cases: The Morass Created by *Allen*," *University of Miami Law Review* 42 (1988): 1023: "a presumption . . . that met the *Leary* [more-likely-than-not] test but not the reasonable doubt test would allow the prosecution to prove its case without proving every element of the crime beyond a reasonable doubt . . . if the prosecution may prove an element of a crime by a presumption, then the presumption of innocence is overcome by proof that has not been established beyond a reasonable doubt."

170. Harold Ashford and D Michael Risinger, "Presumptions, Assumptions, and Due Process in Criminal Cases: A Theoretical Overview," *Yale Law Journal* 79 (1969): 198–199.

171. Generally on empirical evidence regarding juries' understanding of concepts such as the presumption of innocence and beyond reasonable doubt, see Mitchell Frank and Dawn Broschard, "The Silent Criminal Defendant and the Presumption of Innocence: In the Hands of Real Jurors, Is Either of Them Safe?" *Lewis and Clark Law Review* 10 (2006): 237.

172. An example is Ronald Jay Allen, "*Mullaney v Wilbur*, the Supreme Court, and the Substantive Criminal Law—An Examination of the Limits of Legislative Intervention," *Texas Law Review* 55 (1977): 296, who says that states should be broadly free to frame criminal offenses as they wish, subject to *Eighth Amendment* restrictions.

173. *Powell v Texas* 392 US 514, 535 (1968) (Marshall J, for the Chief Justice, Black and Harlan JJ): "this Court has never articulated a general constitutional doctrine of mens rea."

174. Ronald Allen, "The Restoration of *In Re Winship*: A Comment on Burdens of Persuasion in Criminal Cases After *Patterson v New York*," *Michigan Law Review* 76 (1977): 48–50: "the elements theory stipulates that the state must prove beyond reasonable doubt whatever factual issues it labels an element of the offense . . . it is difficult to see just what constitutional interest is served by [that] theory . . . why should the validity of a state statute placing the burden of proving provocation on the defendant depend on whether the state defines murder as intent, causation and no provocation, or simply as intent and causation?"; Henry Hart, "The Aims of the Criminal Law," *Law and Contemporary Problems* 23 (1958): 404: "if one were to judge from the notions apparently underlying many judicial opinions, and the overt language even of some of them, the solution of the puzzle is simply that a crime is anything which is called a crime, and a criminal penalty is simply the penalty provided for doing anything . . . given that name. So vacant a concept is a betrayal of intellectual bankruptcy"; Francis Bowes Sayre, "Public Welfare Offenses," *Columbia Law Review* 33 (1933): 55.

175. As Henry Hart, "The Aims of the Criminal Law," *Law and Contemporary Problems* 23 (1958): 431, asked, "what sense does it make to insist upon procedural safeguards in criminal prosecutions if anything whatever can be made a crime in the first place?."

176. Charles Nesson, "Rationality, Presumptions and Judicial Comment: A Response to Professor Allen," *Harvard Law Review* 94 (1981): 1578: "substantive limitation [may embody] requirements of act, intent and proportionality of punishment. It is difficult, however, to give content to these components."

177. Charles Nesson, "Reasonable Doubt and Permissive Inferences: The Value of Complexity," *Harvard Law Review* 92 (1979): 1190–1191, "legislatures are accorded tremendous latitude in defining a crime . . . this insistence [that only the elements defined by the legislature must be proven beyond reasonable doubt] arguably reflects a fundamental judicial interest, distinct from those legislative concerns reflected in the definition of a particular crime, that the Courts be seen as adjudicating the grounds for criminal liability only according to the most exacting and scrupulous standards."

178. *Mullaney v Wilbur* 421 US 684, 696–700 (1975) (Powell J for the Court); *Patterson v New York* 432 US 197, 226–227 (1977) (Powell J [dissenting], for Brennan and Marshall JJ); *Robinson v California* 370 US 660 (1962); Henry Hart, "The Aims of the Criminal Law," *Law and Contemporary Problems* 23 (1958): 410: "what sense does it make to insist upon procedural safeguards in criminal prosecutions if anything whatever can be made a crime in the first place?"; Herbert Packer, "Mens Rea and the Supreme Court," *Supreme Court Review* (1962): 109, "to punish conduct without reference to the actor's state of mind is both inefficacious and unjust. It is inefficacious because conduct unaccompanied by an awareness of the factors making it criminal does not mark the actor as one who needs to be subjected to punishment in order to deter him or others from behaving similarly in the future, nor does it single him out as a socially dangerous individual who needs to be incapacitated or reformed. It is unjust because the actor is subjected to the stigma of a criminal conviction without being morally blameworthy"; Alan Saltzman, "Strict Criminal Liability and the United States *Constitution*: Substantive Criminal Law Due Process," *Wayne Law Review* 24 (1978): 1637, "it does not make sense to take about a constitutional requirement that the prosecution establish guilt beyond reasonable doubt, unless we are prepared to say what must be proved to establish guilt . . . the *Constitution* contains special limits on the imposition of criminal liability and there must, therefore, be some constitutional rules as to what may be called a crime and how much criminal punishment may be imposed. Those limits must relate to the critical characteristic of crime, that the defendant can be said to have committed a serious wrong, and to the principle that the amount of punishment must be related to the amount of the defendant's blameworthiness"; George Fletcher, "Two Kinds of Legal Rules: A Comparative Study of Burden of Persuasion Practices in Criminal Cases," *Yale Law Journal* 77 (1968): 889; Francis Bowes Sayre, "Public Welfare Offenses," *Columbia Law Review* 33 (1933): 68, "the original objective of the criminal law was to keep the peace; and under the strong church influence of the Middle Ages its function was extended to curb moral delinquencies of one kind or another. For these purposes it developed a suitable procedure, requiring proof of moral blameworthiness or a criminal intent"; Henry Hart, "The Aims of the Criminal Law," *Law and Contemporary Problems* 23 (1958): 401. These matters will be considered in more detail in a subsequent chapter.

179. *Model Penal Code* (1962) s2.02(1), except for non–material elements and strict liability offenses.

180. "It is not intended to deny that criminal liability as well as civil, is founded on blameworthiness. Such a denial would shock the moral sense of any civilized community; or, to put it another way, a law which punished conduct which would not be blameworthy in the average member of the community would be too severe for the community to bear": Oliver Wendell Holmes Jr, *The Common Law* (Barnes and Noble, New York, 2004) 30, cited by all members of the Supreme Court in *Lambert v California* 355 US 225 (1957).

181. Sir William Blackstone, *Commentaries on the Laws of England* (Clarendon Press, London, 1765–1769) 21.

182. In other words, a person cannot be convicted of a crime unless they have committed a guilty act, and had a guilty mind at the time. Susan Pilcher in "Ignorance, Discretion and the Fairness of Notice: Confronting 'Apparent Innocence' in the Criminal Law," *American Criminal Law Review* 33 (1996): 7, notes that this maxim has been a feature of criminal liability since at least the time of Coke and Blackstone.

183. Ronald Allen, "The Restoration of *In Re Winship*: A Comment on Burdens of Persuasion in Criminal Cases After *Patterson v New York*," *Michigan Law Review* 76 (1977): 52–53: "affirmative defenses in the context of serious criminality will not be disturbed except where a statute removes from the definition of a crime those elements that make it serious in the first place . . . the proportionality doctrine [*Eighth Amendment*] is the most sensible explanation of the federal interest in the reasonable doubt standard . . . relating crime to its punishment and viewing it from the perspective of the *Eighth Amendment* has a compelling logical force." And later at 61, "if the punishment provided is not disproportionate in light of the facts established by the state beyond a reasonable doubt, the use of an inference, however tenuous, to 'establish' an additional fact should not impair the constitutionality of the statute defining the offense . . . the [rational connection] test is called for only if a prior eight amendment analysis concludes that the fact in issue is a necessary part of the prosecution's case"; Rollin Perkins, "Criminal Liability Without Fault: A Disquieting Trend," *Iowa Law Review* 68 (1983): 1081: "without fault there is no crime, and to inflict imprisonment on one who has committed no crime is cruel and unusual punishment in violation of the *Eighth Amendment* and of the due process clause of the *Fourteenth*." Similarly, punishment for mere status, as opposed to a positive act, has been held to be contrary to the *Eighth Amendment*: *Robinson v California* 370 US 660 (1962).

184. Clarence Laylin and Alonzo Tuttle, "Due Process and Punishment," *Michigan Law Review* 20 (1922): 614. In *Powell v Texas* 392 US 514, 567 (1968), four justices concluded that "criminal penalties may not be inflicted upon a person for being in a condition he is powerless to change" (relating to the "voluntariness" requirement) (Fortas J, for Douglas Brennan and Stewart JJ). As a result, those justices would have invalidated in its application to an habitually drunk person a statute making public intoxication an offense.

185. *Lambert v California* 355 US 225 (1957).

186. *Robinson v California* 370 US 660 (1962).

187. Francis Bowes Sayre, "Public Welfare Offenses," *Columbia Law Review* 33 (1933): 72.

188. As discussed above, the dissenters suggested concepts of punishment and stigma in adopting a substantive approach to what were in essence elements of a crime, regardless of how the legislature might categorize them.

189. *In Re Winship* 397 US 358, 364 (1970): "it is . . . important in our free society that every individual going about his ordinary affairs have confidence that his government cannot adjudge him guilty of a criminal offense without convincing a proper fact finder of his guilt with utmost certainty" (Brennan J, for the Court); cf Ronald Jay Allen, "*Mullaney v Wilbur*, the Supreme Court, and the Substantive Criminal Law—An Examination of the Limits of Legislative Intervention," *Texas Law Review* 55 (1977): 280: "of what possible concern is it to the Supreme Court of the United States whether a state law tends to instil confidence or distrust in the state's citizenry?"

190. As Larry Laudan noted in "Presumption of Innocence: Material or Probatory?" *Legal Theory* 11 (2005): 352–353: "the system puts no checks on how the juror goes about arriving at that subjective level of confidence [about guilt or innocence]. She is given wholly free rein to make of the evidence what she will and is required at the end only to affirm, if she votes to convict, that she is genuinely persuaded that the accused committed the crime . . . [because] jurors need not be able to articulate their doubts, let alone justify them . . . acquittals remain as arbitrary and subjective as convictions."

191. To like effect, Douglas and Brennan JJ (dissenting) in *Barnes v United States* 412 US 837, 853 (1973): "rather than leaving the jury to determine the element of 'knowledge' . . . the trial court instructed it that it was free to infer the essential element of knowledge from petitioner's unexplained possession of the checks. In my view, that instruction violated the Due Process Clause . . . because it permitted the jury to convict although the actual evidence bearing on knowledge may have been insufficient to establish guilt beyond a reasonable doubt," and Black and Douglas JJ (dissenting) in *Turner v United States* 396 US 398, 429–430 (1970): "government [cannot] be relieved of the constitutional burden of proving the essential elements of its case by a mere congressional declaration that certain evidence shall be deemed sufficient to convict . . . Congress can undoubtedly create crimes and define their elements, but it cannot under our Constitution even partially remove from the prosecution the burden of proving at trial each of the elements it has defined. The fundamental right of the defendant to be presumed innocent is swept away to precisely the extent judges and juries rely upon the statutory presumptions of guilt."

192. This is the position the Court reached in *Sandstrom v Montana* 442 US 510 (1979). There the Court found that the jury may have interpreted the judge's directions as indicating that a presumption of intent was mandatory, unless the accused could overturn such a finding on the preponderance of the evidence standard (517). The Court found that such a result was contrary to the requirements of due process (521): Brennan J, for the Court.

193. 442 US 140, 167 (1979) (Stevens J, for Burger CJ White Blackmun and Rehnquist JJ).

194. 442 US 140, 169 (1979): "if the jury is instructed that it must infer some ultimate fact (that is, some element of the offense) from proof of other facts unless the defendant disproves the ultimate fact by a preponderance of the evidence, then the presumption shifts the burden of proof to the defendant concerning the element thus inferred."

195. 175–176.

196. Francis Bowes Sayre, "Public Welfare Offenses," *Columbia Law Review* 33 (1933): 55, 72 and 79–80; Henry Hart, "The Aims of the Criminal Law," *Law and Contemporary Problems* 23 (1958): 401, 405: "we can say readily enough what a crime is. It is not simply anything which a legislature chooses to call a 'crime.' It is not simply antisocial conduct which public officers are given a responsibility to suppress. It is not simply any conduct to which a legislature chooses to attach a 'criminal' penalty. It is conduct which, if duly shown to have taken place, will incur a formal and solemn pronouncement of the moral condemnation of the community"; Susan Pilcher, "Ignorance, Discretion and the Fairness of Notice: Confronting 'Apparent Innocence' in the Criminal Law," *American Criminal Law Review* 33 (1996): 34: "in a democracy, the legitimacy of law derives from the consent of the governed. Legally authorizing government coercion in areas beyond those delineated by commonly understood social responsibilities leads the governed to question the moral authority of the legal system and diminishes their respect for the power of criminal law in general, thus diluting its distinctive force as a mechanism of social control"; Andrea Tuck-Jackson, "The Defence of Due Diligence and the Presumption of Innocence," *Criminal Law Quarterly* 33 (1991): 19.

197. This reflects the Court's decisions in *McFarland, Supervisor of Public Accounts of Louisiana v American Sugar Refining Company* 241 US 79 (1916) and *Manley v State of Georgia* 279 US 1 (1929).

198. *United States v Gainey* 380 US 63, 88 (1965); similarly in *Leary v United States* 395 US 6, 55 (1969) (Black J); *Turner v United States* 396 US 398, 431 (1970) (Black and Douglas JJ); *Barnes v United States* 412 US 837, 851 (1973) (Douglas J).

199. *United States v Booker* 543 US 220 (2005).

200. Robert Mosher, "Statutory Criminal Presumptions: Reconciling the Practical with the Sacrosanct," *UCLA Law Review* 18 (1971): 172: "a presumption, even under the permissive inference interpretation, removes part of the decision making function

from the jury by imposing on it the legislative decision expressed in the statute . . . [and] the constitutional objection would remain."

201. *Yee Hem v United States* 268 US 178, 185 (1925).

202. *United States v Butler* 297 US 1 (1936).

203. 149 US 60, 66–67 (1893) (Field J, for the Court).

204. *United States v Gainey* 380 US 63, 74 (1965) (Douglas J) and 87 (Black J); *Turner v United States* 398 US 398, 430 (1970) (Black and Douglas JJ).

205. Robert Mosher, "Statutory Criminal Presumptions: Reconciling the Practical with the Sacrosanct," *UCLA Law Review* 18 (1971): 160.

206. Some of these difficulties are discussed in George Christie and Kenneth Pye, "Presumptions and Assumptions in the Criminal Law: Another View," *Duke Law Journal* (1970): 938–940. The authors criticize the "law's niggardly attitude toward criminal discovery" (941).

THREE

Comparative Case Law

Before summarizing and critiquing the law regarding reverse onus provisions in Canada, the United Kingdom and Australia, one important difference between the tradition of these jurisdictions, and that of the United States, must be borne in mind. In the United States the tradition is that the burden of persuasion with respect to affirmative defenses is on an accused, to make out the defense on the balance of probabilities (preponderance of the evidence). In contrast, the United Kingdom common law tradition, mirrored in the other two jurisdictions under discussion in this chapter, is that the prosecution is required to prove all of the elements of the offense, and negate the existence of any defense (once an accused has raised some evidence that might support the defense being applicable to the case at hand) acknowledging the traditional insanity exception.

CANADA

Section 11(d) of the *Canadian Charter of Rights and Freedoms* (1982) enshrines the right to a presumption of innocence for a person charged with an offense. It is not an absolute right, being subject in s1 of the *Charter* to reasonable limits prescribed by law that can be demonstrably justified in a free and democratic society.

The Canadian Supreme Court considered the presumption of innocence in the landmark decision of *R v Oakes*,[1] one of the first cases involving an interpretation of the *Charter*. The case involved the *Narcotic Control Act*. It provided for an offense of drug possession, punishable by a maximum seven-year jail term. It also provided for an offense of possession with a purpose of trafficking, which carried a maximum life sentence. Section 8 of the legislation provided that a person proven to have been in possession of an unlawful drug would be presumed to be in possession for the purpose of trafficking, unless they proved otherwise. If the accused could not show this, they were liable to conviction for the drug-trafficking offense. All members of the Canadian Supreme Court found that the legislation was contrary to s11(d) of the *Charter*, and could not be saved under s1.[2]

The Court noted the presumption of innocence was a "hallowed principle" lying at the heart of Canadian criminal law. It protected the fundamental liberties and human dignity of individuals.[3] The Court noted different kinds of presumptions, including those without basic facts and those with basic facts. Some were mandatory and some were permissive; some were rebuttable, others irrebuttable.[4] The Court interpreted s8 of the *Narcotic Control Act* to impose a mandatory presumption against the accused. The Court also interpreted s8 as imposing a legal, as opposed to evidentiary burden, on the accused to overcome the presumption. In other words, the accused was required to prove that they did not have the drugs for the purpose of trafficking on the civil standard of the balance of probabilities, rather than simply being required to raise some evidence of this.[5]

The majority cited with evident approval a speech made by leading evidence scholar Sir Rupert Cross. Cross had expressed significant concern with legislation casting an onus of proof, even at the civil standard, upon the accused. Cross was particularly concerned about the potential of such provisions to lead to improper convictions. Specifically, he was concerned that a court might convict an accused although there was reasonable doubt as to their guilt. This could occur if, for example, the accused was able to raise a reasonable doubt as to whether one or more of the elements of the offense had been satisfied. Now, if the state had been required to prove that element, the existence of reasonable doubt would of course be fatal to the conviction, and the accused would be acquitted. However, if the onus of proof was on the accused in relation to that matter, and in particular if they were required to prove the matter on the balance of probabilities, grave injustice could arise. Specifically, in the case where the accused could raise some reasonable doubt as to their guilt, but could not meet the balance of probabilities standard, the accused could be convicted of a crime, despite the existence of reasonable doubt as to their guilt.[6]

This possibility gave Sir Rupert Cross and the Canadian Supreme Court significant concern. As a result, the Court found that the provision infringed s11(g).[7] The Court responded to arguments that the "rational connection" be used to support the presumption, as occurred in the United States jurisprudence. The Court found that the rational connection test did not overcome the concern Cross had raised about an accused being convicted despite the existence of reasonable doubt as to their guilt: "a basic fact may rationally tend to prove a presumed fact, but not prove its existence beyond a reasonable doubt. An accused person could therefore be convicted despite the presence of a reasonable doubt. That would violate the presumption of innocence."[8] The Court also found that it was appropriate to apply the rational connection test in the context of the s1 analysis, rather than in determining whether the s11(g) presumption of innocence right had been infringed.[9]

The Court then clarified its approach to s1. If a law were to be saved by it, two criteria had to be met. Firstly, the state would need to show an interest that was of sufficient importance to potentially justify overruling the right. It would have to address "pressing and substantial" concerns. Secondly, the means chosen would have to be shown to be "reasonable and demonstrably justified." Here a balancing exercise involving individual and societal interests was required. Relevant to that proportionality analysis would be three issues:

a. The measures adopted would need to be carefully designed to achieve the relevant objective; they must not be arbitrary, unfair or based on irrational considerations; in other words, they had to be rational;
b. Even if (a) was met, the legislation should impair as little as possible the relevant right or freedom; and
c. There must be proportionality between the effects of the measures responsible for limiting the *Charter* right or freedom and the state's objective.[10]

The Court accepted that parliament's concern with the effects of drug trafficking on society was legitimate. However, the legislation failed the second criterion. Here the rational connection test was of use, but the legislation did not pass the test. Mere possession of a small quantity of marijuana did not rationally suggest a purpose of trafficking.[11] Making such an assumption could defy rationality and lead to unfairness, especially given the maximum life sentence possible for such an offense. As a result, the legislation was invalid, and the Court did not find it necessary to address (b) or (c) above.

In *Vaillancourt v The Queen*[12] the Supreme Court of Canada had to decide whether or not to view the presumption of innocence as merely procedural in nature, or whether it placed constraints on the substance of Canadian criminal law. There the challenged criminal law defined murder in four different ways. Two of these definitions required that the accused have actual subjective foresight (subjective foreseeability) of the likelihood that their actions or omissions would cause death. In the case of the third definition, it was sufficient that the accused knew or ought to know their actions or omissions were likely to cause death (objective foreseeability). The accused was charged under the fourth definition. Under this definition murder was committed where a person caused the death of another while committing various crimes (including robbery), whether or not the person intended to cause death to another, and whether or not the person knew that death was likely to be caused. This would arise in various listed factual circumstances, including one relevant to the accused—the accused used a weapon or had one in their possession, and death resulted as a consequence. In other words, neither subjective nor objective foreseeability was required to be shown in order that the accused be convicted of murder. The accused successfully argued this provision violated the Canadian *Charter*, in particular s7, which protected principles of fundamental justice with respect to situations involving life, liberty or security of a person, and s11(d), protecting the presumption of innocence.

The majority[13] indicated that the *Charter* required the Supreme Court to take a substantive view, at least to some extent, as to the content of Canadian criminal law. This meant that while parliaments had the power to define crimes as they wished, this was subject to judicial review on the question of whether the legislation offended principles of fundamental justice and, if it did, whether it could be saved under s1.[14]

The majority considered the question of whether, in substance, mens rea was required with respect to any offense. It did not have to, and did not, decide whether this was required across the board. However, the majority indicated that, for the purposes of the appeal only, it *might* be possible for the legislature to create a crime that did not require subjective foresight of the result in order to be valid.[15]

The Court said that, in determining the extent to which a particular crime might require mens rea, the nature and seriousness of the crime was relevant. Specifically, the stigma that society traditionally attached to that crime, and the punishment involved, was relevant.[16] Murder was the most serious offense. For the purposes of the particular case, the majority found that given these requirements, a legislature was prohibited by the *Charter* from defining murder in such a way that at least objective foreseeability was not required.[17] This is what the challenged provision did. The majority also suggested, though it was not necessary for the decision reached in this case, that it *might* be that fundamental principles of justice required that a murder conviction be actually based on proof of subjective foreseeability, i.e., that even proof of objective foreseeability would not be enough, in substance.[18] However, it was not necessary to definitively decide that here, because the offense with which the accused had been charged had done away with even a requirement of objective foreseeability.

Next, the Court considered whether the challenged provision violated the presumption of innocence protected by s11(d). In applying s11(d) to the offense, the Court read in the requirement of objective foreseeability to the offense provision with which the accused had been charged.[19] It found that legislatures could sometimes use the device of permitting the state to prove some facts, in order to prove other facts, which were elements of the crime with which the accused had been charged. This could only occur where proof beyond reasonable doubt of the proven fact led beyond reasonable doubt to a finding that the presumed fact existed.[20] This device would not be permitted where it allowed the possibility that an accused could be convicted despite the existence of reasonable doubt as to their guilt.[21] Here the legislation permitted the court to infer from the fact the accused had a weapon at the time the offense was committed that the death of another was objectively foreseeable (as indicated, this requirement was read into the offense). But the fact of one did not prove the other. There were scenarios when an accused who carried a weapon might not objectively foresee death as a result, for example they might have been drunk or under the influence of drugs.[22] As a result, the section as interpreted could lead to the situation of an accused being convicted although there was reasonable doubt as to whether they had the required objective foresight of death, which was not permitted under s11(d).

Further, the provisions could not be saved under s1. Although they might be tailored to achievement of a legitimate objective, that of discouraging the use of weapons, the law went too far in infringing fundamental rights and freedoms. It was not necessary, in order to deter individuals from carrying weapons, to create a murder offense punishable by life imprisonment based on a person's carrying of weapons, and the fact of death.[23]

The Court by majority confirmed in *The Queen v Martineau*[24] that a murder charge required proof of subjective foreseeability. The means by which the majority reached this conclusion are of most interest here. Lamer CJ for the majority noted the stigma and available penalties for the offense in concluding that fundamental principles of justice required mens rea for that offense to be committed.[25] The majority also referred to the "general principle" that criminal liability was not justified except where the actor possessed a "culpable mental state" regarding the result.[26] It also referred to the need for proportionality between the "moral blameworthiness" of the offender and the stigma and punishment attached to the offense.[27] The Court considered the validity of an offense in the following terms:

> Every one who, without lawful excuse, the proof of which lies upon him, has in his possession any instrument suitable for housebreaking . . . under circumstances that give rise to a reasonable inference that the instrument has been used or is or was intended to be used for housebreaking . . . is guilty of an indictable offense and is liable to imprisonment for fourteen years.[28]

A constitutional challenge to the provision was dismissed by a majority of 3–2. In the majority, McIntyre and Le Dain JJ stated that the concept of "reasonable inference" was attended by a requirement of proof beyond reasonable doubt.[29] No presumption was made to assist the prosecution in proving the elements of the offense, so there was no breach of s11(d).[30] In dissent, Dickson CJ and Lamer J adopted a substantive view, finding that intention was an essential element of the offense.[31] They interpreted the words "without lawful excuse" to impose a persuasive burden on the accused to establish an excuse.[32] This meant the provision infringed s11(d), because it permitted an accused to be convicted although there was reasonable doubt. An accused could be asked to do no more than raise a reasonable doubt regarding a defense.[33] No distinction should be drawn between defenses which challenge an element of the offense charged, and those which admit mens rea and actus reus, but seek to raise a defense, for example, of justification.[34] The dissentients read down the provision to impose a merely evidentiary burden on the accused.[35]

Somewhat surprisingly, the Court validated a reverse onus provision in *Whyte v The Queen*.[36] There the accused was charged with having the care and control of a motor vehicle while under the influence of alcohol. Evidence suggested the accused was found in the driver's seat of the car, slumped over the steering wheel. The key was in the ignition but the car was not running. The relevant legislation provided that where it was proven that an accused occupied the seat ordinarily occupied by the driver, they would be deemed to have had the care and control of the vehicle, unless the accused proves they did not enter the vehicle for the purpose of driving it. The Supreme Court unanimously validated the provision. The state tried to distinguish *Oakes* from the present case by arguing that whilst a purpose of trafficking was expressly an element of the offense with which the accused had been charged, here in contrast the requirement that the accused have a purpose of driving the vehicle was not expressly an element of the offense.

Eschewing this technical distinction, the Court suggested that a substantive view would be taken regarding the presumption of innocence, rather than one bound by how the legislature had framed the offense provision and relevant defenses. The Court noted:

> The distinction between elements of the offense and other aspects of the charge is irrelevant to the [presumption of innocence] inquiry. The real concern is not whether the accused must disprove an element or prove an excuse, but that an accused may be convicted while a reasonable doubt exists. When that possibility exists, there is a breach of the presumption of innocence.[37]

The Court noted that when an accused was required, on the balance of probabilities, to prove something to avoid a conviction, the provision violated the presumption of innocence, because it allowed the possibility that an innocent person could be convicted despite the existence of reasonable doubt as to their guilt.[38] It criticized the attempt to divide a trial into stages, with a burden on the accused at an intermediate stage, and an ultimate burden on the state. Here the presumption was infringed—a person could be in the driver's seat without intending to take care and control of the vehicle.[39] The Court noted that the trial judge had found that, in the absence of the presumption, there would have been reasonable doubt as to guilt.[40]

However, the Court saved the section from invalidity by use of s1. It was conceded that the objective of road safety was a legitimate state objective. The interference with the presumption of innocence was carefully drawn, and rationally connected to the legitimate objective. Further, the "rational connection" was satisfied in relation to the presumption:

> There is plainly a rational connection between the proved fact and the fact to be presumed. There is every reason to believe the person in the driver's seat has the care or control of the vehicle. The driver's seat is designed to give the occupant access to all the controls of the car, to be able to operate it. It is true that a vehicle can be occupied by one who does not assume care or control but a person in this state of mind is likely to assume a position in the vehicle intended for a passenger.[41]

The Court found the offense was minimally invasive of the right, and explicable following past cases where the prosecutor had found it difficult to show intention in relation to an intoxicated person.[42]

The case *R v Schwartz*[43] involved a provision of the Canadian *Criminal Code* making it an offense to be in possession of a restricted weapon for which the person did not have a registration certificate. The offense was punishable by a maximum jail term of five years. The legislation specifically cast the onus on to the accused to prove that they had the necessary registration certificate. A majority of the Court found the offense provision did not contravene s11(d).[44]

The majority noted the accused was not required to prove or disprove any element of the offense.[45] The possible vice with reverse onus provisions, that they might allow the conviction of an accused despite the existence of reasonable doubt as to guilt, was not relevant here. The only possible evidence that the accused could produce was the certificate itself—either they could produce it, in which case they would be acquitted, or they could not, in which case they risked conviction. It was not possible in such a situation that an accused could be convicted although there was reasonable doubt as to guilt. Thus, the section did not infringe s11(d).[46] Further, the accused was in the "best position" to resolve the issue regarding whether such a certificate existed.[47] It was irrelevant that possession of a restricted weapon did not rationally prove the absence of a certificate, because possession without a certificate was an offense complete in itself.[48]

Dickson CJ and Lamer J dissented. Again a substantive view was evident, the dissentients noting that "all substantive issues raised in a criminal prosecution are related to the fundamental issue of guilt and innocence . . . they should all be decided by . . . proof beyond reasonable doubt."[49] For the dissentients, this meant it was irrelevant whether lack of registration was an "essential element" or not. It was essential to the verdict.[50] The legislation cast a legal onus on the accused to prove they had the required certificate, contrary to s11(d). The provision was not saved by s1. It would have been easy for the prosecution to show a lack of registration.[51] There was a lack of rational connection between the thing presumed (lack of registration) and the thing proven (possession of a firearm).[52] The legislation did not minimally impair the presumption of innocence—the provision could instead have cast merely an evidentiary burden on the accused.[53] The legislation in effect abrogated the accused's right to silence; they were aware that if they did lead evidence regarding the issue of registration, they were liable to be convicted. This contravened fundamental values in Canadian society.[54]

The validity of a presumption in relation to prostitution charges was considered in *Downey v The Queen*.[55] There the accused had been charged with living on the proceeds of prostitution. The challenged provision stated that a person who lives with or is habitually in the company of prostitutes is, in the absence of evidence to the contrary, deemed to be living on the proceeds of prostitution. All members of the Court found that the provision infringed s11(d) of the *Charter* but, by a majority of 4–3, the provision was validated under s1 of the *Charter*.[56]

The majority read the provision as imposing a mere evidentiary burden on the accused, rather than a legal burden. They merely needed to create some reasonable doubt regarding the commission of the offense. However, the majority stated that even as so interpreted, the provision infringed s11(d). Their constitutional difficulty was with the presumption that a person living with or habitually with a prostitute was living on the proceeds. The majority stated that a presumption permitting one fact to be inferred from a proven fact would only be valid if the proof of the substituted fact led inexorably (beyond reasonable doubt) to proof of the other. However, this test was not satisfied here—the fact that a person was living with a prostitute did not lead inexorably to the conclusion that person was living from the proceeds of prostitution.[57] The majority saved the provision through s1, finding that the objective of the provision was sufficiently important to override the presumption. It was not unreasonable to presume that a person living with a prostitute was living from the proceeds of prostitution.[58] The reality was that if such a presumption was not made, the evidence to obtain a conviction for a living from proceeds prosecution would be very difficult to obtain without the cooperation of the prostitute, which could be difficult to obtain.[59] Infringement of the presumption was minimal—a mere evidentiary burden had been imposed and there was proportionality between the objective and the measures adopted.[60]

The reasons of the dissentients differed. La Forest CJ seemed to adopt a substantive view of the criminal law. He concluded that the facts of the offense "are not intrinsically blameworthy and simply cast too wide a net," including those living with prostitutes but not in a parasitic way.[61] McLachlin and Iacobucci JJ agreed with the position of the majority that the provision infringed the presumption, because living with or habitually being in the company of prostitutes did not lead inexorably to proof of the statutorily required element of living on the proceeds.[62] They shared the view of La Forest CJ that the offense provision was too broad, making it arbitrary, unfair and irrational, thus failing in the proportionality analysis.[63] McLachlin and Iacobucci JJ found that although the "inexorable" concept was suitable when considering whether a provision had breached s11(d), at the stage of s1 analysis, a lesser standard might be acceptable:

> The fact that a presumption fails the inexorable connection test and [violates] s11(d) is by no means determinative of the issue of whether such a presumption will pass the internal rationality test under s1. While the probity of the link between proven fact and presumed fact remains the focus of the inquiry, the balancing of the rights of the accused against deference to the democratic will of the legislature may mandate a less rigorous level of examination at the s1 stage. This may mean that . . . the . . . [requirement] that the substituted fact must prove the presumed fact beyond a reasonable doubt will not prove appropriate in the Canadian context . . . at minimum, proof of the substituted fact must make it likely that the presumed fact is true.[64]

The Court also considered a number of presumptions in relation to drunk driving offenses in *The Queen v St-Onge Lamoureux*.[65] The legislature had responded to cases where those accused of drunk driving offenses had successfully challenged the prosecution on the basis of allegedly faulty breathalyzer equipment. The legislation contained assumptions that (a) the breathalyzer instrument was functional and operated properly; (b) that even where the machine was shown to be faulty, it was not the reason for the accused's blood alcohol reading to apparently exceed the legal limit; and (c) that the accused's blood alcohol limit at the relevant time exceeded the legal limit. These were mandatory rebuttable presumptions.

The Court stated that although the presumptions did not directly concern an element of the offense, they did so indirectly.[66] Something that the prosecution would normally need to establish—the accuracy and the validity of the test results to prove the driving whilst under the influence offense—was instead transferred to the accused.[67] The accused was required to disprove something that the prosecution had not proven as they normally would be required to, under rules of criminal evidence.[68]

The Court found that the presumptions infringed s11(d) of the *Charter*, since they permitted a finding of guilt although there was reasonable doubt as to guilt. The fact finder might have reasonable doubt that the breathalyzer machine readings were accurate, but would have to accept that the reading was valid unless the accused could show otherwise.[69] As a result, the Court concluded the challenged provisions infringed s11(d).

However, this was subject to an s1 analysis. Here relevant factors in assessing the validity of a statutory presumption included the importance of the legislative objective, how difficult it would otherwise be for the prosecutor to prove the disputed fact beyond reasonable doubt, whether it was possible, and readily possible, for the accused to rebut the presumption, and any relevant scientific advances in the field.[70]

Here the presumptions related to a legitimate objective—to give the breathalyzer test results their due scientific value and importance.[71] The requirement that the accused produce evidence questioning of the functionality and operation of the instrument was rationally connected with parliament's objective.[72] It made sense that objections had to have a scientific basis. It was not impossible for the accused to surmount the reverse onus.[73] Requiring the accused to prove such evidence met the minimum impairment requirement. In terms of the proportionality element, the provision made it more difficult for an accused to challenge breathalyzer evidence. They would have to retain an expert in the field.[74]

The provisions requiring an accused to show that the malfunctions led to their unlawful blood alcohol reading were more problematic. This placed a heavy burden on the accused; it was not clear how they would be able to surmount this burden.[75] This provision placed the accused at more expense, with little benefit to the prosecution. The accused had already had to establish the machine was not providing accurate results. The Court found this provision infringed s11(d), and could not be justified under s1.[76]

Further, the requirement that an accused show that their blood alcohol content did not in fact exceed statutory limits was onerous. It was not rationally connected with the legislative objective, being to shore up the credibility of breathalyzer test results.[77] The accused had already had to show the machine was not providing accurate results; it was superfluous to require them also to show that they did not in fact exceed the statutory blood alcohol level.[78]

UNITED KINGDOM/EUROPE

The presumption of innocence is enshrined in United Kingdom law through Article 6(2) of the *European Convention on Human Rights*, and that country's adoption of the *Convention* in the *Human Rights Act 1998* (UK). At the time of writing, it is not known whether, as a result of Brexit, this position will change in the future. The presumption of innocence is also enshrined in the common law of criminal procedure, being famously described as the "golden thread" running through the web of British criminal law.[79] The presumption of innocence is considered to be part of the broader right to a fair trial enshrined in Article 6. Courts interpreting Article 6 have found that while the presumption of innocence is not, per se, absolute,[80] the right to a fair trial is.[81] In other words, if a departure from the presumption of innocence is such as to make a trial unfair, it will be incompatible with the *Convention*. Section 3(1) of the *Human Rights Act 1998* (UK) provides that in the interpretation of legislation, judges should read and give effect to same in a manner that is compatible with *Convention* rights.

The first important case is not strictly a United Kingdom decision, being a decision of the Privy Council based on the Hong Kong *Bill of Rights*, but is worthy of consideration given general remarks made by members of the Privy Council regarding legislation which departs from the presumption of innocence.[82] The challenged legislation there made it an offense for a person to be in possession of anything reasonably suspected of having been stolen, where they did not give an adequate explanation to the court ("stolen property offense"). Separately, another offense provision was challenged. This related to facilitating proceeds of drug trafficking, knowing or having reasonable grounds to believe that the proceeds had been so derived ("facilitating offense"). The accused had a defense if they could show that they did not know or suspect that the arrangement related to drug trafficking.

The Council noted that the question of whether a provision infringed the presumption of innocence principle was a question concerning the substance of the challenged legislation, rather than its form.[83] The Council provided some guidance as to when a reverse onus principle would be acceptable in this context. It pointed out that "common sense" suggested the prosecution not be required to solely shoulder the burden of proof where it was simple for an accused to prove a defense.[84] The relative balance of things the prosecution must prove, compared with things the defense must prove, was relevant.[85] Whether the reverse onus was "reasonably imposed" was relevant.[86] The less significant the departure from normal procedure, the easier it would be to defend the provision.[87] Regarding the use of proven facts to presume other facts relevant to the offense, the Council referred with apparent approval to the United States decision in *Leary v United States*[88] that in such cases, the inferred fact would have to more likely than not flow from the proved fact to be valid.[89] The Council stated that the Canadian approach identified in *Whyte* was "somewhat complex" and would be of general guidance only in difficult cases.[90]

The Court found that the stolen property offense contravened the presumption of innocence. It presumed the most important element of the offense, namely whether possession of the property was innocent, against the accused. It required the prosecution to prove only minor matters.[91] In contrast, the facilitating offense was valid—the prosecution was required to prove the significant matters such as the defendant being involved in a transaction involving the proceeds of drug trafficking, and had the required knowledge or reasonable grounds for belief. In such a case, the imposition of a reverse onus on the accused to disprove knowledge was reasonable.[92]

The question of a reverse onus provision was again considered in *R v Director of Public Prosecutions ex parte Kebilene*.[93] There the challenge involved legislation providing for a terrorism offense. The offense was committed if a person had an article in their possession giving rise to a reasonable suspicion that they had it for a terrorism purpose. It was a defense for the person to show they did not have the item in their possession for a terrorism purpose. Similarly, the act provided that where the relevant item was found on premises that the accused either occupied or habitually used, other than as a member of the public, they were deemed to be in possession of the item, unless they showed they were not aware that the item was on the premises, or if they were, that they did not control the item. Conviction carried a maximum punishment of 10 years in jail. Another offense related to the collection of information, itself innocent, for suspected terrorism use. Again that use was presumed against the accused, unless they could prove otherwise.

The matter was considered by both the Court of Appeal and House of Lords. Strictly, they were dicta comments, because it was established that the *Convention* was not operative in the United Kingdom at the time the accused had been charged. The main Court of Appeal judgment was written by Lord Bingham, who would later be appointed to the House of Lords. As a result, both the Court of Appeal and House of Lords decisions are considered important.

Lord Bingham stated it was the substantive effect of the challenged provision, rather than its form, that was critical. He said the "gravamen" of the offense charged was possession of articles for terrorism purposes. He broke the elements of the crime down to comprise possession (actus reus) and terrorist purpose (mens rea). However, the prosecutor need not prove either of those elements in order to obtain a conviction. An accused who declined to provide evidence could be convicted as a result of the presumptions against them, and on reasonable suspicion that was short of proof. Similarly, the collection offense could be made out although the prosecution had not shown any mens rea regarding the purpose for which the information had been obtained. Again an accused who declined to provide evidence could be convicted. Lord Bingham concluded the provisions undermined the presumption of innocence in a "blatant and obvious way."[94]

Lord Bingham adopted and applied the position of Dickson CJ in *Whyte*, and in particular the question of whether the challenged provisions could result in the conviction of an accused, despite the existence of reasonable doubt as to their guilt. Lord Bingham found this was possible with the challenged provisions—an accused could be convicted although a jury had reasonable doubt as to whether the accused had items in their possession for a terrorism purpose, or had collected information for that purpose.[95]

Lord Bingham acknowledged that in cases where intention was an element of a crime, the accused would be in a better position to lead evidence of their intention. However, this did not relieve the state from the obligation to prove intent.[96]

In the House of Lords, Lord Hope distinguished between statutory presumptions which placed an evidentiary burden on the accused (the accused being required to raise reasonable doubt), and a persuasive or legal burden on the accused (requiring them to prove their innocence on the balance of probabilities).[97] Evidentiary burdens did not breach the presumption of innocence. Legal burdens required further examination. He noted they may be mandatory or discretionary.[98]

Lord Hope suggested various factors were relevant in assessing the validity of reverse onus provisions: (a) what must the prosecution prove in order to transfer the onus to the defense; (b) does the burden on the accused relate to something that is likely to be difficult for them to prove, or is something likely to be within their knowledge; and (c) what is the nature of the threat posed by society to which the legislation is aimed?[99]

Lord Hope concluded it would not impose an unreasonable burden to expect someone in possession of items that could be used for terrorism purposes to explain such possession.[100] Terrorism was an existential threat to society and society had a strong interest in its prevention.[101] Lord Hobhouse merely agreed that in considering whether legislation infringed the presumption of innocence, there was a need to look beyond the bare words of the statute, that the extent to which the prosecution was required to prove "essential criminality" was important, and the justification for casting the onus on the accused.[102]

The Court's interpretation power in s3(1) of the *Human Rights Act 1998* (UK) was of particular importance in *R v Lambert*.[103] The challenged legislation there created an offense of possession of a prohibited substance with intent to supply. The act created a defense if the accused could show that they neither knew nor suspected or had reason to suspect that the substance in their possession was an unlawful drug. The maximum penalty for the offense was seven years' imprisonment. All members of the House of Lords found that the legislation was valid, but a majority found the provision should be interpreted so as to impose merely an evidentiary, rather than legal, onus on the accused.[104]

Some difference of opinion was evident on the Court as to what the offense provision required, and in particular whether it required evidence that the accused knew the substance in their possession was an unlawful substance. The offense in its terms did not require proof that the accused knew the substance was unlawful. Lord Slynn, with whom

Lords Hope[105] and Clyde agreed,[106] concluded that the prosecution did not need to prove knowledge, based on a literal interpretation of the provision.[107] Lord Hope said that parliament could lawfully enact criminal law provisions without requiring a particular mens rea.[108] Lord Clyde agreed parliament could create a criminal offense that did not contain a requirement of intent.[109] Lord Slynn read down the provision to impose an evidentiary burden only.[110] Lord Steyn, on the other hand, found that bearing in mind that the maximum punishment for the offense was life imprisonment, proof of knowledge was required. He agreed that knowledge was the "gravamen" of the offense.[111]

Lord Steyn acknowledged that the distinction between constituent elements of a crime and defenses would sometimes be unprincipled and arbitrary.[112] Drafters had choices as to the framing of offense provisions and defenses. He expressed that this meant a substantive, rather than formalistic, view needed to be applied. He seemed to suggest that proof of matters "closely linked with mens rea and moral blameworthiness" could not be transferred to the accused.[113] Here the question of knowledge related to such matters, such that proof of it could not be transferred to the accused. He expressed agreement with the guide suggested by Dickson CJ in *Whyte*, i.e., that the provision not be interpreted so as to permit an accused to be convicted despite the existence of reasonable doubt as to guilt.[114] Applying this test, a person accused of a crime under this section could be convicted although there was reasonable doubt whether the accused knew of the nature of the substance. This possibility could not be dismissed as unlikely to occur. Thus Lord Steyn agreed that the provision should be read down so as to impose an evidentiary burden only.

Lord Hope, in agreeing that the burden on the accused should be interpreted as an evidentiary, rather than legal, burden, held that in most cases the practical effect of the distinction would be minimal.[115] Lord Clyde, in reading the provision down to impose an evidentiary burden only, noted that the issue to which the presumption related was upon a matter within the accused's knowledge.[116] It would be relatively easy for the accused to lead evidence upon it. Weighted against this was the very serious possible consequences of a conviction under the offense (life imprisonment).[117] Lord Clyde also applied the Dickson CJ test in *Whyte*, that if a legal burden was placed on the accused, it would be possible for an accused to be convicted despite the existence of reasonable doubt as to their guilt.[118] Lord Hutton, in the minority, read the provision as validly imposing a legal burden on the accused. He agreed that the *Convention* meant Parliament did not enjoy complete freedom to define the elements of an offense as it wished.[119] Here the presumption was restricted in scope—it applied only after the prosecution proved some substantive matters, it was not irrebuttable and not unreasonable.[120] If the prosecution were obliged to prove knowledge, it would make convictions very difficult to obtain.[121] There was reasonable proportionality between the legislative objective sought, and the means utilized to achieve it.[122]

A provision which placed a legal burden on the accused was validated against an Article 6(2) challenge in *R v Johnstone*.[123] There the Court reiterated the utility of the Canadian approach, in that reverse onus provisions were problematic where they could result in a person's conviction despite reasonable doubt as to their guilt. It stated that the more serious the punishment which might flow from the conviction, the more compelling must be the justification for the reverse onus. The extent and nature of what the accused had to prove, and their relative importance to what the prosecution had to prove, was relevant. Further, the relative ease (or otherwise) by which the accused would be able to prove that which the legislation required of them would be relevant.[124] Of most importance here were the facts that a statutory presumption was appropriate given the difficulty otherwise in obtaining appropriate evidence regarding a possible breach of the law, and that those in the defendant's position were typically aware of the relevant law in this area, and the risks associated with non-compliance.

The decision *Sheldrake v Director of Public Prosecutions Attorney General's Reference (No4 of 2002)*[125] involved conjoined appeals regarding reverse onus provisions. The first challenge was to provisions of the *Road Traffic Act 1988* (UK). The accused was charged with an offense under the act of being in charge of a motor vehicle while under the influence of alcohol. A sub-section provided a defense if the accused could prove they did not intend to drive the vehicle whilst over the limit. The second challenge was to s11 of the *Terrorism Act 2000* (UK). That provision created an offense of belonging to a proscribed organization. Section 11(2) created a defense if an accused showed that the organization was not proscribed at the time they became a member (or renewed their membership), and had not taken part in activities of the organization at a time when it was proscribed. The maximum penalty for a breach of s11 was ten years' imprisonment. A majority of the House of Lords found that the first provision validly imposed a legal burden on the accused, but that the second provision should be read as imposing only an evidentiary burden on the accused.[126]

Lord Bingham started by noting the "repugnancy" to ordinary notions of fairness for a defendant to be required to disprove an allegation of wrongdoing against them, on pain of punishment and conviction.[127] After discussing various authorities, he summarized the position as that the *Convention* required statutory presumptions to be kept within reasonable limits and not be arbitrary:

> It is open to states to define the constituent elements of a criminal offense, excluding the requirement of mens rea. But the substance and effect of any presumption adverse to a defendant must be examined,

> and must be reasonable. Relevant to any judgment on reasonableness or proportionality will be the opportunity given to the defendant to rebut the presumption, maintenance of the rights of the defense, flexibility in application of the presumption, retention by the court of the power to assess the evidence, the importance of what is at stake and the difficulty which the prosecutor may face in the absence of a presumption.[128]

Lord Bingham took a relatively formalistic view of the *Road Traffic Act* offense, noting that the offense did not require evidence that the accused intend to drive the vehicle whilst under the influence.[129] It was not objectionable to cast an offense in this manner without requiring the prosecutor to prove criminal intent. The defendant had full opportunity to show they did not intend to drive, something that was intimately within their own knowledge at the time, so as to make it appropriate to ask them to prove it.[130] The section had lawfully imposed a legal burden on the accused to prove they did not intend to drive.

In contrast, Lord Bingham had serious concerns with the terrorism offense. Here he appeared to take a more substantive view of what could be the subject of a criminal label, concluding that "If section 11(1) is read on its own, some of those liable to be convicted and punished for belonging to a proscribed organization may be guilty of no conduct which could reasonably be regarded as blameworthy or such as should properly attract criminal sanction."[131]

He expressed concern that the offense could capture a person who joined an organization when it was not proscribed, or joined a proscribed organization ignorant of that status.[132] He was concerned that application of the provision on its terms could lead to a real risk of unfair conviction. A person could be convicted based on conduct which was not criminal at the time of its commission.[133] Given the secretive nature of terrorist organizations, it might practically be very difficult for an accused to show they had not participated in the organization's activities. Such organizations would not typically keep minutes of meetings or other records.[134] For these reasons, Lord Bingham for the majority read the provision down to impose only an evidentiary burden.[135]

A pivot to a more formalistic position to the presumption of innocence was evident in *R v G*.[136] There two justices (with whom other justices agreed) explained that principles of fair trial, including presumption of innocence, did not have any particular substantive content. Legislatures were free to dictate what the elements of particular crimes should be. A crime need not have a particular mens rea element.[137]

AUSTRALIA

Prior to summarizing the Australian case law, two observations must be made by way of explanation. Firstly, while Australia, like Canada, inherited the common law tradition, and while it embraced, like Canada, the idea of a written constitution, the Australian *Constitution* does not contain features strongly supportive of human rights. It was written in the late nineteenth century when legal positivism was at its most influential, espoused by important writers such as Dicey.[138] Ideas of natural law and social contract, so influential in the late eighteenth century, had waned to some extent. Unlike Canada, it has not subsequently addressed the constitutional omission by passage of a national *Charter*, although subnational governments have passed similar human rights instruments. Most recently in 2009, the federal government again considered, but rejected, the idea of a national human rights instrument. Constitutionally, it has the means to do so. The Australian federal government has the constitutional power to implement into legislation international conventions and treaties to which Australia is a signatory. Australia has ratified the *International Covenant on Civil and Political Rights*, but the federal parliament has not implemented the *Convention* into Australian law by way of legislation. Australia subscribes to the theory that unless and until international covenants are implemented by legislation, they do not affect Australian domestic law.[139] Australia has ratified and implemented some human rights conventions, particularly in the area of discrimination on the basis of gender and race. These important pieces of legislation are not enshrined and do not have constitutional status, so they are liable to being amended in the future.

Readers from nations with a long constitutional tradition of protection of fundamental human rights may find it difficult to understand how and why a nation would decline to include fundamental human rights in a constitutional document. The best response is that the experience of the Australian founding fathers had not been burned, as in the case of the United States, by revolution and war. In the case of Australia, the nation was created by a process of evolution, rather than revolution. The lived experience of the founding fathers who wrote the Australian *Constitution* had not taught them the need for strong human rights protection.

While many comment that the Australian *Constitution* is a "Washminster" model, incorporating what were considered the "best" elements of the United Kingdom and United States constitutional arrangements, on the issue of rights protection the founding fathers leaned very far to the (then) United Kingdom model. In this model rights are protected by the rule of law and free and fair elections. Parliament is considered the democratic body. At least in the United Kingdom, a theory of parliamentary supremacy applied, to the effect that any law passed by parliament was valid. A court had no power to declare legislation to be constitutionally invalid. There was no scope for judicial review.

Many assumed that the United Kingdom doctrine of parliamentary supremacy would apply in Australia. However, Australia is a federal nation and has a written *Constitution* which carefully delineates the powers of respective governments. As a result, the Australian High Court has, taking its lead from pivotal *Marbury v Madison*,[140] re-affirmed the fundamental nature of judicial review to Australian constitutional governance, and confirmed that parliamentary supremacy is not applicable to Australian legislatures.[141] Indeed, anyone who reads Dicey's treatise including his discussion of parliamentary supremacy will see that Dicey outlined three characteristics of a parliament that was "supreme" in this sense.[142] At the very least, no Australian parliament meets two out of these three characteristics, and it may well be that no Australian parliament meets any of them.

The other preliminary point must relate to the doctrine of the separation of powers. Like the United States *Constitution*, the Australian *Constitution* clearly contemplates a separation of powers between the legislature (chapter 1 of the *Constitution*), the executive (chapter 2) and the judiciary (chapter 3). Each embraces the Montesquiean theory that each arm of government is to act as a check and balance on the others. In the first three-quarters of the twentieth century, most of the Australian case law on the question of judicial power focused on the question of whether a judicial body was exercising non-judicial power or a non-judicial body was exercising judicial power (both of which would, prima facie, be constitutionally invalid). However, as will be seen shortly, in later years the Court has become constitutionally concerned with laws that confer, or remove, powers from a court such that a court's institutional integrity is threatened. Similarly, a law which denuded a court of the traditional characteristics of judicial process might be constitutionally invalid, because it undermines the institutional integrity of a court, contrary to chapter 3. Through, and only through, this line of reasoning, does the possibility exist that courts might be able to constitutionally protect the presumption of innocence from legislative attack. This would be on the basis that the presumption of innocence is a fundamental characteristic of judicial process, so that legislated departures from it offend the Court's constitutionally entrenched institutional integrity, and so are invalid. And finally, by way of preliminaries, there have been relatively few cases in Australia dealing with reverse onus provisions, in comparison with other jurisdictions studied, so the jurisprudence here is at a more nascent stage.

Early Australian case law considering reverse onus provisions generally held them valid on the basis that the legislature had the constitutional power to make provisions regarding matters of evidence.[143] The Court validated a provision which made it an offense to be in possession of items reasonably suspected of having been unlawfully imported into Australia contrary to the act, unless the defendant had a reasonable excuse, proof of which lay on them.[144] The legislation was held valid on the basis parliament had power to legislate with respect to rules of evidence, including placing the onus of proof wherever it wished.[145]

By the 1990s, comments began to appear in the case law suggesting there might be some constitutional limit on the ability of parliament to legislate away fundamental due process principles like the presumption of innocence. As indicated above, the basis of this is not anything expressed in the *Constitution*, but rather an implication derived from the separation of powers enshrined in the *Constitution*. The Court began to articulate the notion that laws interfering with the institutional integrity of the courts might be invalid, and that one example of law which fits that description was one which departed from traditional characteristics of courts, or of judicial process.

So, for instance, in *Environmental Protection Authority v Caltex Refining Co Pty Ltd*,[146] a case involving the question of whether the privilege against self-incrimination applied to corporations, the Court considered the related right of the presumption of innocence. In a lower court, Gleeson CJ (then of the New South Wales Court of Criminal Appeal, later to be elevated to Chief Justice of the High Court) had referred to the privilege against self-incrimination as "maintaining the integrity of our accusatorial system of criminal justice."[147] In the High Court, Mason CJ and Toohey J approved these comments, referring to the "fundamental principle of the common law that the onus rests on the Crown of proving guilt beyond reasonable doubt."[148] Deane Dawson and Gaudron JJ likewise referred to the fundamental principle of criminal law that the onus of proving a criminal offense lay on the prosecution,[149] and referred to a deeply embedded belief that those alleging the commission of a crime must prove it.[150]

Mason CJ and Toohey J rejected the company's alleged entitlement to the privilege against self-incrimination. However, it is their reasoning, unfortunately expressed in the form of a double negative, that is of most interest to us here. They concluded that although the privilege against self-incrimination could apply to an individual, "It does not follow that the protection is an essential element in the accusatorial system of justice or that its unavailability in this respect, at least in relation to corporations, would compromise that system. The fundamental principle that the onus of proof beyond reasonable doubt rests on the Crown would remain unimpaired."[151] This tantalizing passage raised more questions than it answered. What if the privilege had been made unavailable to an individual? Would this compromise an essential element in the accusatorial system of justice? And if it did, would this justify a finding that the provision was unconstitutional? What would Mason CJ and Toohey J say about a law that did in fact impair the typical requirement that the Crown prove its allegations beyond a reasonable doubt?

Other members of the Court discussed the obligation in common law systems that the prosecutor prove their allegations beyond reasonable doubt in contrast to the inquisitorial process of civil law systems. It reflected the "aversion" of the common law to the inquisitorial method.[152] McHugh J linked the presumption of innocence and privilege against self-incrimination with notions of the integrity of the adversarial system.[153] Though the Court did not specifically refer to chapter 3 requirements in this case, the case provides the first glimmer of hope for those arguing for constitutional protection of presumption of innocence. This is because the High Court has also said that chapter 3 protects fundamental characteristics of judicial process.[154] Here in *Environmental Protection Authority*, members of the Court suggested an adversarial process, including an onus of proof on the prosecution, might be such a characteristic.

Constitutional restrictions on parliament's ability to legislate with respect to rules of evidence were again considered by the Court in *Nicholas v The Queen*.[155] There legislation provided that the court, in determining whether evidence as to drug importation should be admitted, should disregard the fact that it had been obtained through a law enforcement officer committing an offense. Two members of the Court found the legislation was unconstitutional as a breach of separation of powers principle, interfering in the court's role in weighing and assessing the evidence, and preventing abuses of process.[156] Perhaps of most interest though were dicta comments in the judgments of members of the majority pertinent to current discussion.

Brennan CJ stated that a reverse onus provision would be constitutional provided it prescribed a "reasonable approach" to the assessment of the evidence.[157] Toohey and Gaudron JJ could foresee a situation where legislation as to the rules of evidence precluded a fair trial,[158] and indicated there would be constitutional concern with such a trial. In validating the current provision, Gummow J noted it was not a deeming provision:

> Nor does [the section] deem to exist . . . any ultimate fact being an element of the offense with which the accused is charged. A law of that nature, albeit procedural in form, might well usurp the constitutionally mandated exercise of the judicial power for the determination of criminal guilt . . . nor does [the section] change the amount or degree of proof essential to convict [the accused] from that required when the alleged offenses were committed.

Converting the words of Gummow J from a negative to a positive, it seems he might have a constitutional objection to a law which did deem to exist an element of the offense charged. Perhaps in a similar vein, Hayne J noted in validating the legislation that it did not "deal directly with ultimate issues of guilt or innocence."[159] Again the suggestion is that if the legislation did deal directly with ultimate issues of guilt or innocence, it might be constitutionally invalid. And a law of the kind described by Gummow J, deeming or assuming that an element of an offense existed, is surely one that deals directly with ultimate issues of guilt or innocence.

Property forfeiture schemes often contain reverse onus provisions, deeming property to have been unlawfully acquired, and thereby liable to forfeiture, unless the person accused of wrongdoing can show on the balance of probabilities that they acquired the property lawfully. Such a scheme was successfully challenged on constitutional grounds in *International Finance Trust Co Ltd v New South Wales Crime Commission.*[160] The case is somewhat difficult because there were various grounds on which the constitutional challenge was upheld. Despite this, two members of the Court found:

> The result is that the effect of the suspicion by an authorized officer of the Commission . . . which founds a restraining order possibly may be of considerable scope and may be displaced only . . . upon application under s25. But that application cannot succeed unless the applicant proves to the Supreme Court that it is more probable than not that the interest in property for which exclusion is sought is not "illegally obtained property." The making of that proof by the applicant for an exclusion order requires the negating of an extremely widely drawn range of possibilities of contravention of the criminal law found in the common law, and State and Federal statute law . . . the Supreme Court is conscripted for a process which requires in substance the ex parte sequestration of property upon suspicion of wrongdoing for an indeterminate period . . . in addition the possibility of release from sequestration is conditional upon proof of a negative proposition of considerable legal and factual complexity. Section 10 engages the Supreme Court in activity which is repugnant in a fundamental degree to judicial process as understood and conducted throughout Australia.[161]

Thus, the fact that the legislation contained a reverse onus provision which the accused would find difficult to overcome was at least one of the factors which convinced the Court that the legislation was unconstitutional.

These matters were considered again indirectly in a case involving the privilege against self-incrimination.[162] There members of the Court reflected on the adversarial nature of the criminal trial. Hayne and Bell JJ said that the nature of the criminal trial was accusatorial in that the prosecution chose the charge/s, and bore the onus of proof with respect to all elements of that charge.[163] Kiefel J stated that the fact that the prosecutor bore the onus of proof was fundamental to the administration of criminal justice in Australia, and had a constitutional dimension.[164] Dissenting in the result, French CJ and Crennan J agreed that the criminal trial in Australia should be characterized as being adversarial. They conceded parliament could legislate with respect to rules of evidence, including the standard or burden of proof,[165] but seemed to endorse the view of Hayne J in *Nicholas v The Queen*[166] that these changes must not "deal directly with ultimate issues of guilt or innocence."[167]

Most recently in *Lee v New South Wales Crime Commission*,[168] again in the context of the privilege against self-incrimination, Hayne J spoke strongly of the "standard of proof that must be applied in adjudging guilt. If the prosecution cannot prove guilt beyond reasonable doubt, the accused must be found not guilty. Guilt must be determined at trial, not assumed."[169] Again he emphasized the accusatorial process of criminal justice.[170] Kiefel J (with whom Bell J agreed)[171] agreed that presumption of innocence was a fundamental principle of the common law of Australia,[172] and the fact that the onus of proof was on the prosecution as an "essential aspect" of the criminal trial in Australia.[173] Other judges referred more briefly to the accusatorial nature of the criminal trial in Australia.[174]

REFLECTION AND CRITIQUE

Support for Test Based on Whether an Accused Can Be Convicted Despite the Existence of Reasonable Doubt

In the pioneering *Oakes* decision, the Supreme Court of Canada,[175] adopting and applying the views of evidence expert Sir Rupert Cross, stated that the question of the validity of a reverse onus provision should be measured by whether it in effect could permit an accused to be convicted despite the existence of reasonable doubt. This invited attention to the nature of the burden of proof placed on the accused, and in particular whether the burden imposed was legal or persuasive (in which case, the provision was vulnerable to challenge because an accused could be convicted although they raised reasonable doubt), or merely evidentiary (where the provision would be less vulnerable because an accused would only need to raise reasonable doubt). This has continued to be the yardstick in the Canadian case law, and has been embraced by some of the United Kingdom case law.[176]

This approach is supported here. As indicated in chapter 1, one of the prime rationales for the presumption of innocence is to avoid the conviction of innocent people. It is strongly linked to the concept of the burden of proof being on the prosecution, and for the prosecution to meet this burden at the standard of beyond reasonable doubt. As a result, it is perfectly logical and sensible to use the question of whether an accused could be convicted despite the existence of reasonable doubt as a barometer of whether the presumption of innocence has been infringed. A situation where an accused could be convicted despite the existence of reasonable doubt would cause substantial community disquiet, undermining public confidence in the system of criminal justice and causing people to lose respect for the law and legal institutions, as well as being catastrophic for the individual involved, and their family and friends, etc. As a result, a test based on a principle that an accused must not be convicted despite the existence of reasonable doubt is strongly supported and defended here as a bedrock, fundamental principle which must not be breached.

Due to my acceptance of this principle as fundamental, it follows that I cannot accept some of the Canadian decisions. These decisions have found that the challenged legislation permits an accused to be convicted despite the existence of reasonable doubt, and thus breach s11(d) of the *Charter*. However, in some cases judges have proceeded to validate the provision under an s1 proportionality analysis. This occurred in *R v Whyte*[177] and *The Queen v St Onge Lamoureux*.[178] In these cases the Supreme Court found that the challenged provisions breached s11(d) of the *Charter* because as applied they permitted an accused person to be convicted although there was reasonable doubt as to their guilt. However, the Court then proceeded to validate the provisions under s1 analysis, permitting interferences with fundamental freedoms that can be justified in a free and democratic society.

In my own view, there can be no justification in a free and democratic society for conviction of a person where there is reasonable doubt as to their guilt. My own view is that this interest is absolute. I would entertain no exceptions. No governmental interest can justify imprisonment of the innocent, or, more accurately, those not proven beyond reasonable doubt to be guilty. The seriousness of the offense cannot justify it; the fact that the offense is very prevalent cannot justify it. The fact that it is difficult for the prosecution to obtain the required evidence cannot justify it, and nor can the fact that an accused might be able to lead evidence on the matter relatively easily. There is no "moral comfort" in convicting someone in these circumstances. In my view, once a reverse onus provision is interpreted as imposing a legal burden on the accused to disprove guilt, the presumption of innocence is breached, and no s1 analysis can be entertained. That is the end of the inquiry, and the law is invalid. If the reverse onus provision is interpreted as imposing merely an evidentiary burden on the accused, this may be seen as a breach of the presumption of innocence, but could be saved under an s1 analysis. The risk that a person could be convicted despite the existence of reasonable doubt is non-existent in such cases.

Thus, the distinction between a burden considered to be a legal (persuasive) burden, and a burden considered to be a mere evidentiary burden, is absolutely critical. There is a substantial difference between the two, in terms of their basic compatibility with the fundamental principle of presumption of innocence as well as the obligations they practically place on the accused to rebut the reverse onus. In this light, I must respectfully disagree with the assertion of Lord Hope in *R v Lambert* that "the practical effect of reading [the challenged sections] as imposing an evidentiary burden only on the accused and not a persuasive burden . . . is likely in almost every case that can be imagined to be minimal."[179]

Rational Connection Test and Acceptance of Less than Beyond Reasonable Doubt

Like the American case law, the Canadian case law has considered the use of proven facts to infer other facts that are typically elements of a crime. This approach recognizes the difficulty in some cases for a prosecution practically to prove an element of the offense. As a result, it permits them a shortcut, allowing the prosecution to prove another fact (that is presumably easier to prove), and then permitting proof of that fact to serve as a substitute for facts regarding the elements of the actual offense.

Here again, care must be taken. Firstly, the court must not allow backsliding from the presumption of innocence principle. It might do this by, for instance, not requiring that the rational connection between the proven fact and the presumed fact to be proved beyond reasonable doubt. The Supreme Court was alert to this possibility in *R v Oakes*, raising the concern that the rational connection test not be used in a way that directly or indirectly undermined the presumption of innocence. The Privy Council was less circumspect in *Kwong-Kut*, seemingly accepting the United States Supreme Court decision in *Leary v United States* suggesting that a more-likely-than-not test between the proven fact and the presumed face was sufficient.[180] Thankfully, the Supreme Court of Canada in the *Downey*[181] decision and in the *Vaillancourt*[182] decision did require that the proven fact be rationally connected to the presumed fact "inexorably," or at the level of beyond reasonable doubt. This is supported. It led the majority in *Downey* to find that the provision infringed s11(d) of the *Charter*, because the thing presumed (living from the proceeds of prostitution) did not flow inexorably from the proven fact that the accused was living with a prostitute.

However the majority then proceeded to validate the provision under an s1 proportionality analysis, given the provision was deemed reasonable, minimally invasive, and related to something upon which otherwise the prosecution might find it difficult to obtain evidence. My concern is that the accused was convicted of a crime although there was reasonable doubt regarding whether he had committed an element of the crime, namely, was living from the proceeds of prostitution, which was the essence of the crime. The majority concede that there was reasonable doubt as to whether the accused was living off the proceeds, but proceeded to validate the provision under s1. For the same reasons as I gave above, I would not permit a prosecution to succeed where, according to the judges' own assessments, there was reasonable doubt as to whether an accused had committed an element of the offense.

Concern is also raised with the position of two of the dissenting justices, McLachlin and Iacobucci JJ. Those justices indicated that at the s1 stage, a different test than the "inexorable" or "beyond reasonable doubt" standard might be utilized to consider the law. They suggested that, at minimum, the fact that the proven fact made the existence of the presumed fact more likely than not could be sufficient to save the otherwise invalid provision under s1. Again, I am concerned with this approach, since it can also eventually lead to an outcome where an accused is convicted of a crime although the prosecution has not proven all of the elements of that crime beyond a reasonable doubt. We should not permit a conviction where the prosecution has only met the more-likely-than-not standard, either at the stage of considering s11(d) or s1. No interest in a free and democratic society can justify conviction and punishment of those not proven beyond reasonable doubt to have committed each and every element of the crime with which they have been charged.

Substantive versus Procedural View of the Presumption of Innocence

The next question which arises is the extent to which, if at all, the presumption of innocence extends to the substance of the criminal law. In other words, whether legislatures are free to make whatever they wish to make a crime, or whether there are restrictions and, if so, what those restrictions might be. Does the presumption of innocence apply simply to the elements of the crime as defined by the legislature, whatever they are, or does it have a broader, substantive content?

Certainly a range of approaches is evident in the case law. Various United Kingdom decisions refer to the need to consider the substance of the legislation, rather than its form, in this context.[183] Lord Bingham has been consistent on this, in *Kebilene* pointing out that the crime framed there did not contain a requirement of mens rea, and expressing concern with that.[184] Again in *Sheldrake* he referred to conduct that could reasonably be regarded as blameworthy.[185] This indicates concern, at least to some extent, with the substance of the criminal law. To some extent, the comment of Lord Hobhouse in *Kebilene* was similar, questioning the "essential criminality" that the prosecution was required to prove.[186] In *Lambert* Lord Steyn used the concepts of mens rea and "moral blameworthiness" in relation to what the prosecution ought be required to prove,[187] and Lord Hutton said parliament was not completely free in defining offenses.[188] However, several comments in the United Kingdom case law also suggest that the legislature is free to create an offense in whichever manner it wishes, there being no essential requirement such as mens rea, moral blameworthiness, of minimum level of essential criminality.[189]

Concern with the substance of the criminal law has tended to be a minority position in the Canadian case law, where for example Dickson CJ and Lamer J in *R v Holmes* read in a requirement of an intent not expressed in a criminal statute,[190] and in *Downey v The Queen* La Forest CJ refers in this context to the question of whether proscribed conduct was "intrinsically blameworthy."[191] The Court in *Whyte v The Queen* was unanimous in finding that the distinction between elements of an offense and defenses should be ignored,[192] indicative of a substantive approach, as were the comments of Dickson CJ and Lamer J in *R v Schwartz* to the effect that the prosecution had the burden of proof on all substantive issues.[193]

Questions regarding substance also underlay the Court's uncertainty over whether the offense of murder could be defined in a way such that subjective foresight of death was not required. Eventually, the Court adopted a substantive position that such subjective foresight was, as a matter of substance, required.[194] Here, in language reminiscent of some of the United States case law referred to in the previous chapter, the Court referred to concepts such as the moral blameworthiness of the offender, and the stigma and punishment attached to a particular crime. In *Vaillancourt* the Court said that, as a matter of substance, the nature and seriousness of the offense with which the accused had been charged might determine whether mens rea was required.[195] It followed through in *Martineau*, finding that the stigma and punishment attracted by a murder conviction required nothing less than a mens rea finding against the accused, a requirement that could not, consistent with principles of fundamental justice, be read down.[196] In essence, as with the United Kingdom case law, the Canadian decisions have divided over whether, and to what extent, a substantive view can be taken of the requirements of the presumption of innocence, and limits (if any) on the ability of the legislature to define a crime as they wish, and in particular to do away with requirements of intention or (subjective) reasonable foreseeability. At times, concepts of moral blameworthiness, culpability and stigma have been used to suggest limits; at others, these limits have largely been ignored by the Court.

Not surprisingly, academics have strongly divided on the matter. Some have indicated that a substantive view, at least to some extent, should be taken on the presumption of innocence, to include consideration of the substance of criminal law.[197] These scholars argue this is essential to avoid the presumption of innocence being circumvented by the legislature.[198] They argue that mens rea and culpability are, or should be, essential to criminality.[199] Others are completely against this, favoring a purely procedural approach to the presumption, applied to the elements of the offense as defined by parliament.[200] For these scholars, it is not possible to keep any consideration of the substance of the criminal law within workable limits.[201]

As indicated in an earlier chapter, the question of whether a substantive or procedural approach should be taken to presumption of innocence requirements raises a fundamental philosophical question of what a crime is, and whether it is anything that a legislature deems to be a crime, or whether it does, or should, have a required minimum content. This will be the subject of an extended discussion in chapter 4.

Other Rationales for Departure from Presumption of Innocence

I have already discussed in the previous chapter other possible rationales in the case law for a departure from the presumption of innocence. These appear in the case law in the jurisdictions studied in this chapter. For example, that it is legally acceptable to place the onus on the defense because otherwise it would be difficult for the prosecution to prove the matter.[202] Alternatively, that the accused was in the "best" or "better" position to prove a particular thing,[203] or the ease or difficulty for the accused in proving (or disproving) a particular thing.[204] It has also sometimes been suggested that the seriousness of the crime with which the accused has been charged might justify a greater departure from the presumption of innocence,[205] although this is contradicted by other statements that where the punishment for the relevant offense is serious, justification for the departure must be stronger than otherwise.[206] There is substantial academic criticism of relaxation of the presumption of innocence merely because a serious offense is involved,[207] or the accused is thought to be in a position to lead evidence contrary to the presumption.[208] In contrast, relativities, or in other words, the extent to which the prosecution is required to prove substantive matters compared with the extent to which the accused is required to prove matters, may be of some relevance.[209]

State of the Australian Precedent

As indicated, it is harder to make a comparison between the Australian case law and the case law elsewhere given the vastly different legal landscape, and in particular the lack of express protection of the presumption of innocence in a human rights charter. The constitutional principle of the separation of powers holds most promise in the Australian context in terms of protecting the presumption of innocence from statutory interference. It should be acknowledged that in the United States case law discussed in chapter 2, Black and Douglas JJ did discuss the separation of powers implications involved in the use of statutory presumptions, and this was one of the reasons why they (in dissent) found statutory presumptions in cases such as *Gainey*, *Leary*, *Turner* and *Barnes* to be unconstitutional. To that extent at least, there is some overlap between the United States case law and the Australian.

The Australian High Court has not developed any jurisprudence on issues such as whether reverse onus provisions should be read as evidentiary, rather than legal burdens, because it does not have access to the interpretive mechanism available under the *Human Rights Act 1998* (UK), and is not called upon to do the kind of balancing ostensibly required by the Canadian *Charter*. It has not developed any jurisprudence on the question of whether the rational connection principle can be used to infer required facts from proven facts. It has not developed any jurisprudence on the question of whether the legislature can define crimes in any manner it wishes, though the tenor of its largely legal positivism–infused approach suggests that, if called upon to do so, it would probably agree parliament has broad discretion in that regard.

The glimmer of hope on the constitutional horizon for those who would like the presumption of innocence to be defended more robustly are mainly dicta comments to the effect that legislative attempts to deem elements of crimes to be proven, unless the accused shows otherwise, might be an unconstitutional usurpation of judicial power. The High Court has said in a number of cases that the accusatorial nature of criminal process is fundamental to the way the Australian justice system works. It has said in a number of cases that fundamental features of judicial process are protected from legislative interference by the separation of powers principle. The paradox is that, despite these strong sentiments, in only one case has the Court struck out constitutionally a provision containing a reverse onus provision, and the Australian statute book remains littered with provisions which contain reverse onuses on the accused. The High Court has "talked the talk" regarding the accusatorial and adversarial nature of the criminal justice process, but largely has not (yet) "walked the walk" in using that to constitutionally strike out provisions which impose a reverse onus on an accused. Greater judicial will is required.

CONCLUSION

This chapter has discussed the presumption of innocence, and legislative departures from it, in other common law jurisdictions. It has demonstrates a similar pattern to that evident in the United States case law, with legislative attempts to undermine or limit the presumption of innocence through devices such as reverse onus provisions and deeming provisions. A major difference in the non-United States case law has been the development of the principle which considers whether the provision, as applied, can effectively permit an accused to be convicted despite the existence of reasonable doubt as to their guilt. I have indicated my strong support for such a principle. It reflects the prime rationale for the presumption of innocence supported in this book, the need for moral comfort among decision makers that a judgment they have made about another is a sound one, given the stakes involved. The moral comfort that we draw from making correct decisions as to the guilt or otherwise of an individual is fatally compromised when individuals can be convicted although there is reasonable doubt as to whether they are guilty or innocent. The law can also lose its moral force, undermining the public confidence that is essential in order that the legal system play its part in the broader societal structure. Arguments that change the orthodox position on presumption of innocence on the basis that the accused is in a better position to know about the matter in dispute, or would find it easier to rebut an allegation, cannot counter the moral comfort problem involved in convicting someone where there is reasonable doubt about their guilt. Nor can the seriousness of the charge with which the defendant is accused. Just as with the United States case law, there is also evident in the non-United States case law legislative attempts to circumvent difficulties with proof by resort to rational connections and inferences. Again, they do not overcome the moral comfort associated with declining to pass judgment in the absence of compelling proof of guilt.

NOTES

1. [1986] 1 S.C.R. 103.
2. Dickson CJ Chouinard Lamer Wilson and Le Dain JJ; Estey and McIntyre JJ concurring in the result.
3. 119.
4. 115–116.
5. 118.
6. 133.
7. "Mr Oakes is compelled by s8 to prove he is not guilty of the offense of trafficking. He is thus denied his right to be presumed innocent and subjected to the potential penalty of life imprisonment, unless he can rebut the presumption. This is radically and fundamentally inconsistent with the societal values of human dignity and liberty which we espouse and is directly contrary to the presumption of innocence enshrined in s11(d)" (134–135).
8. 134, citing with evident approval the work of Wayne MacKay and T Cromwell, "*Oakes*: A Bold Initiative Impeded by Old Ghosts," 32 C.R. (3d) (1983): 233.
9. 134.
10. 139. This approach has been the subject of critique, for example that it obscures the value-laden inquiry the Court makes, or that its approach is too compartmentalized: see Pamela Chapman, "The Politics of Judging: Section 1 of the *Charter of Rights and Freedoms*," *Osgoode Hall Law Journal* 24 (1986): 857; Robin Elliot, "The Supreme Court of Canada and Section 1: The Erosion of the Common Front," *Queen's Law Journal* 12 (1987): 277; Norman Siebrasse, "The *Oakes* Test: An Old Ghost Impeding Bold New Initiatives," *Ottawa Law Review* 23 (1991): 99.
11. 142.
12. [1987] 2 S.C.R. 636.
13. Lamer J, for Dickson CJ Estey and Wilson JJ; Beetz and Le Dain JJ agreed with the result and reasons of the majority judgment, subject to minor concessions noted in later footnotes, as did La Forest J; McIntyre J dissented.
14. 652.

15. 653; Beetz and Le Dain JJ, while expressing general agreement with the joint reasons, expressly declined to decide whether proof beyond reasonable doubt of subjective foresight would always be required in the case of murder (661). La Forest J also left this open (665).
16. 654.
17. 654.
18. 654; Beetz and Le Dain JJ declined to say whether proof of subjective foresight was required in all cases of murder (661); La Forest J suggested that objective foreseeability and negligence would be sufficient (665). Subsequently in *R v Rodney* [1990] 2 S.C.R. 687, a majority found that proof of subjective foresight of death was required for a murder charge (Lamer CJ, for Dickson CJ Wilson Gonthier and Cory JJ) (there was a change of Chief Justice between hearing and judgment); L'Heureux J (dissenting) (693) found that an objective test of foreseeability of death was sufficient for a murder charge, and Sopinka J said it was not necessary to determine (694). Subsequently in *Sit v The Queen* [1991] 3 S.C.R. 124, 130, all members of the Court concluded that proof of subjective foresight of death was required in order to sustain a murder conviction (Lamer CJ, for the Court).
19. 654–655.
20. 656.
21. 656.
22. 657–658.
23. 660.
24. [1990] S.C.R. 633.
25. 645–646 (Lamer CJ, for Dickson CJ Wilson Gonthier and Cory JJ).
26. 645.
27. 646.
28. *Criminal Code,* R.S.C. 1970, c. C-34 (s309[1]). The case is *R v Holmes* [1988] 1 S.C.R. 914.
29. 944.
30. 948, with whom La Forest J agreed.
31. 924.
32. 925.
33. 936. The dissentients stated that "doubt" here could arise from the insufficiency of Crown evidence regarding elements of the offense, or uncertainty as to "criminal culpability" in general (934).
34. 935.
35. 941.
36. [1988] 2 S.C.R. 3.
37. 18.
38. 18.
39. 19.
40. 26.
41. 21–22.
42. 26.
43. [1988] 2 S.C.R. 443.
44. McIntyre La Forest and L'Heureux-Dube JJ (Beetz J concurring); Dickson CJ and Lamer J dissenting. Estey J did not participate in the judgment.
45. 485.
46. 486.
47. 486.
48. 490.
49. 463.
50. 463.
51. 473.
52. 474.
53. 474.

54. 478.
55. [1992] 2 S.C.R. 10.
56. L'Heureux-Dube Sopinka Gonthier and Cory JJ; La Forest CJ McLachlin and Iacobucci JJ dissenting.
57. 30, a conclusion with which the dissentients agreed.
58. 36.
59. 37.
60. 39.
61. 17.
62. 40.
63. 40.
64. 44.
65. [2012] 3 S.C.R. 187. Earlier the Court had validated a provision containing a presumption of identity between the reading obtained by the test and the accused's actual blood alcohol content at the time of driving. The accused could rebut the presumption by leading "evidence to the contrary," interpreted as imposing a mere evidentiary burden on the accused: *R v St Pierre* [1995] 1 S.C.R. 791.
66. Deschamps J, for McLachlin CJ Le Bel Fish and Abella JJ.
67. 207.
68. 207.
69. 207–209.
70. 210.
71. 211.
72. 212.
73. 213.
74. 215.
75. 216.
76. 216.
77. 221.
78. 221.
79. *Woolmington v Director of Public Prosecutions* [1935] AC 462, 481 (Viscount Sankey LC).
80. *Salabiaku v France* [1988] ECHR 19, noting that the *Convention* did not prohibit the use of presumptions of fact and law, provided they were confined "within reasonable limits" given the interests at stake: [28] (Chamber).
81. *Brown v Scott* [2003] 1 AC 681, 693 (Lord Bingham), 708 (Lord Steyn), 719 (Lord Hope), 727 (Lord Clyde), Ian Kirkwood (730).
82. *Attorney-General of Hong Kong v Lee Kwong-Kut* [1993] AC 951.
83. 968–969 (Lord Woolf for the Council); but contrast *Khan v Trinidad* [2005] 1 AC 374, [14] where a majority of the Council appeared to take a procedural, rather than substantive, view.
84. 969 (Lord Woolf for the Court).
85. 969.
86. 969.
87. 969.
88. 395 US 6 (1969).
89. 972.
90. 972.
91. 973.
92. 973.
93. [2000] 2 AC 326.
94. 344.
95. 344–345.
96. 345. This problem was also noted by the Court of Appeal in *Keogh v R* [2007] EWCA Crim 528. There s2 of the *Official Secrets Act 1989* (UK) made it an offense for a person to make a damaging disclosure of any information, document or article relat-

ing to defense. Section 2(3) provided for a defense if the accused could show that at the time of the offense, they did not know, and had no reasonable cause to believe, that the information, document or article in question related to defense or that its disclosure would be damaging. The Court expressed concern that the offense could be construed in such a way that an accused could be convicted although there was reasonable doubt as to whether they knew or reasonably believed that disclosure could cause damage: [20]. As a result, the Court interpreted the legislation to require the prosecutor to prove the accused had the required mental state for the offense. The prosecutor had to prove the accused knew, or reasonably could have been expected to know, that disclosure would cause harm. The Court concluded that, as read, the provisions infringed Article 6 of the *European Convention on Human Rights*. As a result, it read them down to an evidentiary onus only (Phillips CJ and Clarke J).

97. 379.
98. 379.
99. 386.
100. 387.
101. 387.
102. 398.
103. [2002] 2 AC 545.
104. Lords Slynn, Steyn, Hope and Clyde; Lord Hutton found that the legislation imposed a legal burden on the accused, and validated the provision on that basis.
105. 580.
106. 598–599.
107. 563.
108. 582.
109. 607.
110. 563.
111. 570.
112. 571.
113. 571.
114. 571.
115. 589.
116. 608–609.
117. 609.
118. 609.
119. 619.
120. 620.
121. 620.
122. 621.
123. [2003] 1 WLR 1736.
124. 1750 (Lord Nicholls) (with whom Lords Hope, Hutton and Rodger agreed).
125. [2005] 1 AC 264.
126. Lord Bingham (with whom Lords Steyn and Phillips agreed); Lords Rodger and Carswell dissenting as to the reading down of the second provision.
127. 292.
128. 297.
129. 308.
130. 309.
131. 311–312.
132. 311.
133. 313.
134. 313.
135. In dissent, comments of Lord Rodger and Lord Carswell relate mainly to the practicalities of whether the accused or the prosecutor is in a better position to prove the particular disputed fact, for example Lord Rodger ("who else could do it" [320] in relation to proof that an accused did not know the organization was proscribed and

did not participate in the organization's activities) and Lord Carswell ("the person who knows best whether there was a real risk of that occurring is the defendant" [325], and a reference to practical difficulties for the prosecution in proving particular aspects [326]). Lord Carswell also used the concept of "gravamen" in relation to the definition of an offense: "the ultimate risk may be that the defendant may elect to drive the vehicle, but it is not in my view the gravamen of the offense" (324).

136. [2009] 1 AC 92.

137. Lord Hoffmann (97) and Lord Hope (103). Baroness Hale and Lord Mance expressed agreement with both justices on point.

138. Albert Vere Dicey, *An Introduction to the Study of the Law of the Constitution* (Macmillan, London, 1885).

139. *Bradley v Commonwealth* (1973) 128 CLR 557.

140. 5 US 1 (Cranch) 137 (1803).

141. *Lange v Australian Broadcasting Corporation* (1997) 189 CLR 520, 564: "the *Constitution* displaced, or rendered inapplicable, the English common law doctrine of the unqualified supremacy of the legislature" (all members of the Court).

142. The three characteristics were: (a) there was no law which parliament could not change—constitutional laws could be altered in the same manner as other laws; (b) no clear distinction was made between laws that were not fundamental and those that were; and (c) no person or body could void an act of parliament for constitutional reasons (37–39).

143. *Commonwealth v Melbourne Harbour Trust Commissioners* (1922) 31 CLR 1 (burden cast on a person providing a security to prove certain things in order to have it returned); *Williamson v Ah On* (1926) 39 CLR 95 (person required to prove they were not an immigrant and had not evaded a customs official); *Orient Steam Navigation Co Ltd v Gleeson* (1931) 44 CLR 254 (person deemed to have arrived in Australia unlawfully, unless they could show otherwise).

144. *Milicevic v Campbell* (1975) 132 CLR 307.

145. 316 (Gibbs J), 318 (Mason J).

146. (1993) 178 CLR 477.

147. (1991) 25 NSWLR 127.

148. 501.

149. 527.

150. 532.

151. 503.

152. 528 (Deane Dawson and Gaudron JJ).

153. 551.

154. *Kable v Director of Public Prosecutions* (NSW) (1996) 189 CLR 51, 106 (Gaudron J), 122 (McHugh J), 132 (Gummow J); *Bass v Permanent Trustee Co Ltd* (1999) 198 CLR 334, 359 (Gleeson CJ Gaudron McHugh Gummow Hayne and Callinan JJ).

155. (1998) 193 CLR 173.

156. McHugh and Kirby JJ.

157. 190.

158. 202 and 208–209; see also *Dietrich v The Queen* (1992) 177 CLR 292 where some members of the Court accorded constitutional status to the right to a fair trial (326) (Deane J) and (362) (Gaudron J).

159. 277.

160. (2011) 240 CLR 319.

161. 366–367 (Gummow and Bell JJ); see similarly Heydon J (386).

162. *X7 v Australian Crime Commission* (2013) 248 CLR 92.

163. 135.

164. 153.

165. 120.

166. (1998) 193 CLR 173, 277.

167. 120.

168. (2013) 251 CLR 196.

169. 235.
170. 236.
171. 290; she referred to the adversarial system of criminal justice being based on the assumption the accused was entitled to an acquittal unless the prosecution proved guilt (294).
172. 265.
173. 266.
174. 229 (French CJ), 249 (Crennan J) and 313 (Gageler and Keane JJ).
175. *R v Oakes* [1986] 1 S.C.R. 103.
176. *R v Director of Public Prosecutions Ex Parte Kebilene* [2000] 2 AC 326, 344–345 (Lord Bingham); *R v Lambert* [2002] 2 AC 545, 571 (Lord Steyn) and 609 (Lord Clyde); *Keogh v R* [2007] EWCA Crim 528, [20] (Phillips CJ, Clarke J); cf *Attorney-General of Hong Kong v Lee Kwong-Kut* [1993] AC 951, 972 (Lord Woolf, for the Council); *R v Johnstone* [2003] 1 WLR 1736, 1750 (Lord Nicholls, with whom Lords Hope, Hutton and Rodger agreed).
177. [1988] 2 S.C.R. 3.
178. [2012] 3 S.C.R. 187.
179. [2002] 2 AC 545, 589.
180. *Attorney-General of Hong Kong v Lee Kwong-Kut* [1993] AC 951, 972.
181. *Downey v The Queen* [1992] 2 S.C.R. 10.
182. *Vaillancourt v The Queen* [1987] 2 S.C.R. 636, 656.
183. *Attorney-General of Hong Kong v Lee Kwong-Kut* [1993] AC 951, 969–970 (Lord Woolf, for the Court).
184. He pointed out that neither mens rea nor actus reus had to be proved by the prosecution, in finding the provision breached the presumption of innocence principle: [2000] 2 AC 326, 344.
185. [2005] 1 AC 264, 311: "some of those liable to be convicted and punished for belonging to a proscribed organization may be guilty of no conduct which could reasonably be regarded as blameworthy or such as should properly attract criminal sanctions."
186. [2000] 2 AC 326, 398.
187. [2002] 2 AC 545, 571.
188. 619.
189. *R v Lambert* [2002] 2 AC 545, 563 (Lord Slynn), 582 (Lord Hope) and 607 (Lord Clyde); *Sheldrake* [2005] 1 AC 264. 297 (Lord Bingham, with whom Lords Steyn and Phillips agreed); *R v G* [2009] 1 AC 92, 97 (Lord Hoffmann) and 103 (Lord Hope) (both of whose decisions were approved of by the other two justices).
190. [1988] 1 S.C.R. 914, 924 (dissenting); in contrast, the majority validated a provision criminalizing not possession of an implement proven to have been used in house-breaking, but possession of such an implement in circumstances giving rise to a reasonable suspicion of such use. The framing of an offense in terms of "reasonable suspicion that x," rather than a more traditional framing of x itself as an offense, also caused disquiet in *Kebilene*: 344 (Lord Bingham) and 398 (Lord Hobhouse).
191. [1992] 2 S.C.R. 1, 17 (dissenting).
192. [1988] 2 S.C.R. 1, 18.
193. [1988] 2 S.C.R. 443, 463 (dissenting).
194. *Sit v The Queen* [1991] 3 S.C.R. 124, 130, compared with the earlier decision in *Vaillancourt v The Queen* [1987] 2 S.C.R. 636, 653 where some ambivalence was evident.
195. [1987] 2 S.C.R. 636, 654.
196. *The Queen v Martineau* [1990] S.C.R. 633, 645.
197. Glanville Williams, "Offences and Defences" *Legal Studies* 2(3) (1982): 254: "the definition of an offense in a statute is not a comprehensive and safe guide to the definitional elements of an offense as contrasted with defenses"; Victor Tadros, "The Ideal of the Presumption of Innocence," *Criminal Law and Philosophy* 8 (2014): 449; Victor Tadros and Stephen Tierney, "The Presumption of Innocence and the *Human Rights Act*," *Modern Law Review* 67(3) (2004): 405. Kenneth Campbell said there was an

inherent substantive difference between offenses and defenses; the former were related to things against which the law said there was a prima facie reason, and the latter related to exonerating conditions: "Offence and Defence" in Ian H Dennis ed, *Criminal Law and Justice: Essays from the W G Hart Workshop* (Sweet and Maxwell, London, 1987) 79.

198. Victor Tadros and Stephen Tierney, "The Presumption of Innocence and the *Human Rights Act," Modern Law Review* 67(3) (2004): 415: "the classical theory (that the legislature can frame offenses as it wishes) allows states to evade the putative protections provided by Article 6(2) by creating new offenses from evidential planks of existing offenses. Whilst the burden of proof remains on the prosecution, what it is required to prove is substantially diminished . . . the practical effect . . . is that a conviction . . . can result from the same degree of evidence that would have been required if the burden of proof in the original offense had been reversed . . . fundamental rights (in Article 6[2]) would be capable of being undermined simply by the creation of new criminal offenses."

199. Andrew Ashworth and Lucia Zedner, "Defending the Criminal Law: Reflections on the Changing Character of Crime, Procedure and Sanctions," *Criminal Law and Philosophy* 2 (2008): 33: "only the culpable deserve to be punished, and the public censure and hard treatment involved in punishment are unjustifiably imposed if blame is not established."

200. Paul Roberts, "Drug Dealing and the Presumption of Innocence: The *Human Rights Act* (Almost) Bites," *International Journal of Evidence and Proof* 6 (2002): 22; Paul Roberts, "The Presumption of Innocence Brought Home? *Kebilene* Deconstructed," *Law Quarterly Review* 118 (2002): 50; Andrew Stumer, *The Presumption of Innocence: Evidential and Human Rights Perspectives* (Hart Publishing, Oxford, 2010) 53; Richard Lippke, *Taming the Presumption of Innocence* (Oxford University Press, London, 2016) 54.

201. Paul Roberts, "Drug Dealing and the Presumption of Innocence: The *Human Rights Act* (Almost) Bites," *International Journal of Evidence and Proof* 6 (2002): 36: "once the presumption of innocence is given substantive content, there are no obvious conceptual limits on the scope for judicial reworking of the elements of criminal law offenses."

202. For example, *Whyte v The Queen* [1988] 2 S.C.R. 3, 26; *R v Lambert* [2002] 2 AC 545, 620 (Lord Hutton); Sheldrake [2005] 1 AC 264, 297 (Lord Bingham).

203. *R v Schwartz* [1988] 2 S.C.R. 443, 486; *R v Lambert* [2002] 2 AC 545, 608–609 (Lord Clyde); *R v Johnstone* [2003] 1 WLR 1736, 1750 (Lord Nicholls, with whom Lords Hope, Hutton and Rodger agreed); cf *Kebilene* [2000] 2 AC 326, where Lord Bingham said it was irrelevant that it was easier for the accused to prove the contested matter.

204. *The Queen v St-Onge Lamoureux* [2012] 3 S.C.R. 187, 213; *International Finance Trust Co Ltd v New South Wales Crime Commission* (2011) 240 CLR 319, 366–367 (Gummow and Bell JJ); *Kebilene* [2000] 2 AC 326, 386 (Lord Hope); *Sheldrake* [2005] 1 AC 264, 309 (Lord Bingham).

205. *Kebilene* [2000] 2 AC 326, 386 (Lord Hope).

206. *R v Johnstone* [2003] 1 WLR 1735, 1750 (Lord Nicholls, with whom Lords Hope, Hutton and Rodger agreed).

207. Andrew Ashworth, "Four Threats to the Presumption of Innocence," *International Journal of Evidence and Proof* 10 (2006): 260; Paul Roberts, "The Presumption of Innocence Brought Home? *Kebilene* Deconstructed," *Law Quarterly Review* 118 (2002): 41, 65: "consequentialist thinking is the slow poison of criminal justice . . . it simply does not follow that 'anything goes' in the fight against terrorism. Exclusively result-orientated practices and procedures are fundamentally incompatible with just censure and punishment under the rule of law"; Victor Tadros and Stephen Tierney, "The Presumption of Innocence and the *Human Rights Act," Modern Law Review* 67(3) (2004): 428.

208. Andrew Ashworth, "Four Threats to the Presumption of Innocence," *International Journal of Evidence and Proof* 10 (2006): 267; Victor Tadros and Stephen Tierney, "The Presumption of Innocence and the *Human Rights Act," Modern Law Review* 67(3)

(2004): 426; David Hamer, "The Presumption of Innocence and Reverse Burdens: A Balancing Act," *Cambridge Law Journal* 66(1) (2007): 142.

209. *Attorney-General of Hong Kong v Lee Kwong-Kut* [1993] AC 951, 969 (Lord Woolf for the Court); *R v Johnstone* [2003] 1 WLR 1736, 1750 (Lord Nicholls, with whom Lords Hope, Hutton and Rodger agreed).

FOUR

What Is a Crime and What Is a Defense?

An issue that is tangential to protection of the presumption of innocence is the question of what restrictions, if any, apply to how legislatures can define a crime. Are there any restrictions on the way in which legislatures define a crime, or can lawmakers include as much, or as little, as they like in terms of elements? And relatedly, is legislature completely free in framing defenses to criminal offenses as it wishes? Or are there restrictions on how defenses may be framed? In other words, is there a necessary substantive content to the criminal law? It is necessary to answer these questions because, as we have seen, legislatures have attempted by various means to circumvent or to limit the application of the presumption of innocence principle. They do this, for example, by transferring what would traditionally be considered to be elements of offenses, to be proven by the prosecution, to elements of the defense, by introducing reverse onus provisions, and by "overcriminalizing." By this, I mean criminalizing conduct that would not traditionally be thought of as criminal, and/or by stripping out what might traditionally be thought of as required in order to show "criminality," or "culpability." Often, this is the mens rea requirement that traditionally generally characterized definitions of criminal offenses.

One view, based on legal positivism, is that legislatures are free to define elements of offenses as they wish, with no restrictions. This view may be described as the "procedural" view of criminal law. This view would draw upon the idea that the legislature is democratically elected and, at least broadly and in theory, represents the wishes and will of the people. It is accountable to the people at regular free elections. It may be argued that of all areas of law, the criminal law most closely reflects the wishes and will of the people. According to this theory, the legislature should be completely free to frame offenses, and defenses, as it wishes, (in theory) to reflect the view of voters as to what should be regarded as criminal behavior, what should be recognized as providing a defense or excuse to what would otherwise be criminal behavior, etc.[1] A leading exponent of this procedural view is Paul Roberts. Roberts explains that the protection of the presumption of innocence expressed in the *European Convention on Human Rights*

> has no bearing on the reduction or elimination of mens rea requirements, and is therefore perfectly compatible with offenses of strict or even absolute liability . . . the presumption of innocence is confined to proof of relevant offense criteria, whatever those criteria may be, and in particular whether or not they include (subjective) mens rea conditions as traditionally conceived.[2]

The argument is that the criminal law reflects a delicate balance among a range of competing interests and values, and that the legislature is best placed to make this adjustment.

On the other hand, if the judiciary were to impose limits on how a legislature could frame the criminal law, this would be problematic given that the judiciary is not accountable to the people and does not necessarily reflect the wishes and will of the people. In addition, it may create uncertainty. If some limits on the ability of legislatures to frame the criminal law are accepted, it remains difficult to precisely articulate what those limits are, as will be seen later in the chapter. This difficulty can lead some to acceptance of the procedural view of criminal law—the idea that it is very difficult, if not impossible, to frame appropriate limits.[3]

On the other hand, the procedural view is not free of difficulty. Some argue that if a procedural view is accepted, due process rights that most regard as being fundamental are subject to being removed at the whim of the legislature. This occurs in circumstances where, as has been recognized, given that the chances may only impact on a small minority of individuals, the consequences for such legislative action at the ballot box may be relatively muted. This provides the answer to the question of how the topic of this chapter relates to the overall topic of the book, presumption of innocence. The argument is that if a procedural view of the criminal law is taken, fundamental due process rights like the presumption of innocence may be in peril.[4] Henry Hart called it "a betrayal of intellectual bankruptcy."[5] Dubber called it "patently empty."[6] Courts have been mindful for some time that by tinkering with the elements of offenses, and in particular the mens rea requirement, legislatures may seek to undermine fundamental notions of beyond reasonable doubt, onus of proof on the state, and presumption of innocence.[7]

An example might help to demonstrate the point. As we all know, the offense of murder is typically characterized by an unlawful killing accompanied by an intent to kill, or to do serious injury. As elements of a crime, these facts would typically need to be proven by the prosecutor, at the level of beyond reasonable doubt. If the prosecutor could not meet this standard, the accused would be entitled to be acquitted, based on the presumption that they are innocent.

Say that a legislature is concerned that, as a result of how this law is framed, those guilty of unlawful killing are being acquitted. Prosecutors are finding it difficult to prove their allegations at the required standard. As a result, the legislature re-defines the offense of murder. Under the new definition, murder is committed where the prosecutor has a reasonable suspicion that an accused has killed another. The prosecutor must prove this fact at the level of beyond reasonable doubt. It is a defense for the accused to show either that (a) they did not commit an unlawful killing, or that (b) they did not intend to kill or seriously injure the victim. The defense must prove either of these facts at the level of balance of probabilities.

Some may argue that such an example is far-fetched, and arguments should not be made based on fantastic scenarios. I would remind those who would make that argument of the United Kingdom legislation considered in *Kebilene* in chapter 3 of this book. That legislation created an offense based on the notion that there was a reasonable suspicion that a person had an implement for use in relation to a terrorism offense. This offense was punishable by a lengthy jail term. A defense was created if the defendant could show that in fact they had possession of the implement in issue for a benign purpose. That defense could be read to impose a legal onus, though the Court eventually read down the provision to impose a mere evidentiary onus. However, the point is that legislatures are in fact re-framing offense provisions to make successful prosecutions easier.

Thus, we have adherents of a "substantive" view of the criminal law. Such adherents deny that legislatures have absolute freedom to craft criminal law, including offenses and defenses, entirely as they wish. Limits exist. Such adherents will argue that unless a substantive view of the criminal law is taken, fundamental due process rights such as the presumption of innocence are liable to be effectively neutered by a legislature.[8] A legislature could do this by gutting the requirements to prove a particular offense, removing all or a significant part of the traditional elements of an offense, and transferring them to a defense, requiring the defendant to prove that defense to a particular standard. In this way, while the legislature would on its face have left the presumption of innocence intact, they would effectively have largely neutered it by so radically reducing the scope of what it applies to, in other words the express elements of an offense.

A substantive view is often justified by the argument that the criminal law is distinctive, including its significant sanctions and implications for personal liberty. We discussed this in earlier chapters, and it will be recalled that one of the rationales for doctrines such as the presumption of innocence is the very significant stakes involved in criminal proceedings, namely a person's personal liberty, reputation, and possibly their life. If this justifies special procedures in the criminal law context, it can also justify restrictions on just what a legislature can call a crime. If, in the context of the *Eighth Amendment*, "death is different" (from other types of punishment), a phrase used to justify greater judicial scrutiny of it in the context of a constitutional protection, it is argued by analogy that "the criminal law is different" from non-criminal law, which again justifies greater judicial scrutiny of the context of the criminal law in a way that may not be justified in the non-criminal context. This can also help us to escape comparisons with the Supreme Court's ill-judged foray into substantive due process in a non-criminal sense in the first part of the twentieth century.[9]

It is said that the distinctiveness of criminal law ought not to be lost. That distinctiveness is reflected in the procedural rules governing its enforcement, typically set out in some detail in human rights instruments, and as found in the United States *Bill of Rights*. It is also found in the extensive powers that government authorities have to investigate crime, including search and questioning powers, arrest powers and pre-trial detention powers. The argument is that its distinctiveness must also be reflected in its substance.[10] So the question becomes to what extent legislatures have the power to do this, and/or whether such limits exist.

The difficulty for those who advocate a substantive view of the criminal law is to answer objections that they are engaged in judicial activism, when the judiciary is not democratically elected and not accountable to the people. It is argued that it is beyond the judicial remit to impose limits on the kinds of criminal laws that legislatures can pass, and how legislatures choose to define their own crimes and defenses. Written constitutions, bills of rights and other international human rights instruments do not expressly authorize courts to effectively re-write legislation by re-defining offenses or defenses. Some argue it is above and beyond the scope of judicial power for a court to act in this way.[11] On the other hand, if it is true that a criminal law unrelated to commonly held community ideas about culpability would be "too severe for the community to bear," as Oliver Wendel Holmes said,[12] the fact of a court striking out criminal laws with no inherent underlying culpability attached may be less offensive, and the anti-democratic argument about the judiciary striking down laws muted.

Others argue about parameters. What are the limits on a legislature's ability to frame the criminal law? Is it bound by how a crime has traditionally been characterized, and if so, how does this allow the law to evolve as society evolves? The question of what, in substance, can be made the subject of criminal penalty is a hotly contested one. There are no easy answers or bright line rules.[13] The difficulties posed by the rise of strict liability "offenses" must also be noted in this space. It is not impossible to frame possible limits, but the difficulty in doing so, and the fact it is highly contested, means that for some, a procedural view of criminal law should be taken.[14]

This chapter will proceed on the basis that there should be some limits on the ability of legislatures to define offenses and defenses in criminal law. It is premised on the basis that such limits are essential, because there is substantial concern that if a procedural view is taken, legislatures become free to define offenses precisely how they wish, and they might take advantage of that opportunity to radically reduce the scope of what the prosecution must prove in order that a person be the subject of criminal sanction. Through such a mechanism, the presumption of innocence would lose much of its ability to provide due process to those suspected of criminal behavior. On the other hand, the difficulty in framing appropriate limits on a legislature's ability to define crimes and defenses as it wishes is frankly acknowledged, as is the fact that the legislature is democratically elected and, at least in theory, reflective of general community will and sentiment.

I should respond to the thoughtful work of Louis Billionis, who cautions judges against entering the field of substantive criminal law, on the basis that it is unacceptably entering a field reserved for the legislature. He acknowledges that legislatures may be tempted to legislate highly objectionable criminal laws, but asks why political safeguards are not sufficient to address this potential problem, and tends to suggest that it is "safer" to rely on the inherent limits of the legislature's power in this area, rather than conceive a theory justifying judicial intervention in the field of substantive criminal law.[15]

The obvious response would rely on the work of John Hart Ely,[16] and his observations about the imperfections in the political process, in particular when the laws in issue affect a powerless minority. So called political, ballot box remedies are inefficacious in such circumstances. This has been known for a long time; it gave impetus for the United States *Bill of Rights* and its counter to the "tyranny of the majority." It was recognized most famously in the *Carolene Products* footnote.[17] Clearly there is little "societal love" for those accused of criminal behavior, and given their small minority status and the stigma attaching to a person accused of wrongdoing (regardless of whether it is proven or not), their political strength is likely to be very weak. Stuntz also makes this point: "A lot of constitutional theory has been shaped by the idea, made famous by *Carolene Products* footnote four, that constitutional law should aim to protect groups that find it hard or impossible to protect themselves through the political process. If ever such a group existed, the universe of criminal suspects is it."[18]

The chapter will attempt to balance such considerations by proposing some modest limits on a legislature's ability to define crime, in a way that will protect the substance of the presumption of innocence, will provide certainty to legislatures in their framing of crime, but also permit them discretion in how they draft their criminal laws and tailor them to local community needs and preferences. Specifically, for example, I do not accept the validity of criminal law provisions where the crux of the offense provision is "reasonable suspicion" that an accused has something for a malevolent purpose, and in lieu of an offense provision that a person is proven by the prosecution to in fact have done something for a malevolent purpose.

LITERATURE—SUBSTANTIVE VERSUS PROCEDURAL VIEW OF THE CRIMINAL LAW

There is substantial support in the academic literature for the argument that a substantive, rather than procedural view, needs to be taken to the question of what can comprise a crime. Leading advocates include Kenneth Campbell. Campbell, in favoring a substantive view, suggested that substantively an offense meant something against which the law said there was a prima facie reason. Substantively, a defense referred to exonerating conditions.[19] This approach will be discussed later in the chapter.

Another adherent of a substantive view is Victor Tadros. Tadros advocates looking beyond the bare terms of the criminal law statute. Instead, the court should focus on "conditions of liability"; in other words, what renders a person liable to public condemnation and punishment. It is not necessarily what the criminal statute says.[20] Glanville Williams is somewhat skeptical of the possibility of defining what are, in substance, "offenses" and "defenses." However, he agrees that there is a "single issue of culpability, the burden of proving which rests on the prosecution."[21] Sundby and others takes an intermediate position, agreeing that the label that the legislature has chosen to give something is not determinative. He says what matters is not how the state uses a particular factor, whether a defense, presumption or part of the definition of the offense, but whether it is used as a basis for determining guilt and punishment. If it is, it must be proven by the prosecutor beyond reasonable doubt.[22] Jefferies and Stephan strongly advocate the substantive view of criminal law:

> The trouble lies in trying to define justice in exclusively procedural terms. *Winship*'s insistence on the reasonable doubt standard is thought to express a preference for letting the guilty go free rather than risking conviction of the innocent. This value choice, however, cannot be implemented by a purely procedural concern with burden of proof. Guilt and innocence are substantive concepts. Their content depends on the choice of facts determinative of liability. If this choice is remitted to unconstrained legislative discretion, no rule of constitutional procedure can restrain the potential for injustice. A normative principle for

> protecting the innocent must take into account not only the certainty with which facts are established but also the selection of facts to be proved. A constitutional policy to minimize the risk of convicting the "innocent" must be grounded in a constitutional conception of what may constitute "guilt." Otherwise "guilt" would have to be proved with certainty, but the legislature could define "guilt" as it pleased, and the grand ideal of individual liberty would be reduced to an empty promise.[23]

Pilcher argues that a "rational basis for assigning blame" is a necessary pre-condition for criminal responsibility, sourcing this requirement in social contract theory.[24] She concluded that the intrusion of the criminal law into "socially unexpected realms of conduct" diminished the power of the criminal law as a social institution.[25] The drafters of the American *Model Penal Code* concluded that "crime does and should mean condemnation and no court should have to pass that judgment unless it can declare that the defendant's act was culpable. This is too fundamental to be compromised."[26] The *Model Penal Code* generally required proof of a defendant's mental state, but exceptionally allowed strict liability offenses on condition that they could not lead to imprisonment.

A substantive view of the criminal law may be sourced in general principles of liberalism. This theory would emphasize the inherent freedom of an individual, which the principle of due process reflects.[27] So important is this freedom that the law places curbs on the extent to which legislatures can impinge upon it. This explains the criminal law procedural rights enshrined in the Constitution, but also implies limits on the ability of legislatures to pass particular kinds of laws. Evidently, in the United States it cannot pass ex post facto laws, or laws infringing the principle of double jeopardy. It cannot pass laws which contain or authorize cruel and unusual punishment. These are substantive limits. Further, the argument is that given the general freedom of the individual, laws which deny a person their freedom (criminal laws, and in particular criminal laws which could if applied to a person result in their imprisonment) require particular justification. This theory may buttress a requirement that there are substantive limits on the content of criminal law, including for instance that in respect of any crime punishable by a jail term, that certain minimum requirements, such as mens rea and culpability, are necessary. This is because a decision to criminalize behavior, with all of its implications in terms of possible punishment and stigma, is a serious one, and requires serious justification.[28] And again notions of moral comfort are useful—a decision maker would not be morally comfortable convicting someone of a crime where they do not believe that the behavior "warrants" a criminal label; in other words, that the behavior is not sufficiently "morally blameworthy."

Others argue the very legitimacy of the criminal law is implicated in its finite boundaries:

> The studies suggest that most persons are motivated to obey the law, not because they fear being caught and punished (or shamed), but because they believe in the moral weight of the law. That is, most people obey the law, not because they fear the pain of criminal sanction, but because they want to do what is right. They are driven, in large part, by their perception of themselves as honest, law-abiding people. But the effectiveness of the law in gaining compliance in this way is again a function of the law's credibility for doing justice. If the law closely matches people's shared intuitive notions of justice, it grows in its power to act as a model for their conduct. If the law is seen as being unjust, its power as a moral force is diminished.[29]

One of George Fletcher's insights in this field was his notation of the fact that some confusion arose through the transplantation of models appropriate to civil litigation, in particular the Roman notion that a person who alleges something must prove it. While this might have been justified in the non-criminal sphere, Fletcher notes it was inappropriate to transplant it to the criminal sphere, where different interests, and different stakes, were involved. As a result of doing so, English law for some time placed the burden of persuasion on an accused with respect to what we might broadly call "defenses."[30]

We may more broadly reflect on the distinction between the criminal law and the non-criminal law. So, for instance, while strict liability might be acceptable in some cases in the law of tort, it may be less defensible in the criminal law, given the different interests at stake. In some cases in the past, judges may have been too ready to apply principles developed in, and appropriate to, a non-criminal context to the law of crime, thus eroding fundamental principles of the criminal law.[31]

Fletcher also refers with evident approval to the early twentieth century work of German criminal law scholar Ernst Beling. Beling favored a substantive view of the criminal law. He opined that a prosecutor would have to prove three things in order to obtain a conviction against an accused: (a) that the defendant brought about a result proscribed by the legislature; (b) the act was socially unacceptable; and (c) the defendant was personally blameworthy. The defendant was entitled to the benefit of the doubt on each of the elements. The German statute law did not necessarily expressly embrace these requirements; Beling argued they were inherent in the criminal law. Fletcher explained the relevance of the German classification for criminal law elsewhere:

> The German tripartite structure stands for an analytic and moral claim about the relationship among the issues bearing on the defendant's criminal guilt. The claim is simply that all the substantive issues of liability are on an equal footing: for purposes of determining liability, there is no significant difference between causing harm, intending it, intending it in self-defense, and intending it under duress. That some of these issues may appear in the affirmative and some in the negative

> is irrelevant. The decisive point is that all bear on the defendant's guilt or innocence. If it is agreed that the prosecutor should bear the risk of residual doubt on one of these issues, then he should bear the risk on all of them. In sum, the German tripartite structure builds on two related claims about criminal liability. The first premise is that all defenses bearing on guilt function as challenges to a comprehensive rule of liability; one need never characterize an issue as an exception. And the second premise is that with respect to the risk of residual doubt in trying the defendant's guilt, all issues bearing on his guilt should be treated alike.[32]

Similarly, in the English literature Glanville Williams rejects suggestions of a neat divide between offense elements and defense elements, with offense elements to be proven by the prosecutor beyond reasonable doubt, and with the legislature free to place whatever it wishes within the column of "offense elements" (with possible implications for the burden of proof), as opposed to "defense elements." Instead, he uses the concept of an "offense package" which comprises offense elements and defenses or exceptions. He says they are an indivisible whole. The defendant cannot be convicted unless they are proven to have committed the "offense package."[33] He draws on the work of Julius Stone to state there is "no intrinsic difference" between the elements of an offense and an exception or defense. Adoption of this view would effectively render pointless attempts by the legislature to make convictions easier by moving what were traditionally considered elements of an offense into defenses, perhaps with implications for the burden of proof. However, it would not, in itself, prevent the legislature from paring back the elements of an offense substantially, to achieve a similar end of improving the chances of a successful prosecution, unless the court established a substantive view of criminal law which prescribed at least minimum substantive content.

History—Mens Rea and the Common Law of Crime

Prior to considering the history of mens rea as a component of crime in the history of common law, as least two more general points must be made. The first is that for much of English legal history, crime was not a separate area of law at all, but considered to be part of tort law.[34] This meant that the law was enforced privately rather than by public sanction. The blood feud and private vengeance gave way to a focus on compensation for the victim—in old times the wergild (payment to family of a dead victim) and bot (compensation to a victim for non-lethal injuries). The focus was generally not on the wrongdoer, the old deodand action and outlawry excepted. In such a situation, the precise level of culpability of the wrongdoer was understandably not critical, the focus being on compensation to the victim.[35]

Lastly, like many legal concepts, the precise meaning of mens rea is open to debate, and some argue that its meaning has changed over time. Does it mean, literally, a guilty mind?[36] If so, what does this mean? Is it "general immorality of motive"?[37] Is it a "vicious will"?[38] Is it proof that the alleged wrongdoer knew what they were doing was wrong, something they ought not to do?[39] Does this mean that the prosecutor must prove the accused was subjectively aware of the relevant criminal law provision? If so, how would this fit with another classic legal maxim, that ignorance of the law is no excuse? Or does the concept of "ought not to do" have a less technical meaning; is it sufficient that the accused *ought* to have known that what they were doing was wrong?[40] This would encompass acts that might be considered merely reckless or negligent. And by "wrong," do we mean legally wrong, morally wrong or both? And how do we define what is morally wrong? Is it whatever the legislature prescribes as the mental aspect required for a particular crime, if any? Some difficult questions, to which answers will be suggested at the end of the chapter.

The other preliminary point to make about the importance of history here is that it is often used by the court in assessing what is "fundamental" about our legal system.[41] Specifically, the fact that a concept has a long history in Western legal tradition assists in making the argument that it is a concept of fundamental legal importance, itself important in weighing to what extent due process might require or enshrine it.[42] So, for instance, the Supreme Court held in *Speiser* that legislatures had the power to regulate matters of evidence, including the burden and standard of proof, unless "it offends some principle of justice so rooted in the traditions and conscience of our people as to be ranked as fundamental."[43]

There is some reference to notions of mens rea in early England. For example, the Laws of Alfred (c. 897 AD) state: "Let the man who slayeth another wilfully perish by death. Let him who slayeth another of necessity or unwillingly or wilfully, as God may have sent him into his hands, and for whom he has not lain in wait be worthy of his life, and of lawful 'bot' if he seeks an asylum."[44] Gradually the common law began to turn its eye to the relative gravity of what an offender had done. By the early thirteenth century English common law had embraced the concept of a "felony." This signified the most serious of crimes. Pollock and Maitland trace the word from the French, meaning "full of bitterness or venom."[45] Consideration of the situation of the offender was becoming more common. They also trace at this time recognition of the concept of premeditation, or intention. In the thirteenth century chancery courts exonerated those who had committed homicides by misadventure, rather than through intentional acts.[46] Those in this situation were, alternatively, often pardoned. The amount of compensation payable to the victim began to depend on whether the defendant's actions were intentional or not.[47] Pollock and Maitland describe development of the law in this space thus:

> If once it be granted that a man's death was caused by the act of another, then that other is liable, no matter what may have been his intentions or his motives. To this rigorous principle our evidence directs us, though for an unmitigated application of it we may have to look to a prehistoric time. In a yet early age law begins to treat intentional as worse than unintentional homicide.[48]

Others have traced the common law's increased concern with the nature of the defendant's actions with the influence of ecclesiastical law.[49] That body of law emphasized the morality of a defendant's actions.[50] In turn, numerous passages from the Bible suggest differential punishment according to the circumstances, and in particular the intent, of the wrongdoer. Examples include Numbers 35, which in 16–21 outlines the death penalty for various categories of killing. Verse 20 specifically includes murder with "malice aforethought" in the worst category which attracts the death penalty. But verses 22 and 23 discuss unintentional killings, and it is suggested the penalty for such actions will be less. Numbers 15:30 refers to a person who sins "defiantly" as worthy of aggravated punishment. Deuteronomy 19:16 refers to "malicious" false witnesses. There was even some suggestion that an evil mind alone, without a corresponding act, was enough to attract sanction.[51]

Augustine deserves special mention here. He viewed all earthly beings as sinners, however salvation was possible. In determining who would be entitled to salvation, an individual's will was important. Evil deeds came from an evil will. Good deeds came from a good will. Thus it became critical, in determining the nature of acts, to determine whether they were animated by a good or evil will. He thus derives the maxim *reum linguam non facit, nisi mens rea* (repeated in Leges Henrici 5 No 28).[52] As an example, he used the law of perjury. He said that a witness who is inclined to tell the truth, but who mistakenly gives false information, is not guilty of a sin. In contrast, a witness who is inclined to lie but who in fact describes accurately what occurred was guilty of sin, because of their evil intent. There is further evidence of considerations of mens rea in penitential books. For example, the Penitential of Vinnian seems to suggest that a guilty mind, in itself, warrants punishment even without an act to give it effect. The Penitential of Theodore prescribes reduced penance for unlawful killing during public war, or if done "by chance." The intention of the wrongdoer greatly impacted on the punishment to which they would be subject. Compensation would be payable to the victim regardless of intent, but compensation would often be higher in circumstances of a premeditated, rather than a merely careless, act.[53]

Further, the Roman Law of the Twelve Tables distinguished knowing from unknowing behavior.[54] Old Roman notions of *dolus* and *culpa* and *casus* were introduced to English common law through the door of ecclesiastical law, through writers such as Glanvill and Bracton.[55] For example, Bracton in the mid-thirteenth century claims:

> We must consider with what mind (animo) or with what intent (voluntate) a thing is done, in fact or in judgment, in order that it may be determined accordingly what action should follow and what punishment. For take away the will and every act will be indifferent, because your state of mind gives meaning to your act, and a crime is not committed unless the intent to injure (nocendi voluntas) intervene, nor is a theft committed except with the intent to steal.[56]

Bracton concluded that a person who killed by misadventure, not intending to kill the other, should be acquitted, because a crime would not have been committed in the absence of an intent to injure.[57] He applied the concept to other crimes as well. Some evidence of acceptance of the importance of intention in determining the seriousness of the defendant's wrongdoing is evident in the casebooks of the time.[58]

These views of Bracton were mirrored in the writing of later scholars. Bacon stated in his *Maxims* of the second half of the sixteenth century that "in capital cases . . . the law will not punish in so high a degree, except the malice of the will and intention appear."[59] He contrasted that with civil cases, where the damage done to the victim, rather than the wrongdoer's malice (if any), was important. Hale explained: "If the act that is committed be simply casual and per infortunium, regularly that act, which were it done ex animi intentione, were punishable by death, is not by the laws of England to undergo that punishment; for it is the will and intention, that regularly is required, as well as the act and event, to make the offense capital."[60] In turn, these sentiments are echoed by Coke and Blackstone.[61]

These comments can be interpreted as reflecting both the idea that the criminal law is involved in behavior that is viewed by society as immoral,[62] and sufficiently immoral as to warrant a criminal sanction, including imprisonment and, in previous times (in most societies), the possibility of death. And further, that the question of the existence of a guilty mind influenced the law's view as to the morality of particular behavior. Specifically, conduct committed with a "guilty mind" was viewed as being of a different order of immorality, thus justifying criminal opprobrium and punishment, compared with conduct that was merely innocent, or careless. As Mueller put it, "by employing an ethico-legal term (*mens rea*) as a common denominator for the various possible forms of mental elements in crime, our law has committed itself to an ethical concept of crime."[63]

In other words, morality influenced our view of whether conduct was considered "worthy" of criminal sanction.[64] Of course, many argue that it still should. Now, obviously, questions regarding the relationship between the law and morality are not confined to the criminal law, and have been asked at a much greater level of abstraction with respect to the law generally. This is reflected in the Hart-Fuller debate of the 1950s,[65] and the debate between the philosophical schools of natural law and legal positivism. Even Bentham thought that there should be no criminal liability without fault.[66] It is considered beyond the scope of this project to enter substantially upon that field here. It might be sufficient to note Hart's position that law and morality are not necessarily connected:

> Many actions . . . that if voluntarily done are criminally punishable, although our moral code may be either silent as to their moral quality, or divided. Very many offenses are created by legislation designed to give effect to a particular economic scheme . . . the utility or moral character of which may be genuinely in dispute. An offender against such legislation can hardly be said to be morally guilty or to have intentionally committed a moral wrong.[67]

Despite having these views, Hart also conceded that "a code of criminal law which omitted any reference in the definition of its offenses to mental elements could not possibly be satisfactory."[68] The contrary view is that it is

> important to acknowledge the existence of a relationship between immorality and illegality . . . the fact that conduct that is criminal is not immoral is one good or relevant [but not always sufficient or conclusive] ground for criticizing the law making the conduct criminal. We ought not . . . make a certain kind of action illegal because the action is not blameworthy and because . . . we ought not "brand" someone who does that action as a criminal. The fact that this is so . . . [is] relevant and quite persuasive evidence for believing that the blameworthiness or immorality of an action is linked conceptually to its criminality.[69]

There is also Lon Fuller's point that legal rules derive their efficacy from a general acceptance by members of society that they are right, just and necessary. Now he was talking about fundamental rules, such as constitutional rules, rather than any given law, but the point is well made—that laws derive from efficacy and legitimacy from general acceptance by the people, or in other words at least a general congruence between the values (and morals) of a society, and the rules by which that society is governed.[70]

The traditional distinction between crimes *mala in se* and *mala prohibita* ought also to be recalled here. Though the distinction between the two can be contentious, how one views the purpose of the penalty in issue is relevant. If the purpose of the penalty is to punish, it is a *mala in se* crime; if the purpose of the penalty is merely to "price" behavior, it is a *mala prohibita* crime. The distinction is important because, for many, *mala in se* crimes carry a moral dimension—they are morally wrong.[71] However, it provides the philosophical framework within which arguments occur about what limits, if any, apply to a legislature's ability to define crime, and whether defined crimes must have a moral component or not (and if so, what it is).

It should, however, be acknowledged that the English law accepted from about the mid-nineteenth century the possibility of a successful criminal prosecution in the absence of mens rea.[72] Readers will be aware that the late nineteenth century coincided with the rise of legal positivism, involving a growing separation of law from morality. It may not be a coincidence that the rise of legal positivism took place at the same time as the English criminal law began to downplay the importance of mens rea. This era also reflected growing concern with broader social interests, rather than individual rights, led by utilitarians such as Bentham, who, not coincidentally, also favored a *presumption of guilt* with respect to alleged offenders. It reflects an evolution in the criminal law away from capacity responsibility and towards a focus on the outcomes of a person's behavior.

At first the Court dealt with these provisions by finding that the action was, in substance, civil in nature so that mens rea was not required.[73] Having taken that step, in subsequent cases the validity of a true criminal provision was accepted, although not accompanied by a requirement of mens rea. Though this legislation typically arose in relation to regulatory offenses for which the purpose of the provision was protection of the public collectively, rather than an individual, and thus made most sense where the outcome of the action was that compensation would be ordered or a fine paid, there were also cases where the offense for which the accused was convicted could result in a term of imprisonment.[74]

These examples are sometimes seized upon by those scholars who argue that there is no necessary moral underpinning of the criminal law.[75] Inevitably, once the legal system accepted the possibility that some defined crimes could be committed in the absence of proof of mens rea, the scope of such an exception grew, and the maximum punishment imposed on such offenses increased.[76] Notions of the traditional distinction between *male in se* crimes and *mala prohibita* crimes could have been, and may still be, useful in this analysis. Again the distinction between them has blurred over time, but some argue that the purpose of the provision is relevant—if the purpose of the penalty is to punish, then it is a *male in se* offense, while if the purpose of the penalty is merely to regulate or price, it is a *mala prohibita* crime. Earlier, it was said this distinction was important in the debate about the extent to which law and morality overlapped, because *mala in se* crimes were typically viewed as those that were morally wrong. In the current context of a mens rea discussion, the point is that the traditional view is that mens rea should, at the least, be required with respect to an offense that is (in substance) *mala in se* in nature.[77]

The notion that mens rea is an indispensable part of a criminal offense is repeatedly argued in the literature. It is often argued that there is something special about a criminal sanction that justifies a mens rea requirement that is not necessary in the civil context, given the stakes involved, specifically the deprivation of personal liberty that may follow a criminal conviction, and the likely stigma associated with it. This evidently has parallels with the arguments advanced in chapter 1 for the presumption of innocence in criminal matters, as opposed to civil matters. Packer was a leading advocate of a mens rea requirement:

> The role of *mens rea* in the criminal law has been the subject of much discussion. The consensus can be summarily stated: to punish conduct without reference to the actor's state of mind is both inefficacious and unjust. It is inefficacious because conduct unaccompanied by an awareness of the factors making it criminal does not mark the actor as one who needs to be subjected to punishment in order to deter him or others from behaving similarly in the future, nor does it single him out as a socially dangerous individual who needs to be incapacitated or reformed. It is unjust because the actor is subject to the stigma of a criminal conviction without being morally blameworthy. Consequently, on either a preventive or a retributive theory of criminal punishment, the criminal sanction is inappropriate in the absence of *mens rea*.[78]

Equally, Sayre was adamant that "criminality is and always will be based upon a requisite state of mind as one of its prime factors." He was concerned that if the criminal law imposed punishment in situations where mens rea had not been proven, community confidence in and respect for the legal system would be undermined:

> [T]o inflict substantial punishment upon one who is morally entirely innocent, who caused injury through reasonable mistake or pure accident, would so outrage the feelings of the community as to nullify its own enforcement . . . the moral obloquy and the social disgrace incident to criminal conviction are whips which lend effective power to the administration of the criminal law. When the law begins to permit convictions for serious offenses of men who are morally innocent and free from fault . . . its restraining power becomes undermined.[79]

More recently, scholars have continued to reflect on the essentiality of mens rea in relation to the construction of a criminal offense.[80] Hart, although denying that criminal responsibility depends on moral culpability, defends the use of mental elements in framing criminal law.[81]

At a more general level of abstraction, both the United States Supreme Court and the Canadian Supreme Court have indicated that there would be constitutional difficulty with legislation that "offended some principle of justice so rooted in the traditions and conscience of our people as to be ranked as fundamental."[82] Given the extensive and lengthy history of concepts of mens rea in the legal systems prescribed in the Bible and for centuries in the English common law, it is considered reasonable to argue that mens rea is an inherent requirement of a criminal offense, or at least one that is punishable by a term of imprisonment.[83]

Suggestions of a Mens Rea Requirement in the Case Law

The importance of intention in the criminal law has been asserted strongly since that time. While it is evident in some of the English decisions of the nineteenth century,[84] and continues to be reiterated by some English justices[85] and by the Canadian Supreme Court,[86] recent United Kingdom decisions show a greater acceptance by judges that crimes can lawfully be framed without a requirement of mens rea.[87]

Its importance is reiterated perhaps most strongly by some of the American decisions.[88] For example, the United States Supreme Court in *Morissette v California* noted:

> The contention that an injury can amount to a crime only when inflicted by intention is no provincial or transient notion. It is as universal and persistent in mature legal systems of law as belief in freedom of the human will and a consequent ability and duty of the normal individual to choose between good and evil. A relation between some mental element and punishment for a harmful act is almost as instinctive as the child's familiar exculpatory "but I didn't mean to," and has afforded the rational basis for a tardy and unfinished substitution of deterrence and reformation in place of retaliation and vengeance as the motivation for public prosecution.[89]

The Supreme Court noted in that case that given the importance historically of the mens rea requirement in criminal law, in situations where legislation was silent as to whether a particular offense required proof of mens rea, the court would typically find that mens rea was required, on the basis that the concept was "inherent in the idea of the offense."[90] The Court reiterated that "wrongdoing must be conscious to be criminal,"[91] even as they acknowledged the growth of regulatory type offenses where exceptionally mens rea was not required. However, the Court declined to delineate acceptable boundaries on the use of such regulatory type offenses, beyond an observation that they were typically focused not on the moral character of the defendant's actions, but rather the harm that their activities caused to members of the public.

Somewhat oddly, where elsewhere the Court emphasized the essentiality of a "guilty mind" to essential criminality, it validated an Oregon statute requiring an accused to prove, at the level of beyond reasonable doubt, the defense of insanity.[92] Some might have thought that where there was at least some evidence that an accused was insane at the time of commission of the charge (murder) with which they had been accused, the prosecution would not be able to show the mental element required for a charge, particularly a charge such as murder. Only Frankfurter and Black JJ, dissenting, addressed this argument, striking out the law as unconstitutional.

In striking down a law making it an offense for a convicted felon to fail to register with the police upon arrival into a state, the Court noted the offense was for conduct that was "wholly passive."[93] It acknowledged there that conduct alone without regard to intention could be sufficient to create criminal liability. However, this law was unconstitutional. The Court found actual knowledge of the duty to register, or probability of such knowledge and failure to comply, were minimum requirements.[94]

In *Robinson v California*[95] the Court struck out a law which made it a criminal offense to be addicted to drugs. The Court found the provision offended the *Eighth Amendment* bar on cruel and unusual punishment. Although the judgment is lightly reasoned, the following passage is important:

> It is unlikely that any state at this moment in history would attempt to make it a criminal offense for a person to be mentally ill, or a leper, or to be afflicted with a venereal disease. A state might determine that the general health and welfare require that the victims of these and other human afflictions be dealt with by compulsory treatment . . . but in the light of contemporary human knowledge, a law which made a criminal offense of such a disease would doubtless be universally thought to be an infliction of cruel and unusual punishment in violation of the Eighth and Fourteenth Amendment . . . to be sure, imprisonment for ninety days is not, in the abstract, a punishment which is either cruel or unusual. But the question cannot be considered in the abstract. Even one day in prison would be a cruel and unusual punishment for the "crime" of having a common cold.[96]

It is fair to say that cases in this era, which seemed to herald acceptance of some kind of mens rea concept, did not articulate as clearly as they might have their rejection of the approach suggested in cases such as *Balint* and *Dotterweich*. They did not expressly overrule those decisions, or find they were wrong in their dismissal of culpability as being essential to criminality. The decisions are, with respect, not strongly argued, and not strongly couched in terms supportive of mens rea. Their disparate and sparse reasoning makes them unsuitable candidates as landmark mens rea decisions. Indirectly, this permitted later courts to again make decisions apparently sidelining mens rea and culpability requirements from the criminal law.

The landmark case of *In Re Winship*[97] is of limited use in the mens rea debate. While it strongly re-asserted the importance of the beyond reasonable doubt standard, and the fact the onus of proof was on the prosecutor, this was only in relation to "every fact necessary to constitute the crime with which [the accused] is charged."[98] Thus, the Court did not discuss what "every fact necessary to constitute the crime" meant, and whether it simply applied to every fact necessary as per how the legislature drafted the offense, or whether there were some underlying constitutional "facts" that would be necessary, including a guilty mind. In *Powell v Texas*, to be discussed more fully under the heading of "voluntariness," Marshall J, joined by Warren CJ Black and Harlan JJ, opined that "this Court has never articulated fully a general constitutional doctrine of mens rea,"[99] though conceding that an earlier case, again to be discussed below under the concept of "voluntariness," had brought the Supreme Court "a very small way" into the substantive criminal law.[100]

The high-water mark for advocates of a substantive view to the *Constitution* and the criminal law came in *Mullaney v Wilbur*.[101] There the state criminal code contained the offenses of murder and manslaughter. Both required proof of intent. The onus was on the prosecution to prove the elements of each offense. Malice aforethought was an element of the offense of murder. The legislation provided that where the unlawful killing occurred in the heat of passion, on sudden provocation, without malice aforethought, the killing would be considered manslaughter (only). The section required the defendant to prove the existence of heat of passion. A unanimous Supreme Court found the provision to be constitutionally invalid.

The Court noted that traditionally in the American common law, matters that related to justification, excuse or alleviation were to be proven by the accused. This included matters such as provocation or "heat of passion" type issues. However, statutory law had by and large superseded the common law here, requiring the prosecution to prove the absence of provocation or heat of passion at the level of beyond reasonable doubt. The Court reflected that, since early times, "the single most important factor in determining the degree of culpability attaching to an unlawful homicide" was the presence or absence of heat of passion.[102]

The Court appeared to reject an interpretation of *Winship*'s "every fact necessary to constitute the crime" must be proven by the prosecution beyond reasonable doubt as being merely procedural in nature, applicable only to the offense (and any defense) as drafted by the legislature. They apparently accepted that a substantive view had to be taken of the requirements of due process in this context. It is perhaps the strongest endorsement of a substantive approach to criminal law in any of the United States cases:

> If *Winship* were limited to those facts that constituted a crime as defined by state law, a State could undermine many of the interests that decision sought to protect without effecting any substantial change in its law. It would only be necessary to redefine the elements that constitute different crimes, characterizing them as factors that bear solely on the extent of punishment . . . if petitioner's argument is accepted, [a jurisdiction] could impose a life sentence for any felonious homicide—

> even one that traditionally might be considered involuntary manslaughter—unless the defendant was able to prove that [their] act was neither intentional nor criminally reckless. *Winship* is concerned with substance rather than this kind of formalism.[103]

The Court noted that state criminal law was concerned "not only with guilt or innocence in the abstract but also with the degree of criminal culpability."[104] It noted that the state had chosen to distinguish killing unaffected by provocation and that explained by provocation on the basis that the latter were less blameworthy. The consequences of a conviction for murder were significantly different from the consequences of a conviction for manslaughter. Further, here the burden of proof had been shifted to the defendant. This increased the risk of an erroneous murder conviction, in the case where the defendant could not make out the defense on the balance of probabilities. This fact implicated the due process interests identified in earlier cases around the concepts of beyond reasonable doubt and presumption of innocence. The case certainly placed question marks over the continued use of "affirmative defenses" involving a burden of persuasion on the accused.[105]

Suggestions that *Mullaney* heralded the introduction of a new phase of the Supreme Court's jurisprudence involving a substantive view of the criminal law[106] were soon dashed. Sharp divisions appeared in the Court in *Patterson v New York,*[107] decided just two years after *Mullaney.* There the Court validated a provision which placed the onus on an accused to prove the existence of the affirmative defense of "extreme emotional disturbance" on the balance of probabilities. If the accused could show this, but otherwise the unlawful killing was proven or admitted, the effect would be to render the accused guilty of manslaughter, rather than murder.

The Court retreated from its substantive view in *Mullaney*. The majority observed that legislatures had broad power to regulate the procedure under which its laws were carried out, including the burden and standard of proof.[108] The majority sought to distinguish this defense from the "heat of passion" defense, arguing it was far broader in remit. The majority found that it was not constitutionally required that a state must disprove beyond reasonable doubt every fact relating to any affirmative defense which bore upon the culpability of an accused. Proof of the nonexistence of all affirmative defenses had never been constitutionally required.[109]

Each member of the majority in *Patterson* had been a party to the unanimous decision in *Mullaney,* which some had interpreted as affirmation of a substantive approach to the criminal law. The majority's concession to such a view was succinct: "[Our] view may seem to permit state legislatures to reallocate burdens of proof by labelling as affirmative defenses at least some elements of the crimes now defined in their statutes.

But there are obviously constitutional limits beyond which the States may not go in this regard."[110] The majority provided little elaboration on what these "obvious constitutional limits" might be, apart from a statement that a legislature could not declare a person to be guilty or presumptively guilty of a crime. The majority sought to distinguish *Mullaney* on the basis that, in that case, lack of provocation was part of the definition of a crime, whereas in *Patterson*, it had been defined as a defense. Ironically, in so attempting to distinguish *Mullaney*, the majority provided an example of what all members of *Mullaney* had recently warned against—a redistribution of what were traditionally considered to be elements of crimes to defenses, resulting in a change to the party which must prove the existence or non-existence of a particular circumstance. All members of the Court in *Mullaney* said that a court which permitted a legislature to do so would be allowing the undermining of fundamental values articulated in *Winship*; just two years later, five members of the *Mullaney* court proceeded to do just that.

Powell J, who had written the unanimous judgment in *Mullaney*, wrote a strong dissent, one joined in by Brennan and Marshall JJ, who were also parties to the *Mullaney* decision. The dissentients maintained that a substantive view should be taken of the criminal law. They rejected the suggestion that the only facts that the prosecution needed to prove were necessarily those expressed in the statute. To so provide would be a triumph of form over substance. They found there was no difference in substance between the legislation invalidated in *Mullaney* and that validated by the majority in *Patterson*. While one cast the provision about provocation as an element of the crime, and the other as an affirmative defense, in substance the defenses were materially the same.[111] Logically, the question of their constitutionality should be decided the same way.

The dissentients were alive to the consequences for the presumption of innocence of accepting the procedural view the majority took. They noted it would permit the legislature to "shift, virtually at will, the burden of persuasion with respect to any factor in a criminal case" with appropriate drafting.[112] They derided the majority's statement regarding "obvious constitutional limits" on the basis the limits were far from obvious. The majority's view would permit the undermining of the presumption of innocence, which was supposed to be a bedrock principle whose enforcement lay at the heart of a criminal trial.[113]

The dissentients would permit the legislature broad discretion in the framing of its criminal law offenses and defenses, but with limits. Specifically, it would not permit the legislature to transfer from what would normally be part of an offense, to a defense, things which traditionally[114] made a difference to a situation in terms of punishment and stigma.[115] This was why the legislature could not transfer into a defense the requirement to prove provocation—because traditionally this made a difference to how seriously the law viewed a crime, for instance punishment for manslaughter, as opposed to murder. These limits were apparently accepted and adopted by the Canadian Supreme Court in their clarification that mens rea was a fundamental principle of the criminal law.[116]

A further example of this type of reasoning occurs in *Staples v United States*.[117] In inferring that a criminal provision silent on the matter imported a mens rea requirement, the majority noted that "historically, the penalty imposed under a statute has been a significant consideration in determining whether the statute should be construed as dispensing with mens rea."

A similar division was apparent in *Martin v Ohio*.[118] That case involved a state law which defined aggravated murder as "purposely, and with prior calculation and design," causing the death of another. The criminal law also provided an affirmative defense of self-defense, placing the burden of persuasion on an accused who wished to avail themselves of the defense. The question was whether it accorded with constitutional due process to place the burden of persuasion upon an accused to make good the defense of self-defense. A majority of the Court validated the provision.

In validating the provision, the majority noted, as it had in *Patterson*, that in the history of the common law, the burden of making out an affirmative defense had often been placed on the accused. While almost all states had reformed this position, to cast the burden of disproving such a defense on the prosecutor, there was nothing unconstitutional about the law of the small minority of states which continued to require the accused to satisfy a burden of persuasion with respect to such a defense. The dissentients (Powell Brennan and Marshall JJ, with whom Blackmun J agreed in part) continued with their approach based on concepts of stigma and punishment, on a substantive view of the criminal law. Anything that traditionally made a substantial difference with respect to the stigma and punishment associated with a particular crime had to be proven by the prosecution beyond reasonable doubt.[119] Such an approach was necessary to remove the incentive for a state to simply redefine elements of an offense as elements of an affirmative defense, thereby in effect transferring the burden of persuasion with respect to the matter from the prosecutor to the defendant.[120] On the facts, the state could not transfer the burden regarding self-defense to the accused. Historically, self-defense was one of the most important justifications for what would otherwise be unlawful behavior; it materially impacted on the punishment that an accused offender would receive. As a result, the minority found that the *Constitution* forbade the state from transferring to the defendant the onus of proof with respect to that issue.

Many of the Supreme Court decisions in this area since *Martin* have been decided using principles of statutory interpretation, rather than development of a constitutional doctrine of substantive due process, to ensure some minimum level of mens rea.[121] Mere omissions to provide for mens rea will not be sufficient for the court to dispense with it.[122] The Court has expressed concern with legislation that "punishes seemingly innocent conduct," justifying at least a presumption of a requirement of scienter.[123] Having said that, in these cases there is some acknowledgement at least of the place of culpability in a finding of criminal wrongdoing.[124] It may not be necessary to show that the accused was specifically aware of the illegality of what they were doing, in particular in cases where the unlawfulness of the behavior would be readily apparent to most; in other words, objective mens rea, as opposed to subjective mens rea, may be sufficient.[125]

The Supreme Court again confirmed its deferential approach to state legislatures and their power to frame their criminal law in the manner they see fit in *Clark v Arizona*.[126] The Arizona criminal statute required the accused to prove a defense of insanity on the balance of probabilities. A majority of the Court validated the provision against a due process challenge. The majority seemed to suggest there could be a constitutional minimum, for example, requiring at least that a defense of insanity be available.[127]

The dissentients, Kennedy Stevens and Ginsburg JJ, required that when considering whether the offense element of intent had been satisfied, the jury consider evidence of the possible insanity of the accused. It was not sufficient to permit it only when considering a defense for which the accused had a burden of persuasion. There are renewed suggestions of limits on the ability of legislatures to define crimes as they wish, and to redefine what were traditionally elements of crimes to defenses. For example, the dissentients said that a law which framed murder in terms of intentional killing of another in circumstances that would show intent "but for the defendant's mental illness" would be unconstitutional. The dissentients referred to the "obvious constitutional limits within which the state cannot go" in *Patterson*, citing the above hypothetical as one example of a law that would go beyond what was acceptable. They again expressed the fear that if a state could redefine crimes, it could thus evade fundamental constitutional requirements.[128]

Another way in which arguments for a substantive criminal law, as opposed to a merely procedural view, occurs in the context of the *Eighth Amendment*'s prohibition on cruel and unusual punishment. Now there is a very lengthy jurisprudence on the interpretation of this amendment, which it is not necessary to canvas here. Suffice to say that, at least to some extent, the amendment imports a proportionality requirement, in that laws authorizing grossly disproportionate punishment for given offenses are vulnerable to constitutional challenge. In the latest *Eighth Amendment* cases we once again see members of the Court using the concept of "culpability" in assessing whether a given penalty regime is constitutionally valid or not.[129] This provides some support for the argument in favor of substantive criminal law, that a court is not obliged to simply apply a state's criminal law, including its choices as to definitional elements, defenses (if any), and punishment, but rather that the courts do have a constitutional role regarding the substance of criminal law, and that it should not accept outcomes (whether that be convictions or sentences) that do not reflect the culpability of the particular accused. The Court accepts this reasoning in relation to the *Eighth Amendment*; it should also accept it in relation to due process in the *Fifth* and *Fourteenth*.

The Contours of a Substantive Criminal Law Doctrine

What follows will be an outline of a minimalist substantive criminal law approach. The first point is that it is considered necessary to have such minima, in order to protect fundamental due process rights like presumption of innocence. It accepts the impotence of all of the constitutional due process protections in constitutional law if legislatures are completely free to frame the criminal law as they wish. On the other hand, a court is not a super-legislature, and I accept the broad parameters within which legislatures can frame their criminal law. Above any other area of law, the criminal law is the most likely to reflect community wishes and will, and the democratic legitimacy of legislatures' choices about the mix and balance of principles in its criminal law is fully acknowledged. The delicate balance between the right of a democratically elected legislature to frame and implement its own law, broadly representative of the wishes and will of its constituents, and the right of an individual to quietly go about their business, unimpeded by state authority and not sanctioned without good reason, is not a new one. It will be possible in the space available, and given the object of this book, to provide a sketch of the desired approach, using select issues as examples. It is beyond the scope of the book to offer a fully theorized and articulated structure of substance criminal law; broad brush strokes will be sufficient for current purposes.

Two other preliminary points should be made. It is assumed here that courts will continue to apply principles of statutory interpretation so as to minimize the impact of legislation on human rights. This is known in some jurisdictions as the "principle of legality," whereby any ambiguity in relation to a statutory provision in the human rights area is resolved in a way that the impact of the legislation on fundamental human rights is minimized. Of course, this is only of assistance when courts find that the will and intent of the legislature is not sufficiently clear. It is useless where the legislature makes its intentions clear, for example, to depart from a mens rea requirement in relation to a criminal law attracting possible imprisonment for breach.

Secondly, the suggested structure below is considered applicable to any criminal provision, breach of which may lead to imprisonment. If "death is different," then possible imprisonment is also considered different.[130] Thus, I would allow so-called strict liability offenses that do not have all of the features mentioned below, and in particular offenses that may not be considered "sufficiently blameworthy" to attract criminal sanction.[131] I would allow them on the condition that they cannot lead to a possible jail term in the event of proven breach; for example, they are punished by a fine or some other penalty that does not involve imprisonment. The Supreme Court has already agreed that the penalty imposed by a statute has been and is a significant factor in determining whether mens rea is required.[132] Specifically, it should only permit strict liability offenses to be punishable other than by imprisonment.

In my view, a line is crossed when a criminal provision is punishable by a possible jail term. This line makes the offense of a different substantive order than one punishable by a simple fine. The law originally maintained this line when it accepted the lawfulness of strict liability offenses, but the line has largely disappeared. Courts now routinely accept the validity of strict liability offenses, though the punishment for their breach may well be imprisonment.[133] This is a line that the law should not have crossed. It should accept strict liability only to the extent that a breach of such a provision cannot lead to a term of imprisonment. Merely pointing out the "disfavored status"[134] does nothing, in itself, to curb their use and spread.

In my view, the deprivation of an individual's liberty, and the consequences for them and their family, including stigma, makes offenses punishable by a jail term of a different legal order than ones merely attracting a fine.[135] It seems logical that the substantive rules of criminal law should recognize this different legal order. Boundaries matter. Legislatures are often keen to blur or erase them; courts must be vigilant to uphold them when there is good reason for them, as is the case here.

An Act

Traditionally, a crime has been defined to include an "actus reus," and that requirement is supported here. The state may not criminalize non-acts. For instance, it may not criminalize mere thought, as has occurred at times in history.[136] This can be justified by the harm principle—that merely thinking something cannot, of itself, harm others. It might also preclude the criminalizing of mere status—for instance, the fact of addiction to an illicit substance. As indicated earlier in the book, in previous times the criminal law did apparently seek to criminalize status. The argument is that the mere fact someone is addicted does not indicate they have committed any specific act, and indeed they are not being punished for any specific act.

To the extent that the contours of the criminal law are defined by Mill's harm principle (see below), this supports the argument that mere thought can never be the subject of a crime, because mere thought does not harm anyone. Nor can a person's status.[137] Not coincidentally, Mill was one of the most ardent supporters of freedom of expression.

Voluntariness of the Act/Accused Is Considered Legally Responsible for Act

At minimum, the act that the legislature seeks to criminalize must be "voluntary" in nature.[138] At its simplest, an act committed whilst an individual was sleepwalking could not be criminalized because it was not voluntary in nature. An act committed whilst a person lacked legal capacity, for example they were not of age, would in general not attract criminal sanction, unless there was evidence that the person in fact had the required mental capacity.

In relation to insanity, there would be limits on the ability of states to legislate with respect to this offense. One commonly understood aspect of the legal concept of "insanity" is the inability of a person to control their actions. This aspect of the defense would be constitutionally protected. A person should not face criminal sanction in circumstances where they could not control the actions said to constitute the crime. This ties in with Nicola Lacey's concept of "capacity responsibility."[139]

It is acknowledged that some states have chosen to cast the issue of insanity as a defense, and in some cases cast the onus of proof upon the defendant to prove, at varying levels, the existence of facts supporting the defense. In the model proposed here, the sharp distinction that legislatures seek to draw between offenses and defenses would be abolished. This sharp distinction between accusation and defense, with a suggestion that the accuser bear the onus of proof with respect to the former and the accused the latter, which the common law traditionally adopted,[140] was probably an "inappropriate borrowing" from the civil law.[141] The Supreme Court has acknowledged this.[142] It does not make sense in the criminal law; criminal law is inherently different from non-criminal law; the purpose of the proceedings is fundamentally different; stakes are higher, the parties are different. This is the solution recommended by leading legal philosophers such as Williams.[143] Upon a substantive view, the prosecutor would have to show at the usual standard that the accused was sane, at least if the accused has raised some evidence of the possibility of insanity. The prosecutor would have to prove this at the level of beyond reasonable doubt. It goes to something that is considered essential to criminality—that the person acted in the exercise of free will; in other words, a voluntary act.[144]

This would mean that any statutory presumption that an accused person was sane, casting it upon them to prove the existence of the defense on the balance of probabilities, would be constitutionally invalid. Any attempt to completely remove the issue of insanity from the court's consideration in relation to a criminal charge would likewise be unconstitutional.

Further to this reasoning, questions of self-defense, provocation, extreme emotional disturbance, etc., are also argued to go to the question of free will and voluntariness. As a concept, provocation typically applies to the situation where what the victim did would ordinarily deprive a typical person in society of their ordinary powers of self-control, where the accused acts before their passion cools. This is considered to be an example of an act that is non-voluntary. As such, it would be for the prosecution to prove the absence of circumstances such as this. This would have to be proven at the typical criminal standard of beyond reasonable doubt, at least if the defendant can raise some evidence of the factual basis for such a defense.[145]

This would mean that any statutory presumption that a defendant did not act in self-defense, was not provoked, or did not suffer extreme emotional disturbance would be invalid. Any attempt to remove these issues from the court's consideration in relation to a criminal charge would also be invalid. This theory would find support in the United States Supreme Court decision in *Mullaney v Wilbur*, but a contrary position was taken by the Supreme Court soon after in *Patterson v New York*. The Supreme Court was right in *Mullaney* to insist that the prosecution bear the onus of proof in relation to provocation. Regardless of whether the state defined the offense as requiring absence of it, or defined a defense available in respect of it, the state should be required to prove its absence at the level of beyond reasonable doubt, at least if the defendant can raise some evidence of it.[146] It was wrong in *Patterson* to accept the constitutional validity of the state merely shifting the provocation principle to an affirmative defense, and requiring the accused to meet an onus of proof in respect of it on the preponderance of the evidence.

Knowledge that the Act/s Alleged to Be Criminal Were in Fact Criminal/Ignorance of the Law

The fundamental premise that ignorance of the law is no excuse must be accepted. It cannot be a general defense to a criminal charge for an accused to claim that they were not personally aware of the relevant provisions of the criminal law.

Knew or Ought to Have Known Act/s Alleged to Be Criminal Were "Wrong"

Here an objective test of the mental requirement for the commission of a crime can be accepted. It is, or should be, sufficient for criminality if an accused ought to have known that the acts complained of were against the law.[147] This engages the question of what it is that legislatures can criminalize. We recall acknowledgement of the seriousness and uniqueness of the criminal sanction, and the serious thing that we do when we judge a person to be guilty of a crime. The person becomes liable in many cases to deprivation of liberty, and they and their families will suffer continuing stigma as a result. Their right to be "left alone" is being abrogated. Thus, punishment requires strong justification.[148] Upon what legal basis can imprisonment of an individual be justified in this manner?

The answer is that legislators can only criminalize conduct that is "sufficiently blameworthy" to attract criminal sanction, with its associated costs.[149] Usually, but not always, as will be seen below, there is congruence between the concepts of sufficiently blameworthy and "ought to know" that the conduct was wrong. In most cases, both concepts are useful to justify (or reject) the use of criminal sanction. However, in the odd case, as described below, they may point in different directions. In such cases, I argue that the concept of "sufficiently blameworthy" should override. But this idea, that the criminal law may only criminalize conduct that is sufficiently blameworthy, has been around for many centuries, in the English common law and in civil law systems. It is considered to qualify as one of those "fundamental principles of justice rooted in the traditions and conscience of our people"[150] so as to warrant protection under the auspices of due process.

There is clear concern in the case law[151] and literature[152] with criminalizing conduct that is not sufficiently blameworthy. As indicated earlier in the chapter, there is significant historical evidence of the concern of the law with levels of culpability in the context of criminal law. This is not considered overly prescriptive. Legislators retain broad power to frame offenses as they wish, and to respond to community concern about crime levels. However, there are limits, which are themselves limited. So, for example, it should not be constitutionally acceptable to frame a criminal offense around notions of authorities having reasonable suspicion that a person possesses an otherwise-innocuous thing for purposes of terrorism, together with proof of actual possession. Obviously, this is the very legislation challenged in *Kebilene*. The accused did have a way out if they could prove their possession was innocuous, and the Court read it down to impose merely an evidentiary onus upon the accused. However, in my view it would have been better for the Court to make its decision on the basis that mere reasonable suspicion by authorities of wrongdoing does not belong as an element of a crime, let alone be the substantive basis for a crime (and a serious one at that, punishable by a ten-year jail term). It does not belong as an element of a crime, and the legislature cannot create such a norm of conduct and call it a crime, because it punishes something that is not sufficiently blameworthy to attract a criminal sanction. It is not something that an accused person ought to know not to have done.

This could also explain the orphaned United States Supreme Court decision in *Lambert*. This should be seen as an example of a legislature criminalizing something (failure to register with authorities) that was not sufficiently blameworthy to warrant the attention of the criminal law. Alternatively, it may be seen as a case where a reasonable person ought not to have known that they had to register mere presence in a jurisdiction with authorities. I do not agree that the case should be interpreted as meaning that a person is only in breach of the criminal law when they are aware of the criminal provision of which they have been charged.

Another example may be taken from current criminal law legislation in various Australian states which criminalizes mere acts of association between certain individuals. These are the so-called consorting laws. In relation to certain individuals or groups in society, merely consorting with each other is criminal. There is no need for the prosecutor to prove that the targeted individuals or groups are meeting for an illicit purpose, and in fact it may not be a defense for the individual concerned to show that the purpose for their meeting was in fact benign. Courts should not permit the enforcement of laws of this nature. They should strike them down as unconstitutional and offensive to fundamental principles of justice. This is because they criminalize activity which is not sufficiently blameworthy to attract a criminal sanction.[153] Now, on occasion, these laws are conditioned upon a person first being given a written notice directing them not to consort with certain other individuals. This may arguably provide evidence of the "ought to know that what they were doing was wrong"; however, the fact remains that it criminalizes behavior that is, in my view, not of itself sufficiently blameworthy to attract criminal sanction.

The inevitable concern is that the test is impossibly subjective, and it gives the court too much licence to strike down laws of which it does not approve. To be clear, the intention is not for courts to usurp the role of legislatures. It is not for courts to make the criminal law. However, in a system which cherishes the separation of powers and the idea of checks and balances, there should be no objection to courts circumscribing the ability of legislatures to define behavior as criminal, within limits. The court is intended here to have a minimalist role in judicially reviewing such legislation to ensure it meets minimum requirements of substantive criminal law.[154] This is far from unbridled judicial activism and wholesale rewriting of large slabs of the criminal law. Legislators retain their prime responsibility in this field.

How would a court determine whether conduct was sufficiently blameworthy to attract criminal sanction? Firstly, history would be important. The fact that the common law recognized such behavior as wrong would be highly probative of the right of legislatures to do so in the current context. It is fully acknowledged that history is not a perfect source—systems changed over the centuries, and the evidence can be incomplete. Further, obviously the criminal law cannot be enshrined in stone and reflect earlier societies rather than current ones; the risk with using history is that the scope of the criminal law would ossify. So, for instance, it might be argued that behavior such as commission of so-called revenge porn, where a spurned lover posts online revealing pictures of their ex, should be a crime. Of course, historically the criminal law would not have criminalized such behavior. Conversely, conduct that the law in the past might have been viewed as criminal might no longer be justifiable, because societal standards have changed to such an extent that the conduct can no longer be considered sufficiently blameworthy to criminalize it.[155] So, while not perfect, and while not the only evidence, history should play an important role in defining the parameters of the concept of "sufficiently blameworthy" behavior to attract criminal sanction.

Another important concept, one which would solve the problem identified in the previous paragraph, would be to take into account in determining what was sufficiently blameworthy the harm principle. Mill was famous for this principle, arguing that one justification for laws regulating an individual's behavior in a liberal democracy was harm—that while an individual was generally broadly free to act as they wished, limits could be justified where one person's behavior impacted on the rights of another, causing them injury:

> Every one who receives the protection of society owes a return for the benefit, and the fact of being in society renders it indispensable that each should be bound to observe a certain line of conduct towards the rest. This conduct consists, first, in not injuring the interests of one another . . . as soon as any part of a person's conduct affects prejudicially the rights of others, society has jurisdiction over it.[156]

So in determining whether conduct was sufficiently blameworthy to attract criminal sanction, the fact that it caused harm or could have (or did not or could not) would be relevant.[157] Specifically, the fact that a person has an implement reasonably suspected of being used in relation to terrorist activity does not infringe the harm principle. That would mean that the state could not criminalize it. Similarly, the fact that one individual is associating with another, without more, does not infringe the harm principle. Again, the state would not be constitutionally able to criminalize it.

The concept of "sufficiently blameworthy" can also encompass the kind of proportionality argument made by others.[158] Specifically, not only must conduct be sufficiently blameworthy to attract criminal sanction, it must also be sufficiently blameworthy to attract the degree of criminal sanction that the legislature has actually prescribed. Now the concept of proportionality in criminal sentencing is well-established. It is clear that it is encompassed within *Eighth Amendment* case law.[159] Cruel and unusual punishment is also forbidden in the *Magna Carta* and section 10 of the *Bill of Rights 1688* (Eng). It is beyond the scope of this book to consider in detail courts' jurisprudence regarding cruel and unusual punishment and proportionality, and I have considered this topic elsewhere,[160] but it should be noted here that the work of scholars who have considered proportionality as part of substantive criminal law doctrine is compatible with the suggestion made here.

CONCLUSION

This chapter has considered another threat to the presumption of innocence doctrine, being moves by legislatures to redefine crimes in ways to make it easier to obtain a successful conviction. It has accepted that legislatures have broad discretion to define criminal behavior as they wish, presumably reflective of their community's views and attitudes. However, it has found that a substantive view must be taken, to some extent at least, of criminal law. Unless this occurs, legislatures will be able to effectively circumvent presumption of innocence protections by redefining elements of crimes as defenses.

The challenge for adherents of a substantive view of criminal law has been to carefully articulate the contours of such a doctrine, in ways that accord the legislature broad discretion to frame their criminal law, but also seek to protect the presumption of innocence from effective gutting. This chapter has suggested what these minimal criteria would look like. A legislature could only prescribe something as criminal if it is an act that is voluntary, in the sense described above. Further, it would be necessary to show, at minimum, that the defendant ought to have known that the behavior was wrong. Here a concept of sufficiently blameworthy would be utilized. A person only ought to know behavior is wrong in the eyes of the law if it is sufficiently blameworthy to warrant legal sanction. Here notions of what historically has been considered criminal would be relevant, as would Mill's harm principle, and concepts of proportionality.

NOTES

1. Andrew Stumer, *The Presumption of Innocence: Evidential and Human Rights Perspectives* (Hart Publishing, Oxford, 2010) 63.

2. Paul Roberts, "The Presumption of Innocence Brought Home? *Kebilene* Deconstructed," *Law Quarterly Review* 118 (2002): 50; similarly Paul Roberts, "Drug Dealing and the Presumption of Innocence: The *Human Rights Act* (Almost) Bites," *International Journal of Evidence and Proof* 6 (2002): 22, and Nancy King and Susan Klein, "Essential Elements," *Vanderbilt Law Review* 54 (2001): 1530.

3. Paul Roberts, "Drug Dealing and the Presumption of Innocence: The *Human Rights Act* (Almost) Bites," *International Journal of Evidence and Proof* 6 (2002): 36: "once the presumption of innocence is given substantive content, there are no obvious limits on the scope for judicial reworking of the elements of criminal law offenses." He refers to a court reading down a reverse onus provision to a mere burden of production rather than a burden of persuasion as "judicial legislation" (35); Joseph Kennedy,

"Making the Crime Fit the Punishment," *Emory Law Journal* (2002): 841: "terms like innocence and moral culpability are the bete noir of those concerned by the antimajoritarian aspects of judicial review; such transparently moral terms conjure up in the most direct form possible the nightmare image of a court literally legislating morality."

4. Theodore Gottfried and Peter Baroni, "Presumptions, Inferences and Strict Liability in Illinois Criminal Law: Pre-Empting the Presumption of Innocence?" *John Marshall Law Review* 41 (2008): 739, concludes that the use of strict liability in criminal codes are a "perfect stalking horse for incursions into the defendant's presumption of innocence."

5. Henry Hart, "The Aims of the Criminal Law," *Law and Contemporary Problems* 23 (1958): 404; James Hippard "The Unconstitutionality of Criminal Liability Without Fault: An Argument for a Constitutional Doctrine of Mens Rea," *Houston Law Review* 10 (1973): 1058: "this constitutional right to a presumption of innocence is a hollow right indeed if a legislature can eliminate any substantive element of a crime that suits its utilitarian purposes of the moment."

6. "Towards a Constitutional Law of Crime and Punishment," *Hastings Law Journal* 55 (2004): 524: "the patently empty rule that the state can shift the burden of proof on any issue it designates as a 'defense element' rather than an offense element."

7. [1895] 1 QB 918, 920–921 (Day J).

8. "What sense does it make to insist upon procedural safeguards in criminal prosecutions if anything whatever can be made a crime in the first place?": Henry Hart, "The Aims of the Criminal Law," *Law and Contemporary Problems* 23 (1958): 431; see to like effect Ronald Allen, "*Mullaney v Wilbur*, the Supreme Court and the Substantive Criminal Law—An Examination of the Limits of Legitimate Intervention," *Texas Law Review* 55 (1977): 283–285; Alan Saltzman, "Strict Criminal Liability and the United States *Constitution*: Substantive Criminal Law Due Process," *Wayne Law Review* 24 (1978): 1637–1638: "it does not make sense to talk about a constitutional requirement that the prosecution establish guilt beyond a reasonable doubt, unless we are prepared to say what must be proved to establish guilt . . . the *Constitution* contains special limits on the imposition of criminal liability and there must, therefore, be some constitutional rules as to what may be called a crime and how much criminal punishment may be imposed. These limits must relate to the critical characteristic of crime"; William Stuntz, "Substance, Process and the Civil-Criminal Line," *Journal of Contemporary Legal Issues* 7 (1996): 7: "good procedural rules require good substantive rules in order to accomplish anything," and *The Collapse of American Criminal Justice* (Harvard University Press, Cambridge, 2011) 212: "The *Constitution* is not written with substantive criminal law in mind. More's the pity"; Glanville Williams, "Offences and Defences," *Legal Studies* 2 (1982): 233, 254: "the foregoing argument suggests that the definition of an offense in a statute is not a comprehensive and safe guide to the definitional elements of an offense"; John Calvin Jeffries Jr and Paul Stephan III, "Defenses, Presumptions and Burden of Proof in the Criminal Law," *Yale Law Journal* 88 (1979): 1325, 1347: "guilt and innocence are substantive concepts. Their content depends on the choice of facts determinative of liability. If this choice is remitted to unconstrained legislative discretion, no rule of constitutional procedure can restrain the potential for injustice"; John Stinneford, "Punishment Without Culpability," *Journal of Criminal Law and Criminology* 102 (2012): 657; Donald Dripps, "The Constitutional Status of the Reasonable Doubt Rule," *California Law Review* 75 (1987): 1682.

9. This is obviously often typified by the decision in *Lochner v New York* 198 US 45 (1905).

10. Herbert Packer, "Mens Rea and the Supreme Court," *Supreme Court Review* (1962): 147; William Stuntz, "Substance, Process and the Civil-Criminal Line," *Journal of Contemporary Legal Issues* 7 (1996): 7–9.

11. For example, Louis Billionis, "Process, the Constitution and Substantive Criminal Law," *Michigan Law Review* 96 (1998): 1286, refers to an argument that judges are

"elites who easily confuse their own elitist views for the sense of justice held by the public as a whole."

12. Oliver Wendel Holmes Jr, *The Common Law* (Macmillan, London, 1881) 50.

13. Scott Sundby, "The Reasonable Doubt Rule and the Meaning of Innocence," *Hastings Law Journal* 40 (1989): 477, concludes that the substantive approach is "unrealistic and undesirable" given the Supreme Court's evident wariness to proceed on the path of constitutionally defining the parameters of criminal behavior, and the "inadequacy of tools" to complete the task.

14. As evidence of this difficulty, Charles Nesson observes that on each occasion where the United States Supreme Court has made tentative steps towards recognizing a substantive view of the criminal law, it has quickly retreated: "Rationality, Presumptions and Judicial Comment: A Response to Professor Allen," *Harvard Law Review* 94 (1981): 1581. He refers to the difficulty in giving content to requirements such as act, intention and proportionality. The Court's reluctance to recognize substantive limitations to the criminal law might also reflect its prior bad experience with substantive due process doctrine in the first half of the twentieth century: John Calvin Jeffries Jr and Paul Stephan III, "Defenses, Presumptions and Burden of Proof in the Criminal Law," *Yale Law Journal* 88 (1979): 1367. And some say the distinction itself is problematic: "the substantive-procedural distinction, while it may have applicability in other areas of the criminal law, is inappropriate in classifying questions of responsibility because issues of responsibility often traverse such classificatory lines": Gary Dubin, "Mens Rea Reconsidered: A Plea for a Due Process Concept of Criminal Responsibility," *Stanford Law Review* 18 (1966): 370.

15. "Process, the Constitution and Substantive Criminal Law," *Michigan Law Review* 96 (1998): 1294: "Criminal law choices are controvertible, fundamentally political, and thus best left to the political department. There indeed is a risk that criminal law might drift too far from its moral moorings. Our chief protection against that risk, however, comes not from Platonic guardians (judges), but from the safeguards of the political process and the opportunities for individualized, discretionary justice that are layered institutionally throughout the criminal process. Imperfect? Undoubtedly. But with Platonic guardians in short supply, it is quite possibly safer than the alternative."

16. *Democracy and Distrust* (Harvard University Press, Cambridge, 1980) 85–91.

17. *United States v Carolene Products Co* 304 US 144, 152 n4 (1938), noting "prejudice against discrete and insular minorities . . . which tends seriously to curtail the operation of those . . . [political] processes ordinarily to be relied upon to protect minorities" may justify increased judicial scrutiny of such measures (Stone J, for Hughes CJ Brandeis and Roberts JJ).

18. "Substance, Process and the Civil-Criminal Line," *Journal of Contemporary Legal Issues* 7 (1996): 20.

19. *Criminal Law and Justice: Essays from the W G Hart Workshop* (Sweet and Maxwell, London, 1987) 73.

20. "The Ideal of the Presumption of Innocence," *Criminal Law and Philosophy* 8 (2014): 449; Victor Tadros and Stephen Tierney, "The Presumption of Innocence and the *Human Rights Act," Modern Law Review* 67 (2004): 402.

21. "Offences and Defences," *Legal Studies* 2(3) (1982): 235; see also Glanville Williams, "The Logic of Exceptions," *Cambridge Law Journal* 47(2) (1988): 261.

22. Scott Sundby, "The Reasonable Doubt Rule and the Meaning of Innocence," *Hastings Law Journal* 40 (1989): 465; see also Alan Saltzman, "Strict Criminal Liability and the United States *Constitution*: Substantive Criminal Law Due Process," *Wayne Law Review* 24 (1989): 1630, suggesting the prosecution should be required to prove beyond reasonable doubt any issue, regardless of whether it is labeled as an element of the offense or a defense, "on which liability turns and which relates to defendant's culpability as defined by the lawmaker. It would include all the formal elements and all defenses which relate to culpability." Barbara Underwood concludes that "all facts that define or limit the defendant's criminal guilt" should be on an equal footing, and are implicated in the rationale for the reasonable doubt rule. The central question in a

criminal trial is whether facts have occurred that justify criminal sanction. Again, she says it is irrelevant whether they are formally characterized as parts of an offense or a defense. The question is what facts justify the sanction: "The Thumb on the Scales of Justice: Burdens of Persuasion in Criminal Cases," *Yale Law Journal* 86 (1977): 1347.

23. John Calvin Jeffries and Paul Stephan III, "Defenses, Presumptions and Burden of Proof in the Criminal Law," *Yale Law Journal* 88 (1979): 1347.

24. Susan Pilcher, "Ignorance, Discretion and the Fairness of Notice: Confronting 'Apparent Innocence' in the Criminal Law," *American Criminal Law Review* 33 (1996): 7.

25. 34.

26. 2.02(3) and 2.05 cmt.

27. "The full scope of liberty guaranteed by the Due Process Clause cannot be found in or limited by the precise terms of the specific guarantees elsewhere provided in the *Constitution*. This 'liberty' is not a series of isolated points pricked out in terms of the taking of property; the freedom of speech, press, and religion; the right to keep and bear arms; the freedom from unreasonable searches and seizures, and so on. It is a rational continuum which . . . includes a freedom from all substantial arbitrary impositions and purposeless restraints . . . and which recognizes, what a reasonable and sensitive judgment must, that certain interests require particularly careful scrutiny of the state needs asserted to justify their abridgement": *Poe v Ullman* 367 US 497, 522 (1961) (Harlan J, dissenting).

28. Claire Finkelstein, "Positivism and the Notion of an Offense," *California Law Review* 88 (2000): 369. The United States Supreme Court noted that the fact conduct is criminal had important implications for the dignity of individuals charged in *Lawrence v Texas* 539 US 558, 575 (2003) (Kennedy J, for Stevens Souter Ginsburg and Breyer JJ).

29. Paul Robinson, "Foreword: The Criminal-Civil Distinction and Dangerous Blameless Offenders," *Journal of Criminal Law and Criminology* 83 (1993): 707–708.

30. "Two Kinds of Legal Rules: A Comparative Study of Burden-of-Persuasion Practices in Criminal Cases," *Yale Law Journal* 77 (1968): 897–900, and noting (902) that Blackstone insisted that the defendant's case included issues of justification, excuse and alleviation. He cites *The King v Turner* 5 M and S 206, 105 ER 1026 (1816), as an example of a case where the Court required a defendant to prove an "exception" to liability, specifically noting that the rule had originated in private cases, but was appropriate to criminal cases as well.

31. Glanville Williams, "The Logic of Exceptions," *Cambridge Law Journal* 47(2) (1988): 261, 263 and 271, notes another instance of this, where originally the common law placed the burden of proof upon defendants in criminal matters, because they unthinkingly assumed that the fact that defendants in civil cases had to prove any defenses they raised should also apply to the criminal context.

32. "Two Kinds of Legal Rules: A Comparative Study of Burden-of-Persuasion Practices in Criminal Cases," *Yale Law Journal* 77 (1968): 916–917, and see George Fletcher, "The Meaning of Innocence," *University of Toronto Law Journal* 48 (1998): 163. A similar view is taken by Robert Gordon in "Affirmative Defenses and Due Process: The Constitutionality of Placing a Burden of Persuasion on a Criminal Defendant," *Georgetown Law Journal* 64 (1976): 872: "courts will realize that ultimately every defense bears on the issue of guilt or the degree of the defendant's culpability . . . shifting burdens of persuasion and attempting to separate elements of offenses and defenses are suspect procedures . . . jurisdictions that continue to place the burden of persuasion on a defendant to prove a defense deemed affirmative therefore may contravene due process principles."

33. Glanville Williams, "The Logic of "Exceptions," *Cambridge Law Journal* 47 (1988): 261, 277–280.

34. Martin Gardner notes it was during Henry II's reign in the twelfth century that saw the emergence of punishment for criminal conduct, the decline of compensation as the legal response to wrongdoing, and the increased focus on the culpability of the wrongdoer: "The Mens Rea Enigma: Observations on the Role of Motive in the Criminal Law Past and Present," *Utah Law Review* (1993): 650–651.

35. Francis Bowes Sayer, "Mens Rea," *Harvard Law Review* 45 (1932): 977.
36. *Morisette v United States* 342 US 246, 251 (1952) ("evil mind").
37. Francis Bowes Sayer, "The Present Significance of *Mens Rea* in the Criminal Law," in *Harvard Legal Essays* (Harvard University Press, Cambridge, 1934) 399, 411–412.
38. Sir William Blackstone, 4 *Commentaries on the Laws of England 1765–1769* (Maxwell and Son, London) 21.
39. *Sherras v De Rutzen* [1895] 1 QB 918, 921: "there is a presumption that mens rea, an evil intention or knowledge of the wrongfulness of the act, is an essential ingredient in every offense" (Wright J).
40. This issue is explored in more detail in Gerhard Mueller, "On Common Law Mens Rea," *Minnesota Law Review* 42 (1958): 1059–1063.
41. *Ford v Wainwright* 477 US 399 (1986).
42. "Moral blameworthiness is, and always has been, a precondition for criminal liability . . . it is a principle deeply rooted in the notion of human free will which lies at the heart of our criminal law, and is therefore protected by the Due Process Clause": Jean Gilles Phillips and Rebecca Woodman, "The Insanity of the Mens Rea Model: Due Process and the Abolition of the Insanity Defense," *Pace Law Review* 28 (2008): 494.
43. *Speiser v Randall* 357 US 513, 523 (1958) (Brennan J, for Frankfurter Harlan Brennan and Whittaker JJ, Black Douglas and Burton JJ concurring) (citing *Snyder v Massachusetts* 291 US 97, 105 [1934]).
44. 1 *Ancient Laws and Institutes of England* 47 (Eyre and Spottiswoode, London, 1840), cited in Martin Gardner, "The Mens Rea Enigma: Observations on the Role of Motive in the Criminal Law Past and Present," *Utah Law Review* (1993): 642.
45. Frederick Pollock and Frederic William Maitland, *The History of English Law Vol 2* (Little, Brown and Co, Cambridge, 1895) 463. Ethelrod is said to have distinguished intentional harm from accident, and a doom of Canute stated "if anyone does anything unintentionally, the case is entirely different from that of one who acts deliberately" (cited in Jerome Hall, *Principles of Criminal Law* [Bobbs-Merrill, Indianapolis, 1947] 143). Writing of the late Anglo-Saxon period, Winfield notes there was a "rough appreciation of the distinction between intention, inadvertence and inevitable accident": "The Myth of Absolute Liability," *Law Quarterly Review* 42 (1926): 37.
46. 467.
47. 467.
48. 469. The United States Supreme Court noted that by the start of the sixteenth century, the law of homicide distinguished between intentional (murder) and unintentional homicide (manslaughter): *Mullaney v Wilbur* 421 US 684, 693 (1975).
49. Francis Bowes Sayer, "Mens Rea," *Harvard Law Review* 45 (1932): 974, 980: "The canonists had long insisted that the mental element was the real criterion of guilt and under their influence the conception of subjective blameworthiness as the foundation of legal guilt was making itself strongly felt." He concludes that "under the dominating influence of the canon law and the penitential books the underlying objective of criminal justice gradually came to be the punishment of evildoing; as a result the mental factors necessary for criminality were based upon a mind bent on evildoing in the sense of moral wrong" (1016–1017); Francis Bowes Sayer, "Public Welfare Offenses," *Columbia Law Review* 33 (1933): 68: "the original objective of the criminal law was to keep the peace; and under the strong church influence of the Middle Ages its function was extended to curb moral delinquencies of one kind or another. For these purposes it developed a suitable procedure, requiring proof of moral blameworthiness or a criminal intent."
50. Oliver Wendel Holmes Jr., *The Common Law* (Macmillan, London, 1881) 4: "I do not know any very satisfactory evidence that a man was generally held liable either in Rome or England for the accidental consequences even of his own act."
51. Matthew 5:27–28, who, after repeating the commandment not to commit adultery, stated that "whosoever looketh on a woman to lust after her hath committed adultery with her already in his heart." This finds some legal application in the *Treason*

Act (1351) (Eng), defining treason to include the imagining of the death of the monarch.

52. Paul Raymond, "The Origin and Rise of Moral Liability in Anglo-Saxon Criminal Law," *Oregon Law Review* 15 (1936): 117.

53. These matters are the subject of lengthy discussion in Albert Levitt, "The Origin of the Doctrine of Mens Rea," *Illinois Law Review* 17 (1923): 117; see also H D J Bodenstein, "Phases in the Development of Criminal Mens Rea," *South African Law Journal* 36 (1919): 323.

54. "Whoever destroys by burning a building or a stack of grain placed beside a house . . . shall be bound, scourged, burned to death, provided that knowingly and consciously he has committed this crime": Clyde Pharr ed., *Ancient Roman Statutes* 11 (University of Texas, Austin, 1961).

55. Frederick Pollock and Frederic William Maitland, *The History of English Law Vol 2* (Little Brown and Company, Boston, 1895) 475.

56. Bracton, 2 *De Legibus et Consuetudinibus Angliae* (Twiss trans, 1879) 101b.

57. 136b.

58. Y.B Mich, 6 Edw. IV, f.7, pl 17 (1466) ("there is no felony, for felony is of malice prepense"); Y.B Hil, 13 Hen VII, f.14, pl 5 (1498) ("the question was whether [what happened] should be called mayhem or not . . . and it seems that it was, because he had a bad intent at the beginning"); Y.B Trin, 21 Hen. VII, f.28 pl 5 (1506) (Rede J, stating that a man who mistakenly shot another man while aiming at an inanimate object was not guilty of a felony "as he had no intent to kill him"); I am grateful to Francis Bowes Sayre, "Mens Rea," *Harvard Law Review* 45 (1932): 990–991, for these references.

59. *Maxims*, Reg. 7.

60. Matthew Hale, 1 *Pleas of the Crown* (Atkyns and Atkyns, London, 1682) 38; and earlier "where there is no will to commit an offense, there can be no transgression, or just reason to incur the penalty or sanction of that law" (15); see also William Hawkins, *Pleas of the Crown* (Walthow, London, 1716): "the guilt of offending against any law whatsoever, necessarily supposing a wilful disobedience, can never justly be imputed to those who are either incapable of understanding it or of conforming themselves to it" (1).

61. Third Institute 107; 4 Sir William Blackstone, *Commentaries on the Laws of England 1765–1769* (Clarendon Press, Oxford, 1768) 21: "to make a complete crime, cognizable by human laws, there must be both a will and an act . . . as a vicious will without a vicious act is not civil crime, so, on the other hand, an unwarrantable act without a vicious will is not crime at all. So that to constitute a crime against human laws, there must be, first, a vicious will, and secondly, an unlawful act consequent upon such vicious will."

62. Richard Fuller, "Morals and the Criminal Law," *Journal of Criminal Law and Criminology* 32 (1942): 624, 624: "sociologically speaking . . . a criminal statute is simply the formal embodiment of someone's moral values."

63. Gerhard Mueller, "On Common Law Mens Rea," *Minnesota Law Review* 42 (1958): 1058.

64. Henry Hart, "The Aims of the Criminal Law," *Law and Contemporary Problems* 23 (1958): 405: "[A crime] is not simply anything which a legislature chooses to call a 'crime.' It is not simply antisocial conduct which public officers are given a responsibility to suppress. It is not simply any conduct to which a legislature chooses to attach a 'criminal' penalty. It is conduct which, if duly shown to have taken place, will incur a formal and solemn pronouncement of the moral condemnation of the community."

65. H L A Hart, "Positivism and the Separation of Law and Morals," *Harvard Law Review* 71 (1958): 593; Lon Fuller, "Positivism and Fidelity to Law—A Reply to Professor Hart," *Harvard Law Review* 71 (1958): 630.

66. Jeremy Bentham, *Principles of Penal Law* (Tait, Edinburgh, 1843).

67. H L A Hart, "Legal Responsibility and Excuses," in Sydney Hook ed, *Determinism and Freedom in the Age of Modern Science* (New York University, New York, 1965) 31; H L A Hart, *The Concept of Law* (Clarendon Press, Oxford, 3rd ed, 2012) ch 9. Others have criticized Hart on the basis of inconsistency, that while arguing that laws had no essential moral content, he also praised laws which restricted punishment to those with a particular mens rea (often thought to be conduct that is more morally blameworthy): Richard Wasserstrom, "H L A Hart and the Doctrines of Mens Rea and Criminal Responsibility," *University of Chicago Law Review* 35 (1968): 103.

68. H L A Hart *The Morality of the Criminal Law* (Oxford University Press, London, 1965) 28–29.

69. Richard Wasserstrom, "H L A Hart and the Doctrines of Mens Rea and Criminal Responsibility," *University of Chicago Law Review* 35 (1968): 93; Sanford Kadish talks about the "paradigmatic affront to the sense of justice in the law" involved in convicting a morally innocent person, or imposing blame where there is no reason to do so: "The Decline of Innocence," *Cambridge Law Journal* 26(2) (1968): 283. Francis Bowes Sayre, "Public Welfare Offenses," *Columbia Law Review* 33 (1933): 72, concluded that "to subject defendants entirely free from moral blameworthiness to the possibility of prison sentences is revolting to the community sense of justice, and no law which violates this fundamental instinct can long endure."

70. Lon Fuller, "Positivism and Fidelity to Law—A Reply to Professor Hart," *Harvard Law Review* 71 (1957): 630, 639 and 645; and in the criminal law context, Jerome Hall, *Principles of Criminal Law* (Bobbs-Merrilll, Indianapolis, 1947) 166: "it is just to punish those who have intentionally committed moral wrongs."

71. Sir William Blackstone, 1 *Commentaries on the Laws of England 1765–1769* (Clarendon Press, London) 54–55.

72. *Regina v Woodrow* 11 M & M. 404 (Exch. 1846); cf *Sherras v De Rutzen* [1895] QB 918, in quashing a conviction of a publican who (unwittingly) served alcohol to an on-duty police officer. Relevant liquor legislation prohibited supplying alcohol to an on-duty officer. The court noted the publican "had no intention to do a wrongful act" (Day J, 920) and lacked "guilty knowledge" (Wright J, 922).

73. *Regina v Stephens* LR 1 QB 702, 708–710 (1866): "if this were strictly a criminal proceeding, the prosecution would be met with the objection that there was no *mens rea* . . . inasmuch as the object of this indictment is not to punish the defendant but really to prevent the nuisance from being continued, I think that the evidence which would support a civil action would be sufficient to support an indictment"; *Provincial Motor Cab Co v Dunning* [1909] 2 KB 599, 602: "the doctrine that there must be a criminal intent does not apply to criminal offenses of that particular class which arise only from the breach of a statutory regulation" (Lord Alverstone CJ).

74. *Hobbs v Winchester Corporation* [1910] 2 KB 483–485. This experience was mirrored in the United States, with an early case denying criminal liability in the absence of mens rea, followed subsequently by acceptance of the validity of criminal provisions in the absence of the requirement. See for discussion of the English and American cases Francis Bowes Sayre, "Public Welfare Offenses," *Columbia Law Review* 33 (1933): 56–66.

75. H L A Hart, "Legal Responsibility and Excuses," in S Hook ed, *Determinism and Freedom in the Age of Modern Science* (New York University, New York, 1961, 2nd ed) 81: "many actions . . . that if voluntarily done are criminally punishable, although our moral code may be either silent as to their moral quality, or divided."

76. John Coffee, "Does 'Unlawful' Mean Criminal? Reflections on the Disappearing Tort/Crime Distinction in American Law," *Boston University Law Review* 71 (1991): 198.

77. Francis Bowes Sayre, "Public Welfare Offenses," *Columbia Law Review* 33 (1933): 80; Rollin Perkins, "Criminal Liability Without Fault: A Disquieting Trend," *Iowa Law Review* 68 (1983): 1077; Rollin Perkins, "The Civil Offense," *University of Pennsylvania Law Review* 100 (1952): 833: "there is no offense *malum in se* without some form of *mens rea*." A similar view is taken by Andrew Ashworth and Lucia Zedner, "Defending the Criminal Law: Reflections on the Changing Character of Crime, Procedure and Sanc-

tions," *Criminal Law and Philosophy* 2 (2008): 33: "only the culpable deserve to be punished, and the public censure and hard treatment involved in punishment are unjustifiably imposed if blame is not established."

78. Herbert Packer, "Mens Rea and the Supreme Court," *Supreme Court Review* (1962): 109.

79. Francis Bowes Sayre, "Public Welfare Offenses," *Columbia Law Review* 33 (1933): 55, 56 and 79–80; "in the case of true crimes, however, although the emphasis may shift, courts can never abandon insistence upon the evil intent as a prerequisite to criminality, partly because individual interests can never be lost sight of and partly because the real menace to social interests is the intentional, not the innocent, doer of harm"; see to like effect Sanford Kadish, "Some Observations on the Use of Criminal Sanctions in Enforcing Economic Regulations," *University of Chicago Law Review* 30 (1963): 444: "to the extent that the crucial distinguishing factor of the criminal sanction is the 'judgment of community condemnation which accompanies and justifies its imposition' [quoting Hart], and to the extent that this characteristic contributes substantially to its effectiveness in influencing compliance with proscribed norms, the proliferation of convictions without grounds for condemnation tends in the long run to impair the identity of the criminal sanction and its ultimate effectiveness as a preventive sanction"; Susan Pilcher, "Ignorance, Discretion and the Fairness of Notice: Confronting 'Apparent Innocence' in the Criminal Law," *American Criminal Law Review* 33 (1996): 34: "in a democracy, the legitimacy of law derives from the consent of the governed. Legally authorizing government coercion in areas beyond those delineated by commonly understood social responsibilities leads the governed to question the moral authority of the legal system and diminishes their respect for the power of criminal law in general, thus diluting its distinctive force as a mechanism of social control."

80. John Calvin Jeffries Jr and Paul Stephan III, "Defenses, Presumptions and Burden of Proof in the Criminal Law," *Yale Law Journal* 88 (1979): 1325, 1371: "the other essential of crime definition is culpability. To be culpable, the actor must have a mental attitude, or *mens rea,* indicative of blameworthiness"; Rollin Perkins, "Criminal Liability Without Fault: A Disquieting Trend," *Iowa Law Review* 68 (1983): 1077: "strict liability, while appropriate for offenses mala prohibita, is utterly unacceptable for offenses *mala in se* (and concluding that *mala in se* offenses are those where the penalty provided is enacted with a purpose of punishment, while *male prohibita* offenses are those providing for enforcement of law unrelated to moral behavior)"; Sanford Kadish, "Some Observations on the Use of Criminal Sanctions in Enforcing Economic Regulations," *University of Chicago Law Review* 30 (1963): 437: "the central distinguishing aspect of the criminal sanction appears to be the stigmatization of the morally culpable"; George Fletcher, "Two Kinds of Legal Rules: A Comparative Study of Burden of Persuasion Practices in Criminal Cases," *Yale Law Journal* 77 (1968): 888: "a special theory of justification has emerged from the burden of persuasion decisions of the past 100 years. That theory is that the state may justly punish only those individuals whose violation of the law is morally blameworthy"; Susan Pilcher, "Ignorance, Discretion and the Fairness of Notice: Confronting 'Apparent Innocence' in the Criminal Law" *American Criminal Law Review* 33 (1996): 1, 7: "the traditional association of crime and personal blameworthiness is so powerfully embedded in our culture as to have become part of our social contract, thereby obligating us to recognize substantive limits on the permissible reach of the criminal law. Under this view, a rational basis for assigning blame is an indispensable prerequisite to criminal liability, regardless of the particular mental state prescribed by statute"; James Hippard, "The Unconstitutionality of Criminal Liability Without Fault: An Argument for a Constitutional Doctrine of Mens Rea," *Houston Law Review* 10 (1973): 1040: "criminal liability without fault is a contradiction in terms . . . strict liability crimes are alien to our criminal law; they are unconstitutional anomalies that the Supreme Court should have suppressed long ago"; Gerhard Mueller, "On Common Law Mens Rea," *Minnesota Law Review* 42 (1958): 1046: "everyone will agree that a criminal law, however well intentioned,

which disregards human psyche is as useful for society as a police force of deaf, dumb, blind and lame, though otherwise honorable, citizens."

81. H L A Hart, *The Morality of the Criminal Law* (Oxford University Press, London, 1964) 28–29: "a code of criminal law which omitted any reference in the definition of its offenses to mental elements could not possibly be satisfactory. For there are some socially harmful activities which are now and should always be treated as criminal offenses which can only be identified by references to intention or some other mental element."

82. *Speiser v Randall* 357 US 513, 523; quoted with approval in *Patterson v New York* 432 US 197, 201 (1977) (White J, for Burger CJ Stewart Blackmun and Stevens JJ).

83. The Canadian Supreme Court held in *R v Martineau* [1990] 2 S.C.R. 633, 645 that the "principles of fundamental justice" (enshrined in the Canadian *Charter*) required, at least in the case of murder (due to the stigma attached to the offense), that mens rea be proven (Dickson CJ, for Lamer CJ Wilson Gonthier and Cory JJ).

84. "The general rule of English law is that no crime can be committed unless there is mens rea" (*Williamson v Norris* [1899] 1 QB 7, 14 [Lord Russell CJ]); "it is an essential ingredient in a criminal offense that there should be some blameworthy condition of the mind, sometimes it is negligence, sometimes malice, sometimes guilty knowledge" (*Chisholm v Doulton* 22 Queen's Bench Division 736, 741); "there can be no crime, large or small, without an evil mind" (Joel Bishop, 1 *Criminal Law* [Little Brown and Co, Boston, 8th ed, 1892] 287); *Regina v Page* 8 Car and P 122, 173 ER 425 (1837): "it is an essential ingredient in a criminal offense that there should be some blameworthy condition of the mind"; "it is a sacred principle of criminal jurisprudence, that the intention to commit the crime, is of the essence of the crime, and to hold, that a man shall be held criminally responsible for an offense, of the commission of which he was ignorant at the time, would be intolerable tyranny": *Duncan v State*, 7 Humph 148, 150 (Tenn., 1846).

85. For example, *Kebilene* [2000] 2 AC 326, 344 (Lord Bingham) and *R v Lambert* [2000] 2 AC 545 (Lord Steyn).

86. *The Queen v Martineau* [1990] S.C.R. 633, 645–646 (Lamer CJ Dickson CJ Wilson Gonthier and Cory JJ).

87. *R v Lambert* [2002] 2 AC 545, 563 (Lord Slynn), 582 (Lord Hope) and 607 (Lord Clyde); *Sheldrake* [2005] 1 AC 264, 297 (Lord Bingham, with whom Lords Steyn and Phillips agreed); *R v G* [2009] 1 AC 92, 97 (Lord Hoffmann) and 103 (Lord Hope) (both of whose decisions were approved of by the other two justices).

88. "In order to constitute a crime, a person must have intelligence and capacity enough to have a criminal intent and purpose": *Davis v United States* 160 US 469, 485 (1895); "all punitive legislation contemplates some relation between guilt and punishment. To inflict the latter where the former does not exist would shock the sense of justice of every one" (*Felton v United States* 96 US 699, 703 [1877]). On the other hand, the Court in cases like *United States v Balint* 258 US 250 (1922) and *United States v Dotterweich* 320 US 277, 280 (1943) seemed to accept strict liability, and appeared somewhat to disfavor concepts of culpability.

89. *Morissette v United States* 342 US 246, 250 (1952).

90. 252. An earlier example of this was *Morrison v California* 291 US 82 (1934), where the Court had read into a statute criminalizing conspiracy a requirement that the accused had "guilty knowledge" of wrongdoing (92), as was the case in *United States v United States Gypsum Co* 438 US 422 (1978), where the Court read in a requirement of mens rea with respect to an antitrust offense, because "intent generally remains an indispensable element of a criminal offense" (437). It read *Morrison* as confirming an interpretive presumption with respect to offenses having their origins in the common law that mens rea was required (437), and that a simple omission to state that the crime was conditional upon proof of mens rea was not sufficient to indicate legislative intention to abandon the requirement (437). The Court here stated that strict liability offenses have a "generally disfavored status" in criminal law. A similar approach was

taken in *Staples v United States* 511 US 600 (1994) and *Carter v United States* 530 US 255, 268 (2000) ("presumption in favor of scienter").

91. 252.

92. *Leland v Oregon* 343 US 790 (1952); applied in *Clark v Arizona* 548 US 735 (2006).

93. *Lambert v California* 355 US 225, 228 (1957) (Douglas J, for Warren CJ Black Burton Clark and Brennan JJ). Some read the *Lambert* decision as having broad implications: "*Lambert* established that the *Constitution* imposes limits on the legislative prerogative to declare conduct criminal in the first instance. While not clearly defined, the constitutional limits appear to bar the criminalization of conduct not inherently possessed of (or defined so as to require proof of) indicia of blameworthiness": Susan Pilcher, "Ignorance, Discretion and the Fairness of Notice: Confronting 'Apparent' Innocence in the Criminal Law," *American Criminal Law Review* 33 (1996): 30.

94. 229.

95. 370 US 660 (1962).

96. 370 US 660, 666–667 (1962) (Stewart J, for Warren CJ Black Brennan and Stewart JJ; Douglas and Harlan JJ concurring in the opinion).

97. 397 US 358 (1970).

98. 364 (Brennan J, for five members of the Court).

99. 392 US 514, 535.

100. 533. The Court has applied a substantive approach to due process in relation to executive action, stating that executive action could be vulnerable to a *Fifth* and *Fourteenth Amendment* challenge where it "shocks the conscience" and/or violates traditional ideas of fair play and decency: *County of Sacramento v Lewis* 523 US 833 (1998).

101. 421 US 584 (1975).

102. 696.

103. 699.

104. 697.

105. Anthony Doniger, "Unburdening the Criminal Defendant: *Mullaney v Wilbur* and the Reasonable Doubt Standard," *Harvard Civil Rights–Civil Liberties Law Review* 11 (1976): 390–391.

106. Mark Tushnet, "Constitutional Limitation of Substantive Criminal Law: An Examination of the Meaning of *Mullaney v Wilbur*," *Boston University Law Review* 55 (1975): 775–776.

107. 432 US 197 (1977).

108. 200 (White J, for Burger CJ Stewart Blackmun and Stevens JJ).

109. 210.

110. 210.

111. 221–222.

112. 223.

113. 227.

114. This suggestion finds support in the work of Glanville Williams, who concluded that what could be called a defense depended, among other things, on the "unreasoning force of tradition": "Offences and Defences," *Legal Studies* 2(3) (1982): 256. It also finds support in the work of John Stinneford, "Punishment Without Culpability," *Journal of Criminal Law and Criminology* 102 (2012): 656, who discusses the nature of the common law itself as a gradual accretion of customary law, based on prior practice. The multi–factor approach of Nancy King and Susan Klein in "Essential Elements," *Vanderbilt Law Review* 54 (2001): 1537–1540, also substantially focuses on historical factors and the level of punishment in determining the validity of challenged provisions in this context.

115. 226–227; relatedly, the Supreme Court has also been alive to legislative attempts to circumvent a doctrine closely related to presumption of innocence, beyond reasonable doubt. Legislatures had been re-classifying what were once elements of a crime as "sentencing factors," and requiring proof of them at a level less than beyond reasonable doubt. While the constitutionality of such measures was considered positively in *McMillan* v *Pennsylvania* 477 US 79 (1986), the Supreme Court found in *Apprendi v New*

Jersey 530 US 466 (2000) that every fact that increased the maximum penalty for an offense had to be proven by the prosecution beyond reasonable doubt. In so finding, the majority reasoned that these sentencing factors made a difference to the stigma associated with commission of the offense (484) (Stevens J, for Scalia Souter Thomas and Ginsburg JJ), justifying insistence upon application of a beyond reasonable doubt standard. By parity of reasoning, the Court should not permit a legislature to redefine elements of a crime as defenses to be proven by an accused, particularly where the existence of such an element relates to the stigma associated with the crime with which the accused is charged, and which traditionally would relate to the punishment to be given to someone proven to have committed the crime. Sentencing may be related to mens rea in another way. Joseph Kennedy develops a thesis to the effect that if the sentencing guidelines point to the likelihood that an accused, if convicted, will be jailed, the courts have in such cases required proof of mens rea. He argues that in periods where the Supreme Court did not appear to strongly defend a mens rea requirement, policies of indeterminate sentencing were in place, permitting the court to take into account mens rea issues in determining an appropriate punishment for a convicted offender. He says that moves to determinate (mandatory) sentencing, and to some extent sentencing guidelines, have sharpened the Court's concern with mens rea: "Making the Crime Fit the Punishment," *Emory Law Journal* 51 (2002): 753.

116. *The Queen v Martineau* [1990] S.C.R. 633, 645–646 (Lamer CJ Dickson CJ Wilson Gonthier and Cory JJ).

117. 511 US 600 (1994).

118. 480 US 228 (1987).

119. 241.

120. The dissentients also noted that precedent had established that where an affirmative defense was drafted in such a way as to expressly overlap with stated elements of an offense, the burden of persuasion on such a matter could not constitutionally be shifted to the accused (237) (Powell Marshall and Brennan JJ; this was part of the reasons to which Blackmun J subscribed).

121. *Flores-Figueroa v United States* 556 US 646 (2009).

122. *Posters N Things Ltd v United States* 511 US 513 (1994).

123. *Carter v United States* 530 US 255, 269 (2000) (Thomas J, for Rehnquist CJ O'Connor Scalia and Kennedy JJ); *Liparota v United States* 471 US 419, 426 (1985).

124. For example, in *Arthur Andersen v United States* 544 US 696, 706 (2005), the Court confined a criminal statute to those who were "conscious of their wrongdoing," because they were the ones with the "level of culpability . . . we usually require in order to impose criminal liability" (Rehnquist CJ, for the Court). It criticized a jury direction specifically stating that an accused could be convicted although they believed their conduct was lawful; see to like effect *Ratzlaf v United States* 510 US 135 (1994).

125. *Bryan v United States* 524 US 184 (1998).

126. 548 US 735 (2006).

127. The majority noted that "a central significance of the insanity defense . . . is the separation of non-blameworthy from blameworthy offenders" (768).

128. 798.

129. *Graham v Florida* 560 US 48 (2010); *Miller v Alabama* 567 US —— (2012).

130. See to like effect William Stuntz, "Substance, Process and the Civil-Criminal Line," *Journal of Contemporary Legal Issues* 7 (1996): 24–26.

131. For an extensive critique of strict liability provisions, see John Shepard Wiley, "Not Guilty by Reason of Blamelessness: Culpability in Federal Criminal Interpretation," *Virginia Law Review* 85 (1999): 1021.

132. *Staples v United States* 511 US 600, 616 (1994) (Thomas J, for Rehnquist CJ Scalia Kennedy and Souter JJ).

133. This expansion of strict liability offenses to areas traditionally considered to be part of criminal law, and involving mens rea requirements, is noted in some detail in Joseph Kennedy, "Making the Crime Fit the Punishment," *Emory Law Journal* 51 (2002): 765–785.

134. *United States v United States Gypsum Company* 438 US 422, 438 (1978) (Burger CJ, for Brennan Marshall and White JJ).
135. Support for this position appears in the observation of Joseph Kennedy that in relation to interpretation of the sentencing guidelines, the Supreme Court has been interpreting criminal provisions to require mens rea where the likely result of conviction is a jail term: "Making the Crime Fit the Punishment," *Emory Law Journal* 51 (2002): 754.
136. John Calvin Jeffries and Paul Stephan, "Defenses, Presumptions and Burden of Proof in the Criminal Law," *Yale Law Journal* 88 (1979): 1325, 1348: "the fundamental requirement that every definition of a crime should include a criminal act would (constitutionally) bar a legislature from punishing as criminal the bare desire to have sexual intercourse with an underage person."
137. Nicola Lacey, *In Search of Criminal Responsibility: Ideas, Interests and Institutions* (Oxford University Press, New York, 2016) 157: "it is assumed that it is a fundamental of criminal law in a liberal democracy that criminal responsibility pertains only to voluntary acts . . . and that this is inconsistent with the criminalization of status."
138. Edwin Keedy, "Insanity and Criminal Responsbility," *Harvard Law Review* 30 (1917): 546: "it is a fundamental principle of the criminal law that volition is a necessary element of every crime"; James Stephen, 2 *A History of the Criminal Law of England* (Macmillan, London, 1883) 100: "no involuntary action, whatever effects it may produce, amounts to a crime by the law of England."
139. Nicola Lacey, *In Search of Criminal Responsibility: Ideas, Interests and Institutions* (Oxford University Press, New York, 2016) 27: "only when criminal law is addressed to human beings as choosing subjects capable of conforming their actions to the criminal law can it be compatible with individual freedom."
140. So, for example, Sir William Blackstone stated that the defense had to prove issues of justification, excuse or mitigation: 4 *Commentaries on the Laws of England 1765–1769* (Clarendon Press, London) 201.
141. Robert Gordon, "Affirmative Defenses and Due Process: The Constitutionality of Placing a Burden of Persuasion on a Criminal Defendant," *Georgetown Law Journal* 64 (1976): 881–883; George Fletcher, "Two Kinds of Legal Rules: A Comparative Study of Burden-of-Persuasion Practices in Criminal Cases," *Yale Law Journal* 77 (1968): 894–910.
142. *Davis v United States* 160 US 469, 485–486 (1895).
143. Glanville Williams, "The Logic of Exceptions," *Cambridge Law Journal* 47 (1988): 261, 262 and 280: "the offense package consists of the offense elements and the negative of defenses . . . and it is an indivisible whole. The defendant cannot be convicted unless he committed the offense package . . . [and] if the legislator decrees that the persuasive burden in respect of a defense [however defined] rests on the defendant, he is decreeing that, failing proof of the defense, the defendant can be convicted without proof of the offense package. The defendant can be convicted notwithstanding that there is evidence in favor of the defense and the defense has not been disproved . . . I do not believe that any consideration of policy can justify it"; Glanville Williams, "Offences and Defences," *Legal Studies* 2(3) (1982): 236; see to like effect Scott Sundby, "The Reasonable Doubt Rule and the Meaning of Innocence," *Hastings Law Journal* 40 (1989): 457, 465 and 488, who concludes that the state should be required to prove beyond reasonable doubt every aspect that bears on the defendant's guilt and of their punishment if guilty; labels such as offense and defense would be irrelevant in this analysis; George Fletcher, "Two Kinds of Legal Rules: A Comparative Study of Burden of Persuasion Practices in Criminal Cases," *Yale Law Journal* 77 (1968): 917, concluded that the state's characterization of issues as offenses or defenses was irrelevant, and all issues pertaining to guilt should be treated equally; John Calvin Jeffries and Paul Stephan, "Defenses, Presumptions and Burden of Proof in the Criminal Law," *Yale Law Journal* 88 (1979): 1331–1332: "crime and defense are substantively equivalent . . . the distinction is essentially arbitrary"; Barbara Underwood, "The Thumb on the Scales of Justice: Burdens of Persuasion in Criminal Cases," *Yale Law Journal* 86 (1977):

1347: "all facts that define or limit the defendant's criminal guilt stand on an equal footing with respect to the purposes of the reasonable doubt rule . . . whether it is characterized as an element of crime or a defense, [the reasonable doubt rule should apply]."

144. Francis Bowes Sayre, "Mens Rea," *Harvard Law Review* 45 (1932): 1004: "insanity, which robs one of the power to make intelligent choice between good and evil, must negative criminal responsibility if criminality rests upon moral blameworthiness"; earlier Sayre had emphasized that "blameworthiness or moral guilt is necessarily based upon a free mind voluntarily choosing evil rather than good" (1004). I must concede that in the classic statement of the presumption of innocence and the burden of proof being on the prosecutor, the House of Lords specifically acknowledged that insanity was an exception: *Woolmington v DPP* [1935] AC 462. This may have been to accommodate the decision in *McNaghten's Case* [1843] 1 C and K 130, where the Court seemed to cast the onus on an accused to make out a defense of insanity. Williams calls this exception an "anomaly": "The Logic of Exceptions," *Cambridge Law Journal* 47 (1988): 261, 263.

145. A similar position is taken by Donald Dripps, "The Constitutional Status of the Reasonable Doubt Rule," *California Law Review* 75 (1987): 1706: "in terms of substantive legality, one who kills on reasonable provocation is not guilty of murder, whether state law deems provocation a defense or malice aforethought an element. Similarly one who kills in the reasonable belief that lethal violence is immediately necessary to save her own life committed no crime, whether self-defense constitutes an affirmative defense or negates the element of unlawfulness," and by George Fletcher, "Two Kinds of Legal Rules: A Comparative Study of Burden-of-Persuasion Practices in Criminal Cases," *Yale Law Journal* 77 (1968): 917–918.

146. A similar view is taken by Anthony Doniger, "Unburdening the Criminal Defendant: *Mullaney v Wilbur* and the Reasonable Doubt Standard," *Harvard Civil Rights–Civil Liberties Law Review* 11 (1976): 390, who concludes it is (or should be) unconstitutional to place a burden of persuasion with respect to self-defense upon an accused (406), and similarly that an accused cannot constitutionally be required to bear a burden of persuasion with respect to the insanity defense (412). Robert Gordon reaches a similar position, concluding that due process forbids a defendant from bearing a burden of persuasion with respect to issues such as self-defense, provocation and insanity, at least once raised with some evidence by the accused, and must prove their non-existence at the level of beyond reasonable doubt in order to obtain a conviction: "Affirmative Defenses and Due Process: The Constitutionality of Placing a Burden of Persuasion on a Criminal Defendant," *Georgetown Law Journal* 64 (1976): 871.

147. As Gerhard Mueller puts it, "it is this awareness of evil, the sense of doing something which one ought not, which constitutes the crux or substance of mens rea at common law": "On Common Law Mens Rea," *Minnesota Law Review* 42 (1958): 1060; interestingly, this concept of an accused being conscious "that the act is one he ought not to do" was acknowledged by the House of Lords in *McNaghten* [1843] 1 C and K 130. However, the law has accepted for centuries that wrongdoing which is not intentional but reckless can be made the subject of criminal sanction. I agree with the position of Hart that criminal responsibility for negligence is not to be considered as an example of strict liability: H L A Hart, "Negligence, Mens Rea and Criminal Responsibility," in Anthony G Guest, *Oxford Essays in Jurisprudence* (Clarendon Press, Oxford, 1961) 49.

148. H L A Hart, *Law, Liberty and Morality* (Oxford University Press, Oxford, 1963) 20: "the use of legal coercion by any society calls for justification as something prima facie objectionable to be tolerated only for the sake of some countervailing good"; Claire Finkelstein, "Positivism and the Notion of an Offense," *California Law Review* 88 (2000): 335, 358 and 371: "a criminal prohibition that failed to identify a harm of sufficient magnitude to overcome the presumption against it would be illegitimate, since it would constitute an unjustifiable interference with liberty"; George Fletcher, "Two Kinds of Legal Rules: A Comparative Study of Burden-of-Persuasion Practices in

Criminal Cases," *Yale Law Journal* 77 (1968): 889, asks whether "the defendant's violation of a proscription of the criminal law renders him properly subject to moral censure." He adds that the criminal trial is a "process for determining whether the state's officials may justly deprive an individual of his freedom" (933).

149. As Nicola Lacey describes it: "the burden of legitimating criminal responsibility [has been] borne [by doctrines such as] mens rea and defense" in the late nineteenth and early twentieth centuries: *In Search of Criminal Responsibility: Ideas, Interests and Institutions* (Oxford University Press, New York, 2016) 140.

150. *Patterson v New York* 432 US 197, 202 (1977) (White J) (quoting *Speiser v Randall* 357 US 513, 523 [1958]).

151. For example, *Morissette v United States* 342 US 246, 250 (1952); *Staples v United States* 511 US 600, 614 (1994) (denying that Congress would have intended to criminalize behavior where the accused had a genuine and reasonable belief that what they were doing was wrong); *Carter v United States* 530 US 255, 269 (2000) (Thomas J, for Rehnquist CJ O'Connor Scalia and Kennedy JJ); *Liparota v United States* 471 US 419, 426 (1985), where concern was expressed with legislation that might criminalize "apparently innocent conduct"; *Ratzlaf v United States* 510 US 135, 144–145 (1994) (clear concern that a person charged with the relevant offense may not be engaged in conduct that is "inevitably nefarious," "obviously evil" or "inherently bad"; *Regina v Page* (1837) 8 Car and P, 173 ER 425: "it is an essential ingredient in a criminal offense that there should be some blameworthy condition of the mind"; cf *United States v Balint* 258 US 250 (1923) and *United States v Dotterweich* 320 US 277 (1943).

152. Herbert Packer, "Mens Rea and the Supreme Court," *Supreme Court Review* (1962): 148: "so long as that sanction [criminal conviction] is resorted to, moral blameworthiness should be the indispensable condition precedent to its application"; Francis Bowes Sayre, "Public Welfare Offenses," *Columbia Law Review* 33 (1933): 72: "to subject defendants entirely free from moral blameworthiness to the possibility of prison sentences is revolting to the community sense of justice"; John Stinneford, "Punishment Without Culpability," *Journal of Criminal Law and Criminology* 102 (2012): 658, stating that the constitutional law of crime will remain "radically incomplete" unless and until morality and tradition return as pivotal concepts. He calls the prohibition of punishment without culpability "the most basic limit on the government's power" (663), and he noted that the principle that a person is not criminally guilty unless they have a "guilty mind" has "been so fundamental to the criminal law that courts and commentators treated it as axiomatic for more than 500 years" (684); Sanford Kadish, "The Decline of Innocence," *Cambridge Law Journal* 26 (1968): 283, talks of the "paradigmatic affront to the sense of justice in the law which consists in the deliberate act of convicting a morally innocent person of a crime, of imposing blame when there is no occasion for it"; Sanford Kadish, "Some Observations on the Use of Criminal Sanctions in Enforcing Economic Regulations," *University of Chicago Law Review* 30 (1963): 437: "without moral culpability there is in a democratic community an explicable and justifiable reluctance to affix the stigma of blame"; John Calvin Jeffries and Paul Stephan, "Defenses, Presumptions and Burden of Proof in the Criminal Law," *Yale Law Journal* 88 (1979): 1374: "at least when the offense carries serious sanctions and the stigma of official condemnation, liability should be reserved for persons whose blameworthiness has been established. Otherwise, punishment lacks a moral basis and conviction is unjust"; Andrew Ashworth and Lucia Zedner, "Defending the Criminal Law: Reflections on the Changing Character of Crime, Procedure and Sanctions," *Criminal Law and Philosophy* 2 (2008): 33: "only the culpable deserve to be punished and the public censure and hard treatment involved in punishment are unjustifiably imposed if blame is not established."

153. Sanford Kadish, "The Decline of Innocence," *Cambridge Law Journal* 26 (1968): 274: "surely we should see nothing criminal in joining a group in a public place, apart from the intent to commit unlawful acts."

154. John Shepard Wiley, "Not Guilty by Reason of Blamelessness: Culpability in Federal Criminal Interpretation," *Virginia Law Review* 85 (1999): 1071: "if they act with

self-conscious restraint, judges are competent to make the necessary moral judgments."

155. An example here would be the eventual decriminalization of homosexuality in the United States: *Lawrence v Texas* 539 US 558 (2003), overruling *Bowers v Hardwick* 478 US 186 (1986). In *Powell v Texas* 392 US 514, 535–536 (1968), Marshall J reflected on the evolution of concepts and values informing the criminal law over centuries. A test which focuses on history *as one element* in discerning whether conduct today may properly be proscribed as criminal is not intended to preclude or ignore this reality.

156. John Stuart Mill, *Utilitarianism, On Liberty, Considerations on Representative Government* (Everyman, London, 1972) 143; see also Claire Finkelstein, "Positivism and the Notion of an Offense," *California Law Review* 88 (2000): 335, 372: "a crime in a liberal order is prohibited behavior whose harmfulness justifies restricting a person's liberty in order to prevent or punish that behavior."

157. For example, *Meyer v Nebraska* 262 US 390, 400 (1923), *Pierce v Society of Sisters* 268 US 510, 534 (1925), and *Lawrence v Texas* 539 US 558, 567 (2003), where the Court counseled "against attempts by the State . . . to define the meaning of a relationship or to set its boundaries absent injury to a person or abuse of an institution the law protects" (Kennedy J, for Stevens Souter Ginsburg and Breyer JJ). These cases are discussed in Eric Tennen, "Is the Constitution in Harm's Way? Substantive Due Process and Criminal Law," *Boalt Journal of Criminal Law* 8 (2004): 130.

158. John Calvin Jeffries and Paul Stephan, "Defenses, Presumptions and Burden of Proof in the Criminal Law," *Yale Law Journal* 88 (1979): 1376–1379.

159. *United States v Weems* 217 US 349 (1910).

160. Anthony Gray, "Mandatory Sentencing Around the World and the Need for Reform," *New Criminal Law Review* 20 (2017): 391–432.

FIVE

Civilizing Criminal Behavior

We have seen in earlier chapters various means by which legislatures might seek to obviate the requirement of a presumption of innocence. They may simply seek to remove it with respect to an entire offense. They may provide that a particular element be deemed to be proven in some circumstances, leaving it to an accused to prove otherwise. They may seek to redefine offenses in non-traditional ways, thereby seeking to place the onus of proving more of the facts on the accused by labeling a particular issue part of a defense rather than an offense. We have explored in previous chapters ways in which courts have, and could, respond to such legislative measures which seek to circumvent the sometimes-inconvenient presumption of innocence.

There is another significant way in which legislatures might seek to avoid the strictures of the presumption of innocence doctrine with respect to criminal matters. It might claim that particular proceedings are, in fact, civil in nature, rather than criminal. So, for example, it might claim that the forfeiture of property that is suspected to be crime-derived is a civil, rather than criminal, proceeding. It might claim that the involuntary detention of a past criminal offender, based on an assessment of likely future dangerousness, is a civil, rather than criminal, proceeding. These proceedings may attract a reverse onus. For example, a person in possession of property suspected of being crime-derived may need to show the lawfulness by which they acquired the asset. The prosecution may not need to prove that the person committed any particular crime in order that their property be forfeited to the government.

By this means, again it would be able to circumvent the difficulties of criminal due process requirements, including the presumption of innocence.[1] There can be few objections to placing a burden of proof on a defendant to a civil proceeding. There is nothing in the United States

Constitution, or human rights instruments such as the *European Convention on Human Rights* or Canadian *Charter of Rights and Freedoms,* to prevent this. Understandably, their focus is on criminal matters, where much is at stake. The presumption of innocence relates to a crime. A person is presumed to be innocent of an allegation of criminality made against them. The doctrine says nothing about presumptions in civil matters.

Again, we sometimes see the rational connection argument, which we discussed in chapter 2, in relation to civil forfeiture provisions. Specifically, the argument that there is a rational connection between the fact that a person is in possession of property which they cannot explain the lawful source of, and the conclusion the property was crime-derived.[2] It is said that the conclusion that the property is crime-derived, and liable to forfeiture, flows naturally from the fact that the person cannot prove the lawfulness through which they acquired the property. I will not specifically address this rational connection principle again in this chapter, having critiqued it in chapter 2.

Legislatures have noticed this loophole, and so in several of the jurisdictions studied, there have been attempts to argue that legislation that might bear some hallmarks of being criminal in nature is in fact civil, such that the standard criminal due process protections are not applicable. Two of the contexts in which this phenomenon has been most noticeable have been in relation to forfeiture, and in relation to so-called civil commitment of individuals thought to pose a danger to society. This chapter will discuss examples in each of the jurisdictions being studied in relation to the use of civil proceedings in these contexts, consider the response of the courts, and suggest some principles that should guide courts' consideration of such laws. Courts must be vigilant that legislatures are not dressing up as "civil" proceedings that are, in substance, criminal in nature.[3] Of course, this assumes that courts are interested in, and interesting in enforcing, at least some substantive criminal law principles. It also begs the question of what kinds of proceedings are, in substance, criminal. This chapter will not re-hash the discussion of this in chapter 4, which related to individual crimes and defenses, but will focus on general principles that will be argued to characterize criminal proceedings in general.

FORFEITURE PROCEEDINGS AND UNEXPLAINED WEALTH PROVISIONS

Unexplained wealth provisions are a fairly recent phenomenon in legislation, typically requiring a person whose assets are suspected of having been crime-derived to provide a satisfactory account of how they obtained such assets lawfully. They are analogous to the much older procedure of forfeiture. It is considered necessary to understand some of the history of forfeiture proceedings in the law, prior to consideration of their true nature. The common law essentially recognized three types of forfeiture, being the deodand, in rem forfeiture in admiralty jurisdiction, and attainder forfeiture. The first two, being independent of a criminal conviction of any person involved in possible wrongdoing, are of particular significance to us here.

In classic common law a deodand was something that had caused the death of another. Bizarrely, English law permitted proceedings against the deodand itself, a reflection of religious doctrine.[4] The proceeding was against the deodand as the alleged perpetrator,[5] not the person who allegedly used it and caused the death of another. This was at a time when the law did not allow family members of the victim of the wrong to claim compensation,[6] and criminal law did not exist. The proceeding against the deodand occurred in a criminal court.[7] Blackstone, at least, saw in the proceeding overtones of punishment.[8] If the proceeding were successful, the deodand would be forfeited to the Crown.[9] Deodands were finally abolished in English law in 1846, to coincide with the so-called *Lord Campbell's Act*, which now provided specifically for compensation for family members of a victim who had been killed.

The admiralty jurisdiction recognized the possibility of an in rem proceeding against a ship in the so-called *Navigation Acts*, for example in cases where relevant customs duties or other taxes had not been paid. This was for pragmatic reasons—the owner/s of the ship may well be outside of the jurisdiction of English courts, and sometimes the owner of the ship could not be located. Analogous to the deodand principle, the action here was against the ship as the alleged wrongdoer, rather than its owners.[10] From the earliest days of the United States, the potential for the use of such proceedings to obviate criminal due process was realized, meant in both senses of that word here. The point that punishment should only follow conviction was made during discussions about the United States *Constitution*.[11] The First United States Congress levied customs duties and provided for forfeiture with respect to unpaid dues. The original 1789 act contained a reverse onus provision.[12] Leonard Levy makes the point:

> The personification fiction rationalized punishment of the vessel as a means of diverting attention from the practical fact that in the real world criminal punishment had been summarily inflicted on the innocent owner without allowing him the rights enjoyed by a common felon. In rem proceedings against things, like the deodands to which they were analogous, were make-believe prosecutions of property in order to deprive the owners of their constitutional rights, thereby enabling the governments to make a confiscation not otherwise likely.[13]

This historical basis of forfeiture provisions allows us to understand better the current situation where forfeiture of property continues to occur despite the person holding the forfeiture property never having been charged with, let alone convicted of, the offense/s from which the property is said to be derived, and similarly the fact that such a person was acquitted of such a charge, or had a conviction overturned on appeal, is not bar to the success of civil forfeiture proceedings against them, based on essentially the same wrongdoing. It can only occur because of the persistence of this fiction that the proceeding is against the property, rather than the individual holder of the property, so that it is said that the due process protections to which an accused individual would otherwise be entitled are argued not to be applicable.[14]

From early United States times the dangers of such a proceeding for fundamental civil liberties were noted. One example occurs in the Massachusetts case of *Fisher v McGirr*.[15] There Chief Justice Shaw found an in rem statute for confiscation of alcohol was contrary to that state's due process requirements:

> Supposing the process in rem, when rightly conducted, to be a suitable and proper mode of enforcing obedience to a useful and salutary law, it does it by punishing the offender, who must be the owner, or some person intrusted with the possession by him, or some person for whose unlawful possession of it the owner is responsible; it does this by depriving such owner of his property, at the same time preventing the further noxious and unlawful use of it. Such being the character of the prosecution, in a high degree penal in its operation and consequences, it should be surrounded with all the safeguards necessary to the security of the innocent, having the full benefit of the maxim that every person shall be presumed innocent until his guilt be established by proof. He should have notice of the charge of guilty purpose, upon which his property is declared to be unlawfully held, and in danger of being forfeited, a time and opportunity to prepare his defense, an opportunity to meet the witnesses against him face to face, and the benefit of the legal presumption of innocence.

The question arises as to how the United States Supreme Court has viewed such provisions. Specifically, has it viewed forfeiture provisions as, in substance, criminal in nature, or has it accepted the view of the legislature that such provisions are civil in nature? A consideration of the cases does not yield a simple answer, with authorities to the effect that such provisions are in substance criminal, and others finding them to be civil. It should further be noted that the *Fifth Amendment* specifically prohibits a person from being deprived of property without due process of law, given extended reach by the *Fourteenth Amendment*.

An early example of a case where the Court found the proceedings were in substance criminal in nature was *Boyd v United States*.[16] The legislation there provided for forfeiture in the event of non-payment of customs duties. On the face of the legislation, these proceedings were civil in nature. However, the Court found the substance to be otherwise:

> We have to deal with an act which expressly excludes criminal proceedings from its operation (though embracing civil suits for penalties and forfeitures) and with an information not technically a criminal proceeding and neither therefore within the literal terms of the Fifth (or Fourth) Amendment to the *Constitution* . . . does this relieve the proceedings or the law from being obnoxious to the prohibitions of either? We think not . . . we are also clearly of the opinion that proceedings instituted for the purpose of declaring the forfeiture of a man's property by reason of offenses committed by him, though they may be civil in form, are in their nature criminal.[17]

Numerous other Supreme Court cases have concluded that forfeiture proceedings are in substance criminal. They have often done so in acknowledging that the proceedings typically serve punitive and/or deterrent purposes,[18] purposes associated with the criminal law, as opposed to non-criminal law.

Some non-United States authority appears to confirm the criminal nature of forfeiture provisions. Concerns were expressed with the compatibility of forfeiture of the property of a person not proven beyond reasonable doubt to have committed an offense:

> Confiscation following on from a conviction . . . is a measure inappropriate to assets which are not known to have been in the possession of the person affected, the more so if the measure concerned relates to a criminal act of which the person affected has not actually been found guilty. If it is not found beyond a reasonable doubt that the person affected has actually committed the crime, and if it cannot be established as fact that any advantage, illegal or otherwise, was actually obtained, such a measure can only be based on a presumption of guilt. This can hardly be considered compatible with Article 6(2) [of the ECHR].[19]

On the other hand, the United Kingdom Supreme Court in *Gale v Serious Organized Crime Agency*[20] found that forfeiture proceedings considered there were essentially civil in nature. There the Court considered legislation which permitted the Court to make a forfeiture order with respect to any property derived from unlawful conduct. The Court was required to determine on the balance of probabilities whether it had been proven that any of the matters said to constitute unlawful conduct had actually occurred. It was not necessary to find the person affected guilty of any particular offense. A lower court had found that the person whose property was the subject of this application was involved in drug trafficking, money laundering and tax evasion. He had never been convicted of drug trafficking, and had been acquitted of that charge in another jurisdiction, and other charges involving that crime were dropped. All members of the Court found the United Kingdom legislation was valid, in the face of a challenge under the *European Convention on Human Rights*.

All members of the Court applied the so-called *Engel* factors in determining whether the proceedings were in substance criminal or civil in nature.[21] They are the way in which the domestic law characterizes the proceedings, the essential nature of the proceedings, and the consequences that may follow from the proceedings. These factors assist the European Court in determining whether proceedings are in substance criminal or civil in nature. This has important consequences for the application of Article 6 of the *Convention*. Specifically, Article 6(2) and (3) of the *Convention* apply only to a person "charged with a criminal offense." Article 6(2) specifically enshrines the right to presumption of innocence. Article 6(1) applies both to civil and criminal proceedings, and enshrines the right to fairness. It is possible that even if a proceeding is judged to be civil in nature, questions regarding the onus and standard of proof may be implicated in Article 6(1).

While holding the proceedings were essentially civil in nature, and hence invalid, several members conceded there was "something unattractive" about a prosecuting authority seeking and obtaining a confiscation order on the basis of suspected criminal activity, against a person who had actually been acquitted of that charge.[22] The Court attempted to bypass the suggestions in *Geerings* that such provisions were contrary to the presumption of innocence by denying the link between the earlier criminal proceeding and the subsequent civil proceeding. According to one judge, Lord Dyson, as long as the judges in the subsequent civil proceeding are careful not to express a view that the person affected is actually guilty of the crime, there is no legal difficulty with these proceeds of crime proceedings.[23] So, even though, on the face of the legislation, the court's jurisdiction to make a forfeiture order is enlivened only upon satisfaction "on the balance of probabilities" that unlawful conduct occurred, apparently as long as the court does not expressly make a finding to that effect, there is no difficulty with such provisions in terms of the *European Convention on Human Rights*. The Court did not consider the substantive question of whether forfeiture of property could in fact amount to punishment of the person whose property was to be confiscated.

In a somewhat confused recent judgment (with respect), the Australian High Court appeared to mix the civil and the criminal realms, claiming that "penal ends may be pursued in civil proceedings which result in additional punishment."[24] Of course, it is trite to observe that, traditionally at least, the primary purpose of civil proceedings was to compensate, rather than punish (leaving exceptions such as punitive damages aside). Indeed, a traditional distinction between civil and criminal functions was their different purposes. It is considered important, with respect, to bear these different purposes in mind, in assessing whether a particular scheme is, in substance rather than appearance, criminal or civil in nature.

Other cases support the notion that forfeiture is a penalty or punishment.[25] Further cases connect notions of punishment with the criminal law, and criminal process.[26] This would reflect the familiar idea that the stakes involved in such matters require the strongest protection of due process.[27] There is very significant academic support for the argument that a forfeiture proceeding is, in substance, criminal in nature.[28] Carol Steiker concludes that "Analysis strongly suggests that civil forfeiture as generally practi(c)ed today by the federal government is in fact punishment and thus cannot be imposed separately from and in addition to criminal punishment."[29] Similarly, Piety concludes that "There is little doubt that the principal purpose of civil forfeiture in general . . . is crime deterrence and punishment. As such, they represent essentially penal sanctions, no matter how they are labeled."[30] Relatedly, many scholars have lamented the use of reverse onus provisions in respect of so-called civil forfeiture provisions, requiring a person alleged to be in possession of crime-derived property to prove the lawfulness through which they have acquired the asset.[31]

It should be acknowledged that there is substantial support in the case law for the opposite proposition, that forfeiture proceedings are (or may be, depending on the particular circumstances) civil in nature. For instance, in the early case of *The Palmyra* the Court concluded the proceedings were civil in nature, "independent of and wholly unaffected by any criminal proceeding."[32] Several cases have denied that forfeiture is a kind of punishment.[33] One case specifically held that an acquittal of an individual on criminal charges does not preclude subsequent civil forfeiture proceedings against them.[34] Looking to the non-United States case law, again there are several examples of decisions where courts have accepted that forfeiture provisions are civil, rather than criminal, in nature.[35] A prominent recent example is the decision of the United Kingdom Supreme Court in *Gale*.[36]

Numerous examples exist of legislation which imposes a reverse onus with respect to forfeiture and/or unexplained wealth proceedings. Examples include 19 U.S.C. 1615 (1994). That section relates to the seizure of property for failure to pay customs duties. The government requires probable cause in order to seize the property. However, once it does, the onus is on the person whose property was seized to show that the relevant duties were paid.[37] Another example is 18 U.S.C. 983. There although the general burden is on the government with respect to civil forfeiture proceedings, this is on the preponderance of the evidence standard. Sub-section (d) provides for an innocent owner defense, however the property owner is required to prove this defense, on the preponderance of the evidence.[38] This is problematic when the evidence suggests that most forfeiture proceedings are uncontested.[39]

Further, in Australia, s179E(3) of the *Proceeds of Crime Act 2002* (UK) provides that a person whose property has been tentatively forfeited because of proof of a reasonable suspicion that it is crime-derived must prove on the balance of probabilities the lawfulness by which they acquired the assets. In other words, the legislation contains an express reverse onus provision. The person affected need not have been charged with or convicted of any crime.[40]

The United Kingdom *Criminal Finances Bill 2016* (UK) provides for an application for an unexplained wealth order. Clause 1 would introduce new s362A of the *Proceeds of Crime Act 2002* (UK). In order to obtain an unexplained wealth order, it is necessary for the prosecuting authority to demonstrate reasonable grounds for believing that property has been unlawfully derived.[41] If a person fails to respond to notice of such application, the person is presumed to have unexplained wealth. Property is presumed to be recoverable by the government as crime-derived, unless the person affected can show otherwise.[42]

Eight Canadian provinces currently have civil forfeiture provisions. The constitutional validity of civil forfeiture was upheld by the Canadian Supreme Court in *Chatterjee*,[43] but there remain those who argue that such laws are contrary to the Canadian *Charter*. Each of these eight sets of laws do not require a criminal conviction before the property of a person can be confiscated upon an allegation that it is crime-derived. Most notably, s52(1.1) of the *Victims Restitution and Compensation Payment Act 2001* (Alb) provides that where at least $10,000 cash is found on premises in particular circumstances, it is presumed to be crime-derived unless the person proves to the contrary.[44]

CIVIL DETENTION

Another area of great controversy has been the increased use by legislatures of involuntary detention of an individual based on fears of what they may do in the future. This is often called "preventive detention." Typically legislatures argue that this type of proceeding is civil in nature. The benefits of so doing are obvious—criminal due process standards such as the presumption of innocence, proof of allegations beyond reasonable doubt, double jeopardy, and ex post facto provisions are thereby neutralized. As we will see, courts have sometimes accepted these arguments from legislatures.

The leading United States Supreme Court decision on point is *Kansas v Hendricks*.[45] State legislation there provided for the "civil detention" of particular individuals. It applied, amongst other individuals, to those convicted of a sexually violent offense, who was scheduled for release, or someone charged with such an offense. It applied when such a person suffered from a mental abnormality or personality disorder making them likely to engage in sexually predatory violent behavior. Where an application was made by the state, a court would consider whether the person affected met the above description, at the level of probable cause. A person subject to such order would be segregated from the general prison population. A declaration about a person was subject to regular review, and they were to be released into the community as soon as it was found they no longer met the requirements of detention under the act. By a bare 5–4 majority decision,[46] the Supreme Court validated the legislation against a substantive due process challenge.

The majority found that civil detention of individuals was not unknown to the law. There were appropriate controls—a person so detained had to be proven to be dangerous to themselves or others. Further, it required evidence of a mental condition. The legislation here was valid because it combined a finding of future dangerousness with a finding of lack of volitional control; this distinguished it from other cases which were "perhaps more properly dealt with exclusively through criminal proceedings."[47] The majority accorded great deference to the legislature's categorization of the proceedings, which would only be overturned in rare cases involving the "clearest proof."[48] Here the civil detention laws had been placed in a probate code, as opposed to criminal legislation. The majority found the regime did not relate to the typical criminal law rationales of punishment, retribution or deterrence. It did not impose culpability for past conduct. No finding of scienter was necessary in order that it apply; it was based more on propensity and mental condition. It was not designed for deterrence, given those to whom it applied could not control their behavior.[49] A state was entitled to take measures to restrict the freedom of the "dangerously mentally ill."[50] The duration of confinement was limited to the time when the individual suffered the mental abnormality, emphasizing its non-punitive purpose.[51]

The dissenters accepted that legislatures could define mental illness in a variety of different ways, and the *Constitution* did not totally prohibit civil commitment regimes.[52] However, they found that the legislation here did not, in substance, provide for civil commitment. As a matter of substance, the legislation administered punishment.[53] They noted that the treatment of those subject to the regime was not provided for in the legislation, and details of it did not appear in the statements of the politicians responsible for the introduction of the scheme. Legislation could still be punitive in effect even though it was designed to prevent offenders from re-offending. Any treatment, if it did occur, was scheduled for late in the person's detention period, rather than throughout. There was no evidence that methods less restrictive of the freedom of those detained were to be considered, in relation to a non-punitive purpose.[54] The dissentients noted and applied the so-called *Mendoza-Martinez* factors in determining whether the regime provided for criminal or civil proceedings. Here, the act involved an affirmative restraint on a person's liberty, and that restraint had typically been regarded as punishment, it was imposed on behavior that was already considered a crime, it did require a finding of scienter, it served a traditional aim of punishment (restraint), it did not really serve an alternative purpose, and was excessive.[55]

Subsequently, the Court clarified its *Hendricks* determination, by stating that it would not accept as civil commitment a provision which sought to detain those shown only to be dangerous. It was essential, to justify commitment as being civil, that the state also show that the offender substantially lacked control over their behavior. They expressly emphasized this criterion as being necessary lest "civil commitment become a mechanism for retribution or general deterrence," functions which were properly within the criminal law realm.[56] It was necessary that those subject to civil commitment be segregated from prison inmates who were, at least in theory, involuntarily detained for quite distinct purposes.[57]

There remains some conjecture on the use of the civil standard to authorize the so-called civil commitment of an individual under these kinds of regimes. This would not be an issue for the four dissenting judges in *Hendricks*—given they view the legislation as imposing punishment, they would presumably require proof of the required elements (dangerousness plus lack of control) at the level of beyond reasonable doubt. However, the majority accepted that the involuntary detention there was civil in nature, and validated the provision which required the state to prove (merely) probable cause existed with respect to the required elements. In another context, however, of whether sentencing enhancement factors must be proven beyond reasonable doubt, the Court has said that they do. The finding was that "any fact that increases the penalty for a crime beyond the prescribed statutory maximum must be . . . proved beyond a reasonable doubt."[58]

Certainly, it is possible to argue by way of analogy that an allegation that a convicted criminal should be kept in prison because they are dangerous and cannot control their actions should also be proven at the level of beyond reasonable doubt.[59] No doubt, some might counter by saying that the extra preventive detention period is not a "penalty for a crime" within the above quote. However, the reality is that such provisions apply to those convicted of particular serious crimes. In order to put the person in prison, the prosecutor had to prove they were guilty of a crime at the level of beyond reasonable doubt. There is logic to an argument that just as proof beyond reasonable doubt was required to put the person behind bars (because of the familiar arguments about stigma, seriousness of the infringement upon rights, offense to dignity, respect for the individual, etc.), it should also be required to keep them there beyond their allotted term of imprisonment. Imprisonment remains a very serious intrusion on liberty, offends dignity, imposes stigma, etc. These effects do not disappear because it is a further term of imprisonment, not one imposed immediately after conviction. By the same logic insisting upon the presumption of innocence and beyond reasonable doubt standards at the time alleged commission of the original offense is considered, those standards should also be applied to any subsequent term of imprisonment, even if it is labeled as being "civil" in nature.

In Australia the High Court has considered civil commitment of an individual because of feared future wrongdoing on two occasions. In *Kable v Director of Public Prosecutions* (NSW)[60] it invalidated a law that applied to one named offender, Kable. Kable had been convicted of the manslaughter of his wife, but had nearly served his sentence and was about to be released. He was thought to have made threats to the family of his dead wife about tracking them down when he was released. The legislature responded by passing a law allowing the government to apply to the courts for a preventive detention order. The Court could make the order if it believed it was "more likely than not" that Kable would re-offend if released. The Court was to apply various criteria, but was informed that the most important of these was community protection. Ordinary rules of evidence were specifically held not to be applicable. A majority of the Court invalidated the legislation. It found that it breached separation of powers principles by asking a court to exercise a power that was not judicial in nature. The proceedings were of a kind unknown to the law. It made the Court part of a legislative plan to imprison an individual.

However, a few years later the High Court validated somewhat similar legislation in *Fardon v Attorney-General* (Qld).[61] There the legislation applied to those convicted of serious sexual offenses. Again it allowed the government to apply to the Court for an order for the person's continued detention beyond the end of the term to which they had been sentenced, if there was a "high degree of probability" the person would re-offend if released. On this occasion six of the seven members of the Court validated the legislation. They found there were material differences between the legislation invalidated in *Kable* and the legislation challenged here. The majority did not address the question of whether the legislation provided for civil detention, or was substantially criminal in nature.

Kirby J in dissent did discuss this issue. He found that generally in Australia involuntary detention of an individual was penal or punitive. Human liberty had always been regarded as fundamental.[62] He was also aware of the slippery slope argument—that if the Court accepted the validity of administrative detention of individuals without proof of guilt, the Court could effectively be sidelined when substantial civil liberties were at stake.[63] He noted that in Australia deprivation of liberty was the worst punishment that the legal system could inflict. It could only be administered following proven breach of the law. A person could not be punished for something else.[64] Here what was dressed up as civil detention was not, in fact. In substance, it was punishment. If it were in fact civil detention, those subject to it would be sent to institutions other than a prison, they would receive specific treatment and support to address their specific issue. It was telling that the legislation challenged here provided for no such facilities or treatment.[65] More recently, the Australian High Court has apparently blurred the distinction between criminal and civil proceedings.[66]

The European Court of Human Rights concluded in *M v Germany*[67] that a preventive detention regime was in substance criminal in nature. In doing so, it noted the remarkably similar treatment given in prison to those said to have been detained civilly, compared with others who had been jailed for criminal offenses. It concluded the reality was that individuals being detained under the civil detention regime were being punished; the system did not provide solely for preventive detention. It noted there were no special institutions, systems or treatment in place to cater for the supposed treatment of those said to have been detained civilly, beyond those available to those clearly detained for the purposes of the criminal law. The Court accepted findings from the European Commissioner for Human Rights that those detained civilly were in need of substantial psychological care and support. Genuine civil detention would need to be accompanied by high-level care, involving multi-disciplinary teams who developed specific, tailored treatment programs for particular detainees. It was artificial to try to separate preventive detention and punishment, since prolonged detention, while protecting the community, could also be seen as further punishment of the person detained. It may also deter. There would often be substantial overlap between preventive detention and punishment, contrary to the government's attempts to argue they were separate and distinct. As a result, the Court found the preventive detention imposed on the applicant was in substance punitive and criminal in nature.[68]

CRITERIA FOR WHETHER A PROCEEDING IS CRIMINAL OR CIVIL

As was acknowledged in a previous chapter, civil law existed for a long time in the absence of criminal law, and criminal law was eventually carved out of what we would now consider to be tort law. As is known, the purpose of the law of tort was and is to compensate the wronged individual. So in medieval times the bot and the wergild principles were utilized to compensate the victim or their family respectively for injury caused by the wrongdoer. When the criminal law was carved out of tort law, it had different purposes. They included retribution/punishment, deterrence and, in more recent times, rehabilitation. As a result of these developments, we can say that traditionally a major difference between the criminal law and the civil law has been the purpose of the action.[69] A criminal law prosecution will seek to serve one or more of the purposes of retribution, deterrence and rehabilitation;[70] in contrast, a civil law claim will seek to compensate an innocent person for the wrongdoing of another.[71]

Another distinction relates to the notion of private and public wrongs. A civil law action is taken to obtain redress from a wrong allegedly committed against a private interest. In contrast, a criminal law action is taken in relation to an alleged offense against the community as a whole. No particular victim need be identified. The criminal law action is said to vindicate public, collective interests, as opposed to private, individual interests.[72] Some summarize it by saying the civil law "prices" behavior, while the criminal law "sanctions" it.[73]

As was discussed in chapter 4, traditionally the criminal law attached to behavior that was objectively viewed as morally blameworthy in some way. There was discussion that the serious sanctions contained in the criminal law, usually imprisonment but in extreme cases in some jurisdictions death, should be reserved for the worst kinds of behavior. This was necessary in order to do justice to the party affected, but it was also necessary to preserve proper boundaries. The idea was that the criminal law carried a big stick—imprisonment, death in extreme cases, stigma, long-term personal consequences for offenders and their families. This meant it should only be applied to conduct that truly warranted it. Legislatures could not make innocuous behavior the subject of these kinds of sanctions. If the law were to permit this, the powerful symbolism of the criminal law, and the utility of its serious sanctions, would be lost. Public confidence in the criminal justice system would be lost. Arguably, this also makes the criminal law distinct from the civil law, in what its application says and means for those affected. Criminal law sanctions entail significant opprobrium for those to whom it is applied in a way that marks it as distinctive; there is nothing equivalent in the civil law.[74] Criminal law expresses society's disapproval of what the accused did, and blame for wrongdoing.[75]

Another distinction relates to the parties involved, and their resources. As we discussed in earlier chapters, there is a significant disparity in resources in criminal law cases between the powerful state and the (typical) powerless person accused of wrongdoing. Indeed, one of the justifications for the presumption of innocence is sometimes said to be that it provides some kind of leveling of the playing field between the state, with powerful economic resources, vast experience in the process,[76] and significant powers of investigation, and the accused, who is often impoverished, is likely to have limited to no experience in the process, and without the power to issue warrants to would-be witnesses. These characteristics differ in respect of classic civil matters—at least traditionally in areas of civil law; for example, in the law of contract, the law presumes that parties are of relatively equal bargaining power. This explains the traditional reluctance of the law of contract to rewrite parties' bargains or to otherwise interfere in a voluntary contractual exchange—

the assumption being that the parties were rational, utility maximizers with sufficient bargaining power to look out for their own interests. Now it is beyond the scope of the current article to explore the extent to which that assumption is realistic. The point for present purposes is that the law's assumption about the kinds of parties involved in a criminal matter, and their resources, differs sharply from the law's assumption about the kinds of parties involved in a civil matter.

There is limited overlap, for instance in relation to the remedy of punitive damages in a small range of civil law claims, and accepting that some behavior, such as trespass to the person, can have both criminal and civil consequences. However, the generally distinct purposes of the criminal and civil actions are considered to remain useful to bear in mind in the current context, where legislatures either inadvertently or deliberately seek to blur the lines between the criminal and the civil realm.

A range of criteria have been identified in helping to determine whether a particular proceeding is criminal or civil in nature. Hart suggested five indicia of punishment (which I use as a proxy for "criminal process," given the strong links between punishment and criminal process):

a. It must involve pain or other consequences normally considered unpleasant;
b. It must be for an offense against legal rules;
c. It must be of an actual or supposed offender for his offense;
d. It must be intentionally administered by human beings other than the offender; and
e. It must be imposed and administered by an authority constituted by a legal system against which the offense is committed.[77]

The United States Supreme Court suggested the following factors:

a. Whether the sanction involves affirmative disability or restraint;
b. Whether it has historically been regarded as punishment;
c. Whether its application is conditioned upon a finding of scienter;
d. Whether its application will further purposes of retribution and/or deterrence;
e. Whether the behavior to which it is applicable is already criminal;
f. Whether alternative purposes of the provision can be articulated; and
g. Whether it appears excessive.[78]

The Supreme Court has accorded great deference to the decision of the legislature regarding the nature of a provision. Specifically, it found that "only the clearest proof" that a measure was actually in substance punitive and criminal would override a legislature's view that a measure was civil in nature.[79]

The European Court of Human Rights has cited three factors to help determine whether proceedings are criminal or civil in nature:

a. The classification adopted by the enacting legislature (minor significance only);
b. Nature of the offense; and
c. The severity of the penalty which the defendant faces.[80]

Recently an Australian Parliamentary Joint Committee on Human Rights considered the issue, finding a range of factors were relevant. They included the classification of the penalty, its nature (whether punitive or deterrent, for example), whether the proceedings were initiated by a public authority with statutory enforcement powers, whether the penalty was general in nature, and how severe the penalty was.[81]

Leading criminal law theorist Carol Steiker says that three questions can assist in determining whether proceedings are civil or criminal, a distinction which she supports.[82] They are (a) what does the state intend to do by its action; (b) what is the effect of the state's action on the individual; and (c) what is the public message or social meaning of the state's action? Not all elements must be satisfied in order to find that a proceeding is in substance punishment, and the strength of the existence of one factor may be significant.

She applies her questions to civil forfeiture schemes in the United States. She finds that on the first element, governments generally use civil forfeiture schemes "to promote the blaming function of criminal punishment." Regarding the second element, it is considered a serious thing to have one's property confiscated by the government. And as to the third element, she noted that the social meaning of having one's property confiscated had changed over the years, and was now viewed very seriously by other members of the community. She concludes that "civil forfeiture as generally practiced today by the federal government is in fact punishment and thus cannot be imposed separately from and in addition to criminal punishment."[83]

Application of Tests to Forfeiture and Involuntary Commitment Schemes

Forfeiture Provisions

In terms of Hart's five factors, forfeiture of one's property is certainly considered to be a painful and unpleasant consequence. The forfeiture occurs for a suspected offense. It is usually, but not always, administered against the wrongdoer, given that an innocent third party in receipt of crime-derived property may be affected. It is intentionally administered by, and imposed by, the state. On at least four of Hart's criteria, and on all five of them when it is the owner of the property to be forfeited that is accused of wrongdoing, forfeiture is punishment, and should be subject to a criminal process, with the relevant due process protections in place. Forfeiture should only occur once the person suspected of wrongdoing is proven beyond reasonable doubt to have committed the crime, and good faith defenses must protect an innocent possessor of that property.

In terms of the United States Supreme Court's approach, forfeiture of one's property involves affirmative disability or restraint. Historically, it has often been regarded as punishment, evidenced by, for example, the view of Blackstone. It does not require a finding of scienter in order to be applied. It will often in substance serve to achieve purposes of retribution and deterrence, purposes typically associated with the criminal law. It does not serve a compensatory purpose, as civil proceedings typically would. It may be considered to be excessive, in particular when the person whose property is seized is not themselves guilty of wrongdoing. As indicated, the Supreme Court accords great deference to any expressed view of a legislature that particular forfeiture proceedings are civil in nature. With respect, it should be more prepared to consider the question in substance, and adopt the view of the European Court of Human Rights, that the label placed on the provision by the legislature is of marginal importance only. Most of these factors suggest that forfeiture is criminal in nature, as a matter of substance.

The European Court, as indicated, will take into account the legislature's view as a minor point only. It considers the nature of the wrongdoing alleged. The examples cited above from the United Kingdom indicate that forfeiture is typically used when serious allegations of wrongdoing are being made. Confiscation of a person's property may be considered significant, and in the case of the proposed new United Kingdom provisions, they involve property of substantial value. The factors again point to forfeiture proceedings being in fact criminal in nature, despite the label. It has been pointed out that Carol Steiker applied her own factors, concluding that civil forfeiture proceedings are in substance criminal in nature. In sum, of all of the tests cited to determine whether forfeiture proceedings are in substance criminal in nature, they are all taken to suggest that they are. Obviously, the result is that criminal due process provisions such as the presumption of innocence should be applied, and protections against double jeopardy, double punishment and ex post facto laws in the criminal context respected.

Involuntary Commitment of Those Believed to Be Dangerous

In terms of Hart's factors, involuntary detention is certainly considered to involve pain and unpleasant consequences. The government might argue the detention is not for an offense; rather, it is designed to be preventive in nature. However, the legislation only applies to those already convicted of past criminal activity, and thus there remains a connection to the anterior offense. It is applied to an actual or supposed offender. It is intentionally administered and imposed by the state. At least four of Hart's five criteria would suggest that systems of preventive detention in fact render punishment.

In terms of the *Mendoza* factors, involuntary commitment involves affirmative disability and restraint. Historically, while most involuntary detention involved punishment, there is a history of detaining those considered to be mentally ill, those with an infectious disease, etc. Thus, it must be conceded that involuntary detention has not always been considered punishment historically, though it usually has been. There can be debate about "scienter" here—one argument may be that someone who suffers from mental abnormality or insanity is not capable of forming the "scienter" required for criminal activity. Regarding the purpose of the commitment, the government often alleges that its purposes are rehabilitative in nature. However, the realities must be considered. In the typical case where those involuntarily detained under these regimes are not obtaining treatment for their conditions and/or are placed in the general prison population, it is hard to argue that the purpose of their detention is for treatment. Rather, it looks as if the individual is being punished (further). So it is possible that on this limb the government could show the detention really is for non-criminal punitive purposes, but clear evidence would be required. As these detention periods can be particularly long, the total length of incarceration can appear excessive in terms of proven behavior. While again deference is due to the classification by the legislature, most of these factors tend to suggest that involuntary commitment statutes based on the dangerousness of the offender are in fact criminal and punitive in nature. However, the court should keep an open mind in respect of any regimes which can be shown by cogent and clear evidence to actually be treatment and rehabilitation based, as opposed to punishment based.

In regards to the *Engel* factors from Europe, again the classification adopted by the legislature is of low importance. These regimes are typically applied to those convicted in the past of very serious wrongdoing. The penalty imposed can be serious—as noted in cases like *M v Germany*, individuals may be incarcerated for many years under so-called preventive detention statutes, though there is sometimes very little evidence that tailored, specific treatment is actually given, and the prospects of a person's release from such incarceration may actually be very limited. This regime looks like punishment, in substance.

Steiker's factors point in a similar direction. If the person so detained is not in fact receiving treatment for the condition said to justify their preventive detention, the purpose of the detention looks to be punitive, in substance. That is certainly its effect on the individual—depriving a person of their liberty is one of the worst punishments that can be inflicted. Involuntary detention will attract significant opprobrium from other members of the community, future employers, family and friends, etc. Steiker's factors suggest that involuntary detention because of alleged future dangerousness should not be considered as, in substance, civil.

CONCLUSION

Another way in which legislatures might seek to circumvent the presumption of innocence typically attaching to criminal process is to deny that a particular process is criminal. Again, courts should not accept at face value assertions by a legislature that a particular proceeding is civil in nature, if the substance appears otherwise. Courts should use specific substantive criteria to ascertain the true nature of proceedings, and apply the "due process" that is required by their true nature. Criteria have been developed in this regard by Hart, Steiker and by the courts themselves. Applying these criteria, it has been suggested that existing regimes said to be civil in nature, including preventive detention regimes and property forfeiture schemes, are in fact substantively criminal, involving objectives typically associated with the criminal law. As a result, criminal due process protections, including the presumption of innocence, must be applied. A government seeking to forfeit an individual's property should only be able to do so once they have proven beyond a reasonable doubt that the property is crime-derived. A government seeking to incarcerate, or further incarcerate, a person on the basis of alleged future criminality should be required to prove the truth or likelihood that their suspicions are accurate at the beyond reasonable doubt level. We must not assume likely future criminality based on past behavior.

NOTES

1. Tamara Piety, "Scorched Earth: How the Expansion of Civil Forfeiture Doctrine Has Laid Waste to Due Process," *University of Miami Law Review* 45 (1991): 924: "the operation of the civil forfeiture statutes allow the government to bypass entirely the cumbersome criminal justice system, with its tedious set of impediments to investigation, prosecution and conviction, and substitute a control system consisting of civil sanctions" (quoting Steven Wisotsky, "The Emerging 'Drug Exception' to the Bill of Rights," *Hastings Law Journal* 38 [1987]: 925).

2. Harold Ashford and Michael Risinger, "Presumptions, Assumptions and Due Process in Criminal Cases: A Theoretical Overview," *Yale Law Journal* 79 (1969): 165; Margaret Lewis, "Presuming Innocence, or Corruption, in China," *Columbia Journal of Transnational Law* 50 (2012): 310.

3. Kenneth Mann, "Punitive Civil Sanctions: The Middle Ground Between Criminal and Civil Law," *Yale Law Journal* 101 (1992): 1801: "while legislatures . . . have busily created punitive civil sanctions for the state to impose, they have gone to great lengths to avoid labeling them as 'punitive' to circumvent the application of criminal-type procedural rules."

4. "When an ox gores a man or a woman to death, the ox shall be stoned, and its flesh shall not be eaten, but the owner of the ox shall not be liable": Exodus 21:28.

5. *Calero-Toledo v Pearson Yacht Leasing Co* 416 US 663, 681 (1974) (Brennan J, for the Court).

6. "In a civil court, the death of a human being cannot be complained of as an injury": *Baker v Bolton* (1808) 170 ER 1033 (Lord Ellenborough).

7. Daniel Boudreaux and A C Pritchard, "Innocence Lost: *Bennis v Michigan* and the Forfeiture Tradition," *Missouri Law Review* 61 (1996): 601–602.

8. Sir William Blackstone 1 *Commentaries on the Laws of England 1765–1769* (Clarendon Press, Oxford, 1768) 30, claiming that deodands were "grounded [on the] additional reason that such misfortunes [accidental death] are in part owing to the negligence of the owner [of the thing forfeited] and he is therefore properly *punished* by such forfeiture" (my emphasis).

9. Sir Matthew Hale, *Pleas of the Crown* (Atkyns and Atkyns, London, 1736) 419–421: "tho the killing of another per infortunium be not in truth felony . . . yet the party forfeits his goods . . . for tho it was not his crime but his misfortune, yet because the king hath lost his subject, and that men may be more careful, he forfeits his goods"; Jacob Finkelstein, "The Goring Ox: Some Historical Perspectives on Deodands, Forfeitures, Wrongful Death and the Western Notion of Sovereignty," *Temple Law Quarterly* 46(2) (1973): 181–182.

10. *The Palmrya* 25 US 1, 24–25 (1827); *Mitchell qui tam v Torup*, Parker 227, 232, 233, 145 ER 764, 766 (Ex. 1766); Stefan Cassella, "An Overview of Asset Forfeiture in the United States," in Simon Young ed, *Civil Forfeiture of Criminal Property* (Edward Elgar Publishing, Cheltenham, 2009) 25; Lawrence Harper, *The English Navigation Laws: A Seventeenth Century Experiment in Social Engineering III* (Columbia University Press, New York, 1975).

11. "Need I mention it as a rule, that punishments ought to be inflicted upon those persons only, who have committed crimes—that the innocent ought not to be blended in cruel and ruinous confusion with the guilty? Yes it is necessary to mention this as a rule; for however plain and straight it is, when viewed through the pure and clear ether of reason and humanity, it has not been seen by those whom pride and avarice have blinded . . . the doctrine of forfeiture and corruption of blood have found their ingenious advocates, as well as their powerful patrons": James Wilson, *The Works of James Wilson* (Lorenzo Press, Philadelphia, 1804) 630–631.

12. Marc Stahl, "Asset Forfeiture, Burdens of Proof and the War on Drugs," *Journal of Criminal Law and Criminology* 83 (1993): 294.

13. *A License to Steal: The Forfeiture of Property* (University of North Carolina Press, Chapel Hill, 1996) 51; see also Todd Barnet, "Legal Fiction and Forfeiture: An Historical Analysis of the *Civil Asset Forfeiture Reform Act*," *Duquesne Law Review* 40 (2002): 98.

14. David Benjamin Ross, "Civil Forfeiture: A Fiction That Offends Due Process," *Regent University Law Review* 13 (2001): 263: "civil forfeitures, which proceed in rem, are used to circumvent the protections of the Due Process Clause"; Issachar Rosen-Zvi and Talia Fisher, "Overcoming Procedural Boundaries," *Virginia Law Review* 94 (2008): 83: "the government regularly brings civil forfeiture actions alongside criminal prosecution in order to avoid granting defendants criminal procedural protections"; Tamara Piety, "Scorched Earth: How the Expansion of Civil Forfeiture Doctrine Has Laid Waste to Due Process," *University of Miami Law Review* 45 (1991): 917: "the civil posture of a forfeiture action is nothing more than a procedural fiction"; Todd Barnet, "Legal Fiction and Forfeiture: An Historical Analysis of the *Civil Asset Forfeiture Reform Act*," *Duquesne Law Review* 40 (2002): 95: "by employing this fiction the courts have been able to sidestep the question of whether civil forfeiture imposes a punishment on the owner of the property seized, because the proceedings take place against the property itself."

15. 67 Mass (1 Gray) 1, 35–36 (1854); see also *Hibbard v People* 4 Mich 125, 129 (1856), where, speaking of a civil forfeiture regime, the Court concluded "that this is clearly a criminal proceeding, within the meaning of the Constitution, we can entertain no doubt. It is instituted for the purpose of forfeiting the property . . . such forfeiture is imposed as a part of the punishment for such offense. It makes no difference in its

character, that the form of proceeding for the recovery of the pecuniary penalty or forfeiture is assimilated to that of a civil action. The issue is, guilty or not guilty, and the penalty is imposed as a punishment for an offense."

16. 116 US 616 (1886).

17. 633–634.

18. *Calero-Toledo v Pearson Yacht Leasing Co* 416 US 663, 687 (1974), referring to forfeiture as furthering the purpose of the underlying criminal statute by preventing further use of the forfeited thing, and imposing an economic penalty on the (true) wrongdoer; *Austin v United States* 509 US 602, 617 (1993), where the Court noted that forfeiture "historically [has] been understood, at least in part, as punishment" (Blackmun White Stevens O'Connor and Souter JJ); and the Court's conclusion in *United States v Halper* 490 US 435, 448 (1989): "a civil sanction that cannot fairly be said to serve a remedial purpose, but rather can only be explained as also serving either retributive or deterrent purposes, is punishment as we have come to understand the term" (Blackmun J, for all members of the Court). The deterrent purpose of forfeiture was emphasized in *Bennis v Michigan* 516 US 442, 452 (1996); see also *In Re Winship* 397 US 358, 366 (1970): "civil labels and good intentions do not themselves obviate the need for criminal due process safeguards" (Brennan J, for the majority).

19. *Geerings v Netherlands* [2007] ECHR 877, [39].

20. [2011] UKSC 49.

21. *Engel v Netherlands* [1976] ECHR 3.

22. [42] (Lord Phillips, with whom Lords Mance, Judge and Reed agreed).

23. Speaking of European Court authorities which had struck out subsequent "civil" proceedings following upon an acquittal, Lord Dyson said "the rationale for these decisions appears to be that voicing any suspicions of guilt in proceedings following an acquittal is incompatible with the presumption of innocence" ([128]).

24. *Attorney-General (NT) v Emmerson* (2014) 253 CLR 393, 435 (French CJ Hayne Crennan Kiefel Bell and Keane JJ).

25. *Attorney-General (NT) v Emmerson* (2014) 253 CLR 393, 416: "the statutory scheme in question exemplifies the acceptance by legislatures in Australia and elsewhere of the utility of the restraint and forfeiture of property, not only as a strong and drastic sanction vindicating a law and encouraging its observance, but also as a means of depriving criminals of profits" (French CJ Hayne Crennan Kiefel Bell and Keane JJ); see also *Re Director of Public Prosecutions; Ex Parte Lawler* (1994) 179 CLR 270, 290 (Brennan J identified forfeiture as a penalty); and *Cheatley v The Queen* (1972) 127 CLR 291, where members of the Court noted forfeiture was punishment: Barwick CJ (297), McTiernan J (300), Menzies J (304), Walsh J (307), Mason J (310–311); *Johnson v Attorney-General (Alberta)* [1954] SCR 127.

26. *Han and Yau Martins and Martins Morris v Commissioner of Customs and Excise* [2001] EWCA Civ 1048; *Clingham v Royal Borough of Kensington and Chelsea* [2003] 1 AC 787, Lord Steyn [31], Lord Hope [61], Lord Hutton [103], with whom Lords Hobhouse and Scott agreed. In *Witham v Holloway* (1995) 183 CLR 525, 534 members of the Australian High Court connected punishment with the use of criminal due process, finding that in cases which could lead to punishment the allegations had to be proven at the criminal standard of proof (Brennan Deane Toohey and Gaudron JJ).

27. Andrew Ashworth and Lucia Zedner, "Defending the Criminal Law: Reflections on the Changing Character of Crime, Procedure and Sanctions," *Criminal Law and Philosophy* 2 (2008): 49.

28. Tamara Piety, "Scorched Earth: How the Expansion of Civil Forfeiture Doctrine Has Laid Waste to Due Process," *University of Miami Law Review* 45 (1991): 911; Liz Campbell, "Theorising Asset Forfeiture in Ireland," *Journal of Criminal Law* 71 (2007): 441; Kenneth Mann, "Punitive Civil Sanctions: The Middle Ground Between Criminal and Civil Law," *Yale Law Journal* 101 (1992): 1795; Carol Steiker, "Punishment and Procedure: Punishment Theory and the Criminal-Civil Procedure Divide," *Georgetown Law Journal* 85 (1997): 814; Andrew Ashworth and Lucia Zedner, "Defending the Crim-

inal Law: Reflections on the Changing Character of Crime, Procedure and Sanctions," *Criminal Law and Philosophy* 2 (2008): 45–48.

29. "Punishment and Procedure: Punishment Theory and the Criminal-Civil Procedural Divide," *Georgetown Law Journal* 85 (1997): 817.

30. Tamara Piety, "Scorched Earth: How the Expansion of Civil Forfeiture Doctrine Has Laid Waste to Due Process," *University of Miami Law Review* 45 (1991): 920; Susan Klein, "Redrawing the Criminal-Civil Boundary," *Buffalo Criminal Law Review* 2 (1999): 718: "some 'civil' sanctions, such as the forfeiture of an individual's residence because that individual is determined by a judge or jury to be a drug trafficker, are quite stigmatizing" (stigma is usually attached to proceedings that are criminal in nature).

31. Jeffrey Boles, "Criminalizing the Problem of Unexplained Wealth: Illicit Enrichment Offenses and Human Rights Violations," *New York University Journal of Legislation and Public Policy* 17 (2014): 867: "illicit enrichment statutes, through their burden-shifting provisions, plainly intrude upon the presumption of innocence, and by adopting such statutes, governments violate the human rights of criminal defendants." Boles points out that the United States and Canadian governments declined to adopt the *Inter-American Convention Against Corruption* (IACAC) Article IX precisely because its offense of illicit enrichment placed a legal burden upon the person accused of wrongdoing. Officials from both countries pointed out the provision was inconsistent with the presumption of innocence (869); Alexandra Rogin, "Dollars for Collars: Civil Asset Forfeiture and the Breakdown of Constitutional Rights," *Drexel Law Review Online* (2014): 66: "the civil forfeiture claimant is in the same position in many respects as a criminal defendant, but is required to prove innocence—that is, to prove a negative—in that he must prove the absence of his connection to a crime to win his proceeding. Civil forfeiture's burden-shifting framework directly defies our justice system's presumption of innocence that places the burden of proof on the government"; Todd Barnet, "Legal Fiction and Forfeiture: An Historical Analysis of the *Civil Asset Forfeiture Reform Act*," *Duquesne Law Review* 40 (2002): 94.

32. 25 US 1, 14–15 (1827).

33. *United States v Bajakajian* 524 US 321, 327 (1998); *United States v Ursery* 518 US 267, 293 (1996); *Van Outer v Kansas* 272 US 465, 467–468 (1926); *Taylor v United States* 44 US 197 (1845); and *One Lot Emerald Cut Stones v United States* 409 US 232 (1972).

34. *United States v One Assortment of 89 Firearms* 465 US 354, 366 (1984).

35. *Gilligan v Criminal Assets Bureau* [1997] I.E.H.C. 106, [1998] 3 Irish Reports 185 (confiscation of property suspected of having being crime-derived valid although owner of property had not been charged with an offense); similar facts and outcome in the Canadian decision *Chatterjee v Ontario (Attorney-General)* [2009] 1 S.C.R. 624; *Air Canada v United Kingdom* [1995] ECHR 15. In *International Finance Trust Co Ltd v New South Wales Crime Commission* (2009) 240 CLR 319, 345, former Australian Chief Justice Robert French seems to accept a blurring of the criminal and the civil, referring to the "utility of civil forfeiture laws as a means of deterring serious criminal activity."

36. *Gale v Serious Organized Crime Agency* [2011] UKSC 49, [17] (Lord Phillips, with whom Lords Mance, Judge, Reed and Brown agreed), [124] (Lord Dyson).

37. Evidence suggests about 80 percent of forfeitures are uncontested by the person affected: David Pimentel, "Forfeitures Revisited: Bringing Principle to Practice in Federal Court," *Nevada Law Journal* 13 (2012): 1.

38. As others have noted, it can be difficult to prove a negative: Alexandra Rogin, "Dollars for Collars: Civil Asset Forfeiture and the Breakdown of Constitutional Rights," *Drexel Law Review Online* 7 (2014): 78. The Supreme Court has found an innocent owner defense is not constitutionally required: *Bennis v Michigan* 516 US 442 (1995). Others have noted that those whose property is seized through such processes are often themselves innocent of wrongdoing: "often the forfeited property's true owner is innocent of any wrongdoing . . . for example commercial mortgage lenders, lessors of boats and airplanes, and parents or others who have loaned children their cars [are often not aware of wrongdoing]": Scott Nelson, "The Supreme Court Takes a Weapon from the Drug War Arsenal: New Defenses to Civil Drug Forfeiture," *St*

Mary's Law Journal 26 (1994): 183. See also Eric Moores, "Reforming the Civil Asset Forfeiture Reform Act," *Arizona Law Review* 51 (2009): 779; Thomas Johnson, "Restoring Civility—The Civil Asset Forfeiture Reform Act of 2000: Baby Steps Towards a More Civilized Civil Forfeiture System," *Indiana Law Review* 35 (2002): 1045; David Benjamin Ross, "Civil Forfeiture: A Fiction That Offends Due Process," *Regent University Law Review* 13 (2000): 259.

39. David Pimentel, "Forfeitures Revisited: Bringing Principle to Practice in Federal Court," *Nevada Law Journal* 13 (2013): 27.

40. Ben Clarke, "A Man's Home Is His Castle—Or Is It? How to Take Houses from People Without Convicting Them of Anything," *Criminal Law Journal* 28 (2004): 285: "it is difficult for those who recognize the inherent worth of time-honored common law principles of justice to be anything but alarmed by non-conviction-based confiscation laws"; Peter Wright, "Criminal Punishment Without Civil Rights: The Criminal Proceeds and Instrument Bill's Punitive Civil Sanctions," *Victoria University of Wellington Law Review* 37 (2006): 623.

41. Proposed new s362B *Proceeds of Crime Act 2002* (UK).

42. Proposed new s362C *Proceeds of Crime Act 2002* (UK).

43. *Chatterjee v Ontario (Attorney-General)* [2009] 1 S.C.R. 624; see Kevin Davies, "The Effects of Forfeiture on Third Parties," *McGill Law Journal* 48 (2003): 183; Michelle Gallant, "Alberta and Ontario: Civilizing the Money-Centered Model of Crime Control," *Asper Review of International Business and Trade Law* 4 (2004): 13.

44. See similarly the conclusion of the United States Court of Appeal (11th Circuit) in *United States v $121,100.00 in United States Currency* 999 F.2d 1503, 1507: "the quantity of cash seized in this case is highly probative of a connection to some illegal activity."

45. 521 US 346 (1997).

46. Thomas J, for Rehnquist CJ O'Connor Scalia and Kennedy JJ; Breyer Stevens Souter and Ginsburg JJ dissenting.

47. 360.

48. 361.

49. 362.

50. 363.

51. 363.

52. 380.

53. 383.

54. 388.

55. 394.

56. *Kansas v Crane* 534 US 407, 412 (2002) (Breyer J, for Rehnquist CJ Stevens O'Connor Kennedy Souter and Ginsburg JJ).

57. *Selling v Young* 531 US 250, 261 (2001).

58. *Apprendi v New Jersey* 530 US 466, 490 (2000) (Stevens J, for Scalia Souter Thomas and Ginsburg JJ).

59. Existing authority suggests that the appropriate standard to apply in such contexts is something between the traditional criminal and civil standards, namely clear and convincing evidence: *Addington v Texas* 441 US 418 (1979).

60. (1986) 189 CLR 51.

61. (2004) 223 CLR 575.

62. 632.

63. 633.

64. 634.

65. 635–636.

66. "Penal ends may be pursued in civil proceedings which result in additional punishment": *Attorney-General (NT) v Emmerson* (2014) 253 CLR 393, 435 (French CJ Hayne Crennan Kiefel Bell and Keane JJ).

67. [2009] ECHR 2071, [127]–[133].

68. This made it contrary to Article 7 of the *European Convention on Human Rights,* which forbids a heavier "punishment" being imposed than the one that was applicable at the time the offense was committed. See to like effect *K v Germany* [2012] ECHR 957, [80] and *Glien v Germany* [2013] ECHR 1206, [125].

69. Kenneth Mann, "Punitive Civil Sanctions: The Middleground Between Criminal and Civil Law," *Yale Law Journal* 101 (1992): 1799; Susan Klein, "Redrawing the Criminal-Civil Boundary" *Buffalo Criminal Law Review* 2 (1999): 686; *Halper v United States* 490 US 435, 449 (1989): "a civil sanction that cannot fairly be said solely to serve a remedial purpose, but rather can only be explained as also serving either retributive or deterrent purposes, is punishment"; *Austin v United States* 509 US 602 (1993), concluding the legislation could not "fairly be said to serve a remedial purpose, but rather could only be explained as also serving either retributive or deterrent purposes" (and thus forfeiture there was punitive and criminal in substance).

70. David Benjamin Ross, "Civil Forfeiture: A Fiction That Offends Due Process," *Regent University Law Review* 13 (2001): 269: "punishment cannot be a legitimate government objective [when] the owner has done no wrong" (in the context of civil forfeiture); "it is beyond dispute that among the aims of civil forfeiture under [the relevant federal forfeiture provision] are deterrence and retribution": Tamara Piety, "Scorched Earth: How the Expansion of Civil Forfeiture Doctrine Has Laid Waste to Due Process," *University of Miami Law Review* 45 (1991): 946.

71. *State Farm Mutual Auto Insurance v Campbell* 538 US 408, 416 (2003).

72. Sir William Blackstone, 4 *Commentaries on the Laws of England 1765–1769* (Clarendon Press, Oxford, 1768) 6–7.

73. Robert Cooter, "Prices and Sanctions," *Columbia Law Review* 84 (1984): 1523; John Coffee, "Paradigms Lost: The Blurring of the Criminal and Civil Law Models—And What Can Be Done About It," *Yale Law Journal* 101 (1992): 1884.

74. This argument can challenge so-called civil forfeiture because "civil sanctions, such as the forfeiture of an individual's residence because that individual is determined by a judge or jury to be a drug trafficker, are quite stigmatizing" (stigma being a standard feature of criminal proceedings): Susan Klein, "Redrawing the Criminal-Civil Boundary," *Buffalo Criminal Law Review* 2 (1999): 718. Interestingly, the United States Supreme Court referred to the "stigma" associated with involuntary commitment to a mental institution in *Addington v Texas* 441 US 418, 426 (1979).

75. Joel Feinberg, "The Expressive Function of Punishment," in Joel Feinberg, Jules Coleman and Christopher Kutz, *Philosophy of Law: Crime and Punishments* 9th ed (Cengage, Kentucky, 2014).

76. Marc Galanter, "Why the Haves Come Out Ahead: Speculation on the Limits of Legal Change," *Law and Policy Review* 9 (1974): 95.

77. H L A Hart, *Punishment and Responsibility* (Oxford University Press, Oxford, 1968) 4–5. Stanley Benn and Richard Stanley Peters, *The Principles of Political Thought* (Free Press, New York, 1959), found that the unpleasantness referred to by Hart would need to be an essential aspect of what was intended, rather than incidental to a different prime objective (202).

78. *Kennedy v Mendoza-Martinez* 372 US 144 (1963); *United States v Ward* 448 US 242 (1980).

79. *United States v Ward* 448 US 242, 248–249 (1980).

80. *Engel v Netherlands* [1976] ECHR 3; *Gale v Serious and Organized Crime Agency* [2011] UKSC 49.

81. *Offence Provisions, Civil Penalties and Human Rights* (Guidance Note 2); Parliament of Australia (2014). The Australian Law Reform Commission in its recent report, *Traditional Rights and Freedoms—Encroachments by Commonwealth Laws,* Report 129 (2015), noted that "some aspects of proceeds of crime laws may be considered to involve civil penalties that are criminal in nature" (282).

82. "Punishment and Procedure: Punishment Theory and the Criminal-Civil Procedural Divide," *Georgetown Law Journal* 85 (1997): 817. She is more equivocal on so-called civil commitment, concluding that she suspects the provisions are being used to

impose further punishment on offenders sentenced at a time when sentencing of such offenders was not as harsh as today, but also acknowledges that the provisions may genuinely have preventive, rather than punitive, purposes (817–818).

83. See also Stefan Cassella, "An Overview of Asset Forfeiture in the United States," in Simon Young ed, *Civil Forfeiture of Criminal Property* (Edward Elgar Publishing, London, 2009) 32: "asset forfeiture constitutes a form of punishment. While taking the instrumentalities of crime out of circulation, obtaining funds for restitution, taking the profit out of crime and achieving some measure of deterrence all constitute remedial aspects of forfeiture, it cannot be denied that depriving a wrongdoer of the accoutrements of an expensive lifestyle . . . can serve, in some cases, as a form of punishment or retribution exacted by the criminal justice system. Forfeiture, in other words, gives the criminal his just desserts."

Conclusion

This book has sought to re-assert the fundamental importance of the presumption of innocence in our criminal justice system, and to highlight various ways in which it is being progressively undermined by legislatures. The presumption has been a hallmark of the criminal law in common law systems for at least a couple of centuries, and perhaps much longer. Its strongest theoretical rationale is the moral anxiety that decision makers, and society more generally, should feel about judgment of another. Even if the supernatural context in which that anxiety originally appeared has largely disappeared from the legal systems studied here, moral comfort around making correct decisions around guilt, and most egregiously, punishing the innocent, provides a firm foundation for recognition and protection of the presumption of innocence from attack. It also forms an integral piece in the puzzle of the kind of due process we have come to accept is owed to an accused. If we take that piece out, others parts become more fragile.

Notwithstanding its longstanding roots, compelling rationale and recognition in international human rights instruments, the presumption is currently in a precarious state. This book has documented ways in which it has been circumvented, limited and marginalized by determined legislatures in a range of jurisdictions. Techniques that have been explored at some length here have included reverse onus provisions, casting the onus on an accused to prove innocence, rational connection provisions, permitting an element of a crime to be inferred from proof of something else (presumably, sometimes easier to prove), redefining old crimes in novel ways, transferring what would normally be considered elements of crimes into the defense category, defining crimes with no regard to mens rea, and claiming that proceedings which some might regard as being substantively criminal in nature are civil. Through one or a combination of these techniques, legislatures have undermined the presumption, and courts have, by and large, permitted them to do so.

This book has argued that courts must re-assert the prime importance of the presumption of innocence. They must be cognizant of, and be prepared to do something about, clear legislative efforts to subvert the principle. They should recall the moral opprobrium which should properly attach to the incorrect verdict. They must feel the moral discomfort associated with convicting innocent people, or rather, those not shown beyond reasonable doubt to be guilty. I have indicated support for a guiding principle that no provision should be accepted and applied by courts where it can demonstrably lead to a result whereby an accused can be convicted although there is reasonable doubt as to their guilt. Simply, courts must not permit this.

However, of itself, this is not sufficient to protect the presumption of innocence. It would not stop legislatures redefining crimes, transferring offense elements to defense elements, and denuding criminal definitions of all traces of culpability. Thus, I have argued in this book that courts must take a substantive view of the criminal law. Anything does not go, in terms of legislatures defining criminal behavior. Where jail terms are possible punishments for commission of an offense, that offense must include minimum levels of culpability. Specifically, it must concern an act that is voluntary, where the accused can be taken to know of its criminal nature, and that they ought to have known that the acts involved were wrong. In other words, the act criminalized must reach a certain minimum level of "moral blameworthiness" such that the criminal label is, in substance, warranted. The harm principle, historical practice, and proportionality principles are of some use here.

Similarly, legislatures are not free to deem proceedings to be civil in nature, neatly sidestepping due process protections that are designed to protect the person accused of criminal wrongdoing. Again a substantive view must be taken of what are truly criminal proceedings and what are truly civil proceedings. Labels must never be a substitute for substance.

It is not too late for the common law to feel once again the moral comfort associated with punishing only those who are truly guilty of that of which they are accused, and who are deserving of all of the moral opprobrium and practical consequence of being criminally punished. And it must remember the moral discomfort, and long-term unsustainability, of a system whereby an accused is found guilty, and punished accordingly, although there is reasonable doubt as to their guilt. A justice system worthy of the name cannot countenance this. As the gatekeepers of the justice system, our judges must be vigilant. They have often been too meek in responding to legislative incursion into fundamental due process rights. They must re-assert their gatekeeper role, to protect the very great interests involved.

References

Allen, Robert Jay, "*Mullaney v Wilbur*, the Supreme Court and the Substantive Criminal Law—An Examination of the Limits of Legislative Intervention," *Texas Law Review* 55 (1977): 269–301.

———. "The Restoration of *In Re Winship*: A Comment on Burdens of Persuasion in Criminal Cases After *Patterson v New York*," *Michigan Law Review* 76 (1977): 30–63.

Allen, Ronald, and Hastert, Ethan, "From *Winship* to *Apprendi* to *Booker*: Constitutional Command or Constitutional Blunder?" *Stanford Law Review* 58 (2006): 195–216.

Aristotle, *Problems* (W S Hett trans, Harvard University Press, Cambridge, 1937).

Ashford, Harold, and Risinger, Michael, "Presumptions, Assumptions and Due Process in Criminal Cases: A Theoretical Overview," *Yale Law Journal* 79 (1969): 165–208.

Ashworth, Andrew, "Four Threats to the Presumption of Innocence," *International Journal of Evidence and Proof* 10 (2006): 241–279.

Ashworth, Andrew, and Zedner, Lucia, "Defending the Criminal Law: Reflections on the Changing Character of Crime, Procedure and Sanctions," *Criminal Law and Philosophy* 2 (2008): 21–51.

Australian Law Reform Commission, *Traditional Rights and Freedoms—Encroachments by Commonwealth Laws Report 129* (2015).

Bacon, Francis, *The Works of Francis Bacon* (F C and J Rivington, London, 1819).

Barnet, Todd, "Legal Fiction and Forfeiture: An Historical Analysis of the *Civil Asset Forfeiture Reform Act*," *Duquesne Law Review* 40 (2002): 77–109.

Bartlett, Robert, *Trial by Fire and Water: The Medieval Judicial Ordeal* (Oxford University Press, New York, 1986).

Beattie J M, *Crime and the Courts in England 1660–1800* (Princeton University Press, New Jersey, 1986).

———. "Scales of Justice: Defense Counsel and the English Criminal Trial in the Eighteenth and Nineteenth Centuries," *Law and History Review* 9 (1991): 221–267.

Benn, Stanley, and Peters, Richard Stanley, *The Principles of Political Thought* (Free Press, New York, 1959).

Bentham, Jeremy, *Principles of Penal Law* (Tait, Edinburgh, 1843).

Bewley, Peter, "The Unconstitutionality of Statutory Criminal Presumptions," *Stanford Law Review* 22 (1970): 341–355.

Bigelow, Melville Madison, *History of Procedure in England from the Norman Conquest* (Rotham Reprints, New Jersey, 1987).

Billionis, Louis, "Process, the Constitution and Substantive Criminal Law," *Michigan Law Review* 96 (1998): 1269–1334.

Binnall, James, "EG 1900 . . . The Number They Gave Me When They Revoked My Citizenship: Perverse Consequences of Ex-Felon Civil Exile," *Willamette Law Review* 44 (2008): 669–697.

Bishop, Joel, *Criminal Law* (Little, Brown and Co, Boston, 1892).

Blackstone, Sir William, *Commentaries on the Laws of England 1765–1769* (Clarendon Press, London, 1768).

Bodenstein, H D J, "Phases in the Development of Criminal Mens Rea," *South African Law Journal* 36 (1919): 323–349.

Boles, Jeffrey, "Criminalizing the Problem of Unexplained Wealth: Illicit Enrichment Offenses and Human Rights Violations," *New York University Journal of Legislation and Public Policy* 17 (2014): 835–880.

Boudreaux, Daniel, and Pritchard, A C, "Innocence Lost: *Bennis v Michigan* and the Forfeiture Tradition," *Missouri Law Review* 61 (1996): 593–632.
Bowring, John, ed., *The Works of Jeremy Bentham* (Tait, Edinburgh, 1829).
Bracton, Henry de, *De Legibus et Consuetudinibus Angliae* (1268).
Branch, Thomas, *Principia Legis and Aequitatis* (J and W T Clarke, London, 1753).
Campbell, Kenneth, *Criminal Law and Justice: Essays from the W G Hart Workshop* (Sweet and Maxwell, London, 1987).
Campbell, Liz, "Theorizing Asset Forfeiture in Ireland," *Journal of Criminal Law* 71 (2007): 441–460.
Campbell, Morten, et al., *Harvard Legal Essays* (Harvard University Press, Cambridge, 1934).
Cascarelli, Joseph, "Presumption of Innocence and Natural Law: Machiavelli and Aquinas," *American Journal of Jurisprudence* 41 (1996): 229–269.
Cassella, Stefan, "An Overview of Asset Forfeiture in the United States," in Simon Young ed., *Civil Forfeiture of Criminal Property* (Edward Elgar Publishing, Cheltenham, 2009).
Chapman, Pamela, "The Politics of Judging: Section 1 of the *Charter of Rights and Freedoms*," *Osgoode Hall Law Journal* 24 (1986): 867–896.
Christie, George, and Pye, Kenneth, "Presumptions and Assumptions in the Criminal Law: Another View," *Duke Law Journal* (1970): 919–942.
Clark, Sherman, "The Juror, the Citizen and the Human Being: The Presumption of Innocence and the Burden of Judgment," *Criminal Law and Philosophy* 8 (2014): 421–429.
Clarke, Ben, "A Man's Home Is His Castle—Or Is It? How to Take Houses from People Without Convicting Them of Anything," *Criminal Law Journal* 28 (2004): 263–286.
Coffee, John, "Does 'Unlawful' Mean Criminal? Reflections on the Disappearing Tort/Crime Distinction in American Law," *Boston University Law Review* 71 (1991): 193–246.
———. "Paradigms Lost: The Blurring of the Criminal and Civil Law Models—And What Can Be Done About It," *Yale Law Journal* 101 (1992): 1875–1893.
Cohen, Jonathan, "The Logic of Proof," *Criminal Law Review* (1980): 91–103.
Collier, Charles, "The Improper Use of Presumptions in Recent Criminal Law Adjudication," *Stanford Law Review* 38 (1986): 423–462.
Cooke, Lord, *The Third Part of the Institutes of the Laws of England* (E and R Brooke, London, 1797).
Cooter, Robert, "Prices and Sanctions," *Columbia Law Review* 84 (1984): 1523–1560.
Cross, Rupert, *The Golden Thread of the English Criminal Law: The Burden of Proof* (Cambridge University Press, New York, 1976).
Davis, Kevin, "The Effect of Forfeiture on Third Parties," *McGill Law Journal* 48 (2003): 183–224.
Demosthenes, *Against Meidias, Androtion, Aristocrates, Timocrates, Aristogeiton* (J H Vince trans, Harvard University Press, Cambridge, 1935).
Dennis, Ian, "The *Human Rights Act* and the Law of Criminal Evidence: Ten Years On," *Sydney Law Review* 33 (2011): 333–357.
———. *Criminal Law and Justice: Essays from the W G Hart Workshop* (Sweet and Maxwell, London, 1987).
Dicey, Albert Vere, *An Introduction to the Study of the Law of the Constitution* (Macmillan, London, 1885).
Doniger, Anthony, "Unburdening the Criminal Defendant: *Mullaney v Wilbur* and the Reasonable Doubt Standard," *Harvard Civil Rights–Civil Liberties Law Review,"* 11 (1976): 390–432.
Dripps, Donald, "The Constitutional Status of the Reasonable Doubt Rule," *California Law Review* 75 (1987): 1665–1718.
Dubber, Markus, "Towards a Constitutional Law of Crime and Punishment," *Hastings Law Journal* 55 (2004): 509–572.

Dubin, Gary, "*Mens Rea* Reconsidered: A Plea for a Due Process Concept of Criminal Responsibility," *Stanford Law Review* 18 (1966): 322–395.

Edmond, Gary, and Roberts, Andrew, "Procedural Fairness, the Criminal Trial and Forensic Science and Medicine," *Sydney Law Review* 33 (2011): 359–394.

Elliot, Robin, "The Supreme Court of Canada and Section 1: The Erosion of the Common Front," *Queen's Law Journal* 12 (1987): 277–340.

Ely, John, *Democracy and Distrust* (Harvard University Press, Cambridge, 1980).

Ewald, Alec, "Civil Death: The Ideological Paradox of Criminal Disenfranchisement Laws in the United States," *Wisconsin Law Review* (2002): 1045–1132.

Farinacci, *Praxis et Theoricae Criminalis Libri duo in Quinque Titulos Distributi* (Frankfurt, 1606).

Farmer, Lindsay, *Making the Modern Criminal Law: Criminalization and Civil Order* (Oxford University Press, Oxford, 2016).

Feinberg, Joel, Coleman, Jules, and Kutz, Christopher, *Philosophy of Law: Crime and Punishment* (Cengage, Kentucky, 2014).

Finkelstein, Claire, "Positivism and the Notion of an Offense," *California Law Review* 88 (2000): 335–394.

Finkelstein, Jacob, "The Goring Ox: Some Historical Perspectives on Deodands, Forfeitures, Wrongful Death and the Western Notion of Sovereignty," *Temple Law Quarterly* 46(2) (1973): 169–290.

Fletcher, George, "Two Kinds of Legal Rules: A Comparative Study of Burden of Persuasion Practices in Criminal Cases," *Yale Law Journal* 77 (1968): 880–935.

———. "The Meaning of Innocence," *University of Toronto Law Journal* 48 (1998): 157–174.

Fox, Marvin, *Interpreting Maimonides: Studies in Methodology, Metaphysics and Moral Philosophy* (University of Chicago Press, Illinois, 1992).

Fraher, Richard, *Ut Nullus Describatur Reus Prius Quam Convincatur: Presumption of Innocence in Medieval Canon Law* (Proceedings of the Sixth International Congress of Medieval Canon Law, 1985).

Frank, Mitchell, and Broschard, Dawn, "The Silent Criminal Defendant and the Presumption of Innocence: In the Hands of Real Jurors, Is Either of Them Safe?" *Lewis and Clark Law Review* 10 (2006): 237–285.

Fuller, Allen, and Urich, Robert, "An Analysis of the Constitutionality of Statutory Presumptions That Lessen the Burden of the Prosecution," *University of Miami Law Review* 25 (1971): 420–434.

Fuller, Lon, "Positivism and Fidelity to the Law—A Reply to Professor Hart," *Harvard Law Review* 71 (1958): 630–672.

Fuller, Richard, "Morals and the Criminal Law," *Journal of Criminal Law and Criminology* 32 (1942): 624–630.

Galanter, Mark, "Why the Haves Come Out Ahead: Speculation on the Limits of Legal Change," *Law and Society Review* 9 (1974): 95–160.

Gallant, Michelle, "Alberta and Ontario: Civilizing the Money-Centered Model of Crime Control," *Asper Review of International Business and Trade Law* 4 (2004): 13–33.

Gardiner, Martin, "The Mens Rea Enigma: Observations on the Role of Motive in the Criminal Law Past and Present," *Utah Law Review* (1993): 635–750.

Godbey, Allen, "The Place of the Code of Hammurabi," *The Monist* 15 (1905): 199–226.

Goldgar, Bertrand A, ed., *The Covent Garden Journal and a Plan of the Universal Register-Office* (Oxford University Press, Oxford, 1988).

Gordon, Robert, "Affirmative Defenses and Due Process: The Constitutionality of Placing a Burden of Persuasion on a Criminal Defendant," *Georgetown Law Journal* 64 (1976): 871–894.

Gottfried, Theodore, and Baroni, Peter, "Presumptions, Inferences and Strict Liability in Illinois Criminal Law: Pre-Empting the Presumption of Innocence," *John Marshall Law Review* 41 (2008): 715–740.

Gray, Anthony, "Securing Felons' Voting Rights in America," *Berkeley Journal of African-American Law and Policy* 16 (2014): 3–31.

———, "Mandatory Sentencing Around the World and the Need for Reform," *New Criminal Law Review* 20 (2017): (forthcoming).

Groot, Roger, "The Jury of Presentment Before 1215," *American Journal of Legal History* 26 (1982): 1–24.

Guest, Anthony G, *Oxford Essays in Jurisprudence* (Clarendon Press, Oxford, 1961).

Hale, Matthew, *Pleas of the Crown* (Atkyns and Atkyns, London, 1682).

Hall, Jerome, *Principles of Criminal Law* (Bobbs-Merrill, Indianapolis, 1947).

Hamer, David, "The Presumption of Innocence and Reverse Burdens: A Balancing Act," *Cambridge Law Journal* 66(1) (2007): 142–171.

Harper, Lawrence, *The English Navigation Laws: A Seventeenth Century Experiment in Social Engineering III* (Columbia University Press, New York, 1975).

Harper, Robert, *The Code of Hammurabi: King of Babylon* (Chicago University Press, Chicago, 1904).

Harris, Leslie, "Constitutional Limits on Criminal Presumptions as an Expression of Changing Concepts of Fundamental Fairness," *Journal of Criminal Law and Criminology* 77 (1986): 308–357.

Hart, Henry, "The Aims of the Criminal Law," *Law and Contemporary Problems* 23 (1958): 401–441.

Hart, H L A, "Positivism and the Separation of Law and Morals," *Harvard Law Review* 71 (1958): 593–629.

———. *The Concept of Law* (Clarendon Press, Oxford, 2012).

———. *The Morality of the Criminal Law* (Oxford University Press, London, 1965).

———. *Law, Liberty and Morality* (Oxford University Press, London, 1963).

———. *Punishment and Responsibility* (Oxford University Press, London, 1968).

———. "Legal Responsibility and Excuses," in Sydney Hook ed., *Determinism and Freedom in the Age of Modern Science* (New York University, New York, 1961).

———. "Negligence, Mens Rea and Criminal Responsibility," in Anthony G Guest, *Oxford Essays in Jurisprudence* (Clarendon Press, Oxford, 1961).

Hawkins, William, *Pleas of the Crown* (Walthow, London, 1716).

Hippard, James, "The Unconstitutionality of Criminal Liability Without Fault: An Argument for a Constitutional Doctrine of *Mens Rea*," *Houston Law Review* 10 (1973): 1039–1058.

Hoffmann, Morris, "The Myth of Factual Innocence," *Chi-Kent Law Review* 82 (2007): 663–690.

Holdsworth, William, *A History of English Law* (Little, Brown and Co, Boston, 1956).

Holland, N Huntley, and Chamberlin, Harvey, "Statutory Criminal Presumptions: Proof Beyond a Reasonable Doubt?" *Valparaiso University Law Review* 7 (1973): 147–167.

Holmes, Oliver Wendel Jr., *The Common Law* (Barnes and Noble, New York, 2004).

Hook, Sydney, ed., *Determinism and Freedom in the Age of Modern Science* (New York University, New York, 1965).

Hostettler, John, *The Criminal Jury Old and New: Jury Power from Early Times to the Present Day* (Waterside Press, Hampshire, 2004).

Howard, M N, et al., *Phipson on Evidence* (Sweet and Maxwell, London, 1990).

Ireland, R W, "The Presumption of Guilt in the History of English Criminal Procedure," *Journal of Legal History* 7 (1986): 243–255.

Jacobson, Shari, "Mandatory and Permissive Presumptions in Criminal Cases: The Morass Created by *Allen*," *University of Miami Law Review* 42 (1988): 1009–1032.

Jeffries, John Calvin Jr., and Stephan, Paul, III, "Defenses, Presumptions and Burden of Proof in the Criminal Law," *Yale Law Journal* 88 (1979): 1325–1407.

Johnson, Thomas, "Restoring Civility—The Civil Asset Forfeiture Reform Act of 2000: Baby Steps Towards a More Civilized Civil Forfeiture System," *Indiana Law Review* 35 (2002): 1045–1084.

Jong, Ferry de, and Van Lent, Leonie, "The Presumption of Innocence as a Counterfactual Principle," *Utrecht Law Review* 12(1) (2016): 32–49.

Kadish, Sanford, "The Decline of Innocence," *Cambridge Law Journal* 26(2) (1968): 273–290.
———. "Some Observations on the Use of Criminal Sanctions in Enforcing Economic Regulations," *University of Chicago Law Review* 30 (1963): 423–449.
Keedy, Edwin, "Insanity and Criminal Responsibility," *Harvard Law Review* 30 (1917): 535–560.
Keeton, W Page, "Statutory Presumptions—Their Constitutionality and Legal Effect," *Texas Law Review* 10 (1932): 34–50.
Kennedy, Joseph, "Making the Crime Fit the Punishment," *Emory Law Journal* 51 (2002): 753–876.
King, Nancy, and Klein, Susan, "Essential Elements," *Vanderbilt Law Review* 54 (2001): 1467–1555.
Klein, Susan, "Redrawing the Criminal-Civil Boundary," *Buffalo Criminal Law Review* 2 (1999): 679–721.
Lacey, Nicola, *In Search of Criminal Responsibility* (Oxford University Press, New York, 2016).
Langbein, John, *The Origins of Adversary Criminal Trial* (Oxford University Press, Oxford, 2003).
Laudan, Larry, "The Presumption of Innocence: Material or Probatory?" *Legal Theory* 11 (2005): 333–361.
Laylin, Clarence, and Tuttle, Alonzo, "Due Process and Punishment," *Michigan Law Review* 20 (1922): 614–645.
Leeson, Peter, "Ordeals," *Journal of Law and Economics* 55 (2012): 691–714.
Levitt, Albert, "The Origin of the Doctrine of Mens Rea," *Illinois Law Review* 17 (1923): 117–137.
Levy, Leonard, *A License to Steal: The Forfeiture of Property* (University of North Carolina Press, Chapel Hill, 1996).
Lewis, Margaret, "Presuming Innocence, or Corruption, in China," *Columbia Journal of Transnational Law* 50 (2012): 287–369.
Lippke, Richard, *Taming the Presumption of Innocence* (Oxford University Press, London, 2016).
MacKay, Wayne, and Cromwell, T, "*Oakes*: A Bold Initiative Impeded by Old Ghosts," C.R. (3d) 32 (1983): 221–235.
Maitland, Frederic, *The Constitutional History of England* (Cambridge University Press, Cambridge, 1968).
Mann, Kenneth, "Punitive Civil Sanctions: The Middle Ground Between Criminal and Civil Law," *Yale Law Journal* 101 (1992): 1795–1873.
May, Allyson, *The Bar and the Old Bailey 1750–1850* (University of North Carolina Press, Chapel Hill, 2003).
McAuley, Finbarr, "Canon Law and the End of the Ordeal," *Oxford Journal of Legal Studies* 26(3) (2006): 473–514.
McKeon, Richard, ed., *The Basic Works of Aristotle* (Random House, New York 1941).
Meyer, Hermine, "Constitutionality of Pre-Trial Detention," *Georgetown Law Journal* 60 (1972): 1139–1194.
Mill, John Stuart, *Utilitarianism, On Liberty, Considerations on Representative Government* (Everyman, London, 1972).
Mommsen, Theodor, Krueger, Paul, and Watson, Alan, eds., *The Digest of Justinian Vol IV* (University of Pennsylvania Press, Philadelphia, 1985).
Moores, Eric, "Reforming the Civil Asset Forfeiture Reform Act," *Arizona Law Review* 51 (2009): 777–803.
Morano, Anthony, "A Reexamination of the Development of the Reasonable Doubt Rule," *Boston University Law Review* 55 (1975): 507–528.
Mosher, Robert, "Statutory Criminal Presumptions: Reconciling the Practical with the Sacrosanct," *UCLA Law Review* 18 (1971): 157–187.
Mueller, Gerhard, "On Common Law Mens Rea," *Minnesota Law Review* 42 (1958): 1043–1104.

Nance, D A, "Civility and the Burden of Proof," *Harvard Journal of Law and Public Policy* 17 (1994): 647–690.

National Research Council of the National Academies, *Strengthening Forensic Science in the United States: A Path Forward* (2009).

Nelson, Scott, "The Supreme Court Takes a Weapon from the Drug War Arsenal: New Defenses to Civil Drugs Forfeiture," *St Mary's Law Journal* 26 (1994): 157–201.

Nesson, Charles, "Reasonable Doubt and Permissive Inferences: The Value of Complexity," *Harvard Law Review* 92 (1979): 1187–1225.

———. "Rationality, Presumptions and Judicial Comment: A Response to Professor Allen," *Harvard Law Review* 94 (1981): 1574–1590.

Nichols, Francis, *Britton—An English Translation and Notes* (Byrnes and Co, Washington, DC, 1901).

Olson, Trisha, "Of Enchantment: The Passing of the Ordeals and the Rise of the Jury Trial," *Syracuse Law Review* 50 (2000): 109–196.

O'Reilly, Gregory, "England Limits the Right to Silence and Moves Towards an Inquisitorial System of Justice," *Journal of Criminal Law and Criminology* 85(2) (1994): 402–452.

Packer, Herbert, "*Mens Rea* and the Supreme Court," *Supreme Court Review* (1962): 107–152.

Palmer, Robert, "Conscience and the Law: The English Criminal Jury," *Michigan Law Review* 84 (1986): 787–800.

Pennington, Kenneth, "Innocent Until Proven Guilty: The Origins of Legal Maxim," *The Jurist* 63 (2003): 106–124.

———. *The Prince and the Law 1200–1600: Sovereignty and Rights in the Western Legal Tradition* (University of California Press, Berkeley, 1993).

Perkins, Rollin, "Criminal Liability Without Fault: A Disquieting Trend," *Iowa Law Review* 68 (1983): 1067–1081.

———. "The Civil Offense," *University of Pennsylvania Law Review* 100 (1952): 832–851.

Pharr, Clyde, *Ancient Roman Statutes* (University of Texas, Austin, 1961).

Phillips, Jean Gilles, and Woodman, Rebecca, "The Insanity of the Mens Rea Model: Due Process and the Abolition of the Insanity Defense," *Pace Law Review* 28 (2008): 455–494.

Piety, Tamara, "Scorched Earth: How the Expansion of Civil Forfeiture Doctrine Has Laid Waste to Due Process," *University of Miami Law Review* 45 (1991): 911–978.

Pilcher, Susan, "Ignorance, Discretion and the Fairness of Notice: Confronting 'Apparent Innocence' in the Criminal Law," *American Criminal Law Review* 33 (1996): 1–55.

Pimentel, David, "Forfeitures Revisited: Bringing Principle to Practice in Federal Court," *Nevada Law Journal* 13 (2012): 1–59.

Pollock, Frederick, and Maitland, Frederic, *The History of English Law II* (Little Brown and Co, Boston, 1895).

Quintard-Morenas, Francois, "The Presumption of Innocence in the French and Anglo-American Legal Traditions," *American Journal of Comparative Law* 58 (2010): 107–149.

Ranney, James,"Presumptions in Criminal Cases: A New Look at an Old Problem," *Montana Law Review* 41 (1980): 21–37.

Raymond, Paul, "The Origin and Rise of Moral Liability in Anglo-Saxon Criminal Law," *Oregon Law Review* 15 (1936): 93–117.

Roach, Kent, "Wrongful Convictions in Canada," *University of Cincinnati Law Review* 80 (2012): 1465–1526.

Roberts, Paul, "Drug Dealing and the Presumption of Innocence: The *Human Rights Act* (Almost) Bites," *International Journal of Evidence and Proof* 6 (2002): 17–37.

———. "The Presumption of Innocence Brought Home? *Kebilene* Deconstructed," *Law Quarterly Review* 118 (2002): 41–71.

Robinson, Paul, "Foreword: The Criminal-Civil Distinction and Dangerous Blameless Offenders," *Journal of Criminal Law and Criminology* 83 (1993): 693–717.

Rogin, Alexander, "Dollars for Collars: Civil Asset Forfeiture and the Breakdown of Constitutional Rights," *Drexel Law Review Online* (2014): 45–82.
Rosen-Zvi, Issachar, and Fisher, Talia, "Overcoming Procedural Boundaries," *Virginia Law Review* 94 (2008): 79–155.
Ross, David Benjamin, "Civil Forfeiture: A Fiction That Offends Due Process," *Regent University Law Review* 13 (2001): 259–277.
Saltzman, Alan, "Strict Criminal Liability and the United States Constitution: Substantive Criminal Law Due Process," *Wayne Law Review* 24 (1978): 1571–1640.
Saunders, Kurt, "Race and Representation in Jury Service Selection," *Duquesne Law Review* 36 (1997): 49–77.
Sayre, Francis Bowes, "Public Welfare Offenses," *Columbia Law Review* 33 (1933): 55–88.
———. "Mens Rea," *Harvard Law Review* 45 (1932): 974–1026.
———. "The Present Significance of Mens Rea in the Criminal Law," in Campbell, Morton, et al., *Harvard Legal Essays* (Harvard University Press, Cambridge, 1934).
Sentencing Project, *Felony Disenfranchisement Laws in the United States* (2011).
———. *The Impact of Felony Disenfranchisement Laws in the United States* (2011).
Shapiro, Barbara, *Beyond Reasonable Doubt and Probable Cause* (University of California Press, Berkeley, 1991).
Sheldrick, Byron, "Shifting Burdens and Required Inferences: The Constitutionality of Reverse Onus Clauses," *University of Toronto Faculty of Law Review* 44(2) (1986): 179–208.
Sheppard, Steve, "The Metamorphoses of Reasonable Doubt: How Changes in the Burden of Proof Have Weakened the Presumption of Innocence," *Notre Dame Law Review* 78 (2003): 751–793.
Siebrasse, Norman, "The *Oakes* Test: An Old Ghost Impeding Bold New Initiatives," *Ottawa Law Review* 23 (1991): 99–137.
Simon, Rita James, and Mahan, Linda, "Quantifying Burdens of Proof," *Law and Society Review* 5 (1971): 319–330.
Smith, Bruce, "The Presumption of Guilt and the English Law of Theft, 1750–1850," *Law and History Review* 23 (2005): 133–171.
Stahl, Marc, "Asset Forfeiture, Burdens of Proof and the War on Drugs," *Journal of Criminal Law and Criminology* 83 (1993): 274–337.
Starkie, Thomas, *A Practical Treatise of the Law of Evidence and Digest of Proofs in Civil and Criminal Proceedings* (T and W Johnson, Philadelphia, 1824).
Steiker, Carol, "Punishment and Procedure: Punishment Theory and the Criminal-Civil Procedural Divide," *Georgetown Law Journal* 85 (1997): 775–819.
Stephen, James Fitzjames, *A General View of the Criminal Law of England* (Macmillan and Co, London, 1863).
———. *History of the Criminal Law of England* (Macmillan and Co, London, 1883).
Stewart, Hamish, "The Right to Be Presumed Innocent," *Criminal Law and Philosophy* 8 (2014): 407–420.
Stinneford, John, "Punishment Without Culpability," *Journal of Criminal Law and Criminology* 102 (2012): 653–724.
Stumer, Andrew, *The Presumption of Innocence: Evidential and Human Rights Perspectives* (Hart Publishing, Oxford, 2010).
Stuntz, William, "Substance, Process and the Civil-Criminal Line," *Journal of Contemporary Legal Issues* 7 (1996): 1–41.
———. *The Collapse of American Criminal Justice* (Harvard University Press, Cambridge, 2011).
Sundby, Scott, "The Reasonable Doubt Rule and the Meaning of Innocence," *Hastings Law Journal* 40 (1989): 457–510.
Tadros, Victor, "The Ideal of the Presumption of Innocence," *Criminal Law and Philosophy* 8 (2014): 449–467.
Tadros, Victor, and Tierney, Stephen, "The Presumption of Innocence and the *Human Rights Act*," *Modern Law Review* 67(3) (2004): 402–434.

Tapper, Colin, *Cross and Tapper on Evidence* (Oxford University Press, New York, London, 2007).

Tennan, Eric, "Is the Constitution in Harm's Way? Substantive Due Process and Criminal Law," *Boalt Journal of Criminal Law* 8 (2004): 3.

Thayer, James, "The Presumption of Innocence in Criminal Cases," *Yale Law Journal* 6 (1897): 185–212.

———. *Preliminary Treatise on Evidence at the Common Law* (Little Brown and Co, Boston, 1898).

Thorne, Samuel, ed., *Bracton on the Laws and Customs of England III* (Harvard University Press, Cambridge, 1977).

Tribe, Laurence, "Trial by Mathematics: Precision and Ritual in the Legal Process," *Harvard Law Review* 84 (1971): 1329–1393.

Tuck-Jackson, Andrea, "The Defence of Due Diligence and the Presumption of Innocence," *Criminal Law Quarterly* 33 (1991): 11–42.

Tushnet, Mark, "Constitutional Limitation of Substantive Criminal Law: An Examination of the Meaning of *Mullaney v Wilbur*," *Boston University Law Review* 55 (1975): 775–802.

Underwood, Barbara, "The Thumb on the Scales of Justice: Burdens of Persuasion in Criminal Cases," *Yale Law Journal* 86 (1977): 1299–1348.

Van Caenegem, Raoul, *Legal History: A European Perspective* (Cambridge University Press, Cambridge, 1991).

———. *The Birth of the English Common Law* (Cambridge University Press, Cambridge, 1988).

Volokh, Alexander, "n Guilty Men," *University of Pennsylvania Law Review* 146 (1997): 173–216.

Wasserstrom, Richard, "H L A Hart and the Doctrines of Mens Rea and Criminal Responsibility," *University of Chicago Law Review* 35 (1968): 92–126.

Weinstein, J B, "Jury Nullification: When, May and Should a Jury Reject the Law to Do Justice?" *American Criminal Law Review* 30 (1993): 239–254.

Whitman, James, *The Origins of Reasonable Doubt* (Yale University Press, Connecticut, 2008).

Wiley, John Shepard, "Not Guilty by Reason of Blamelessness: Culpability in Federal Criminal Interpretation," *Virginia Law Review* 85 (1999): 1021–1162.

William of Ockham, *Dialogue* (1476).

Williams, Glanville, "The Mathematics of Proof," *Criminal Law Review* (1979): 297–312.

———. "Offences and Defences," *Legal Studies* 2(3) (1982): 233–256.

Wilson, James, *The Works of James Wilson* (Lorenzo Press, Philadelphia, 1804).

Winfield, Percy, "The Myth of Absolute Liability," *Law Quarterly Review* 42 (1926): 37–51.

Wisotsky, Steven, "The Emerging 'Drug Exception' to the Bill of Rights," *Hastings Law Journal* 38 (1987): 889–926.

Wright, Peter, "Criminal Punishment Without Civil Rights: The Criminal Proceeds and Instrument Bill's Punitive Civil Sanctions," *Victoria University of Wellington Law Review* 37 (2006): 623–641.

Young, Simon, *Civil Forfeiture of Criminal Property* (Edward Elgar Publishing, Cheltenham, 2009).

Index

About the Author

Professor **Anthony Gray** is a researcher in constitutional and human rights law. Based in Australia, he has published extensively in refereed legal journals in that country, as well as in journals in Europe and the United Kingdom, the United States, and Canada. He has more than 100 refereed journal articles of which he was the sole author, and has authored books in the area of criminal due process and human rights.

www.ingramcontent.com/pod-product-compliance
Ingram Content Group UK Ltd.
Pitfield, Milton Keynes, MK11 3LW, UK
UKHW041629031026
15587UKWH00001B/162

9 781498 554107